# Studies in the History of Pl

C000293715

## Volume 27

The aim of the series *Studies in the History of Philosophy of Mind* is to foster historical research into the nature of thinking and the workings of the mind. The volumes address topics of intellectual history that would nowadays fall into different disciplines like philosophy of mind, philosophical psychology, artificial intelligence, cognitive science, etc. The monographs and collections of articles in the series are historically reliable as well as congenial to the contemporary reader. They provide original insights into central contemporary problems by looking at them in historical contexts, addressing issues like consciousness, representation and intentionality, mind and body, the self and the emotions. In this way, the books open up new perspectives for research on these topics.

This book series is indexed in SCOPUS.

For more information, please contact the publishing editor at christi.lue @ springer.com

More information about this series at http://www.springer.com/series/6539

Anselm Oelze

# Animal Minds in Medieval Latin Philosophy

A Sourcebook from Augustine to Wodeham

 Springer

Anselm Oelze
Leipzig, Sachsen, Germany

ISSN 1573-5834          ISSN 2542-9922   (electronic)
Studies in the History of Philosophy of Mind
ISBN 978-3-030-67014-6          ISBN 978-3-030-67012-2   (eBook)
https://doi.org/10.1007/978-3-030-67012-2

This Springer imprint is published by the registered company Springer Nature Switzerland AG
The registered company address is: Gewerbestrasse 11, 6330 Cham, Switzerland

# Acknowledgements

Giving a modern meaning to old texts is not an easy task. For me, taking on this task would have been even more difficult, if not impossible, without the help of various people and institutions. First of all, I am grateful to Dominik Perler and Bernd Roling who immediately supported my idea for this kind of volume when I first mentioned it to them in late 2015. From their remarks I profited immensely. In 2016 and 2017, I was glad to be a member of José Filipe Silva's ERC project "Rationality in Perception: Transformations of Mind and Cognition 1250–1550" at the University of Helsinki (ERC Grant Agreement No. 637747). It was a source of funding, time, and inspiration. Moreover, I would like to thank Manuel Bohn and the students who participated in seminars in Leysin, Münster, and Munich in 2017 and 2019. They made me see many aspects of animals' mental life of which I had been ignorant before. Several people, including Peter Adamson, Jari Kaukua, Christian Kny, Martin Pickavé, Paolo Rubini, Christoph Sander, and Juhana Toivanen, supported me in one way or another. Without their help, this book would not have come to fruition. Thanks to Henrik Lagerlund and Mikko Yrjönsuuri, who accepted it for publication in this series, and also thanks to the valuable comments of two anonymous referees, it may hopefully provide some insights into the minds of different kinds: of medieval thinkers but also, and mainly, of human and nonhuman animals.

Leipzig                                                                                     Anselm Oelze
November 2020

# Contents

# About the Author

**Anselm Oelze** (PhD, Humboldt University of Berlin, 2017) worked as a postdoctoral researcher at the University of Helsinki and as a teaching fellow in philosophy at the LMU Munich. He is author of the book *Animal Rationality: Later Medieval Theories 1250–1350* (Brill, 2018) and of articles on animal cognition and animal ethics in the Middle Ages.

# Chapter 1
# Introduction: Modern and Medieval Philosophy of Animal Minds

**Abstract**  How do animals see the world? Do they have feelings? Can they willingly control their behaviours? Such questions are asked and answered in contemporary philosophy of animal minds. If one looks at the history of this discipline there seems to exist no medieval precursor because a mind or the rational part of the soul was usually denied to nonhuman animals. Yet, as this sourcebook aims to show, there is still a medieval version of our modern philosophy of animal minds to be discovered. In a broader sense of the term 'mind', medieval thinkers did indeed discuss the mental life of other animals, namely, insofar as they scrutinised their cognition, emotions, and volitions. The introduction highlights the most important concepts of the contemporary debate and explains how they compare to the medieval discussion.

## A Day at the Zoo or A Contemporary Point of View

Imagine you spend a day at the zoo. You observe the elephants taking a bath, laugh about the funny warning whistles of the meerkats, and finally go to see the chimpanzees. The very moment you arrive at the great ape house, Kofi, an adult male chimp, takes a twig and starts to extract raisins from small holes in a chock block.[1] You literally feel how challenging this is, but Kofi easily manages to pick one raisin after another. While you watch him doing this you begin to wonder what is going on in Kofi's head right now. For instance, what does he *perceive*? Does he see twigs, chock blocks, and raisins like you do, or does he simply perceive various undefined objects of different shapes, sizes, and colours? Moreover, what does he *feel* while he engages in this kind of task? Does he feel happy when he succeeds in getting a raisin? Or is he frightened of being attacked by one of his fellow chimpanzees which are roaring in the background? Finally, does he do what he does willingly and

---

[1] This example is inspired by Wild (2013), 19–22.

© The Author(s), under exclusive license to Springer Nature
Switzerland AG 2021
A. Oelze, *Animal Minds in Medieval Latin Philosophy*, Studies in the History of
Philosophy of Mind 27, https://doi.org/10.1007/978-3-030-67012-2_1

intentionally? Put differently, does he *want* to extract raisins or is he merely subject to some natural impulses and instincts?

These are legitimate questions, and all of them obviously concern what can be called Kofi's *mental life*. The life of the mind contains various aspects. First, there is the aspect of *cognition*. When you wonder whether Kofi sees raisins you are interested in the nature of his perceptions. But you might as well ask about more sophisticated cognitive skills such as the capacity of problem solving that it may take to find the right tool for removing raisins. Second, there is the aspect of *emotion*. Kofi's state of mind is not only characterised by what he cognises but also by what he feels. He might feel joy, happiness, anger, fear, or hope, and so he might have as large a spectrum of emotions as you have. The third aspect of mental life is the aspect of *volition*. This concerns, for instance, Kofi's intentions or desires. No matter whether you think that all Kofi wants is raisins, you grant him the capacity to will something, and this is an ability you may not as easily ascribe to other nonhuman beings, say, machines. So, the sheer impression that an animal like Kofi is mentally not so far removed from you is what makes him such a fascinating object of study.

As fascinating as Kofi's mental life may be, there is a serious problem: how can you actually tell that Kofi has a mental life at all, let alone what it looks like in detail? The behaviourist's or skeptic's answer would be: you cannot (not seriously, at least). The argument behind this negative reply revolves around what is sometimes called the 'unobservability thesis'.[2] According to this thesis, mental states are not directly observable. We cannot see or read others' thoughts, feelings, or intentions from the outside, neither in human nor in nonhuman animals. Even when we employ the latest techniques of brain imaging we only get pictures of neural states which then need to be interpreted as showing a certain mental activity. Thus, we can observe the mental life of others only indirectly, namely, by observing their behaviours.[3] When you watch Kofi extracting raisins you could, for instance, start by asking whether he would be capable of doing this without having any kind of perceptions. Furthermore, you might wonder whether one can coherently account for Kofi's behaviour without ascribing certain intentions to him. If you conclude that one cannot give a satisfactory explanation of what Kofi does without granting him a certain degree of mental activity you have already begun to access his mental life via the observation of his behaviour.

Unsurprisingly, the indirect access to the mental states of others leads to a whole range of possible theories and explanations of what those mental states look like in particular. Whether Kofi intentionally uses the stick or whether he feels happy when successfully picking a raisin is a matter of debate. An argument that is often used in this context in favour of ascribing mental states to others, and nonhuman animals in particular, is the *argument from analogy*.[4] What this argument claims is basically

---

[2] For a discussion, see Overgaard (2015).

[3] That the observation of behaviour provides one of the most important, if not the only, means by which we can acquire knowledge about others' mental life is a position widely shared in and beyond animal psychology; see Wasserman and Zentall (2006), esp. 6f.

[4] See Wild (2013), 84–89.

this: whenever we observe a certain behaviour B in an animal A, and whenever we explain it by a mental state M we have good reasons to suppose that the same kind of mental state is responsible for the same kind of behaviour in another animal. The following example may help to illustrate this. Imagine we get Kofi and an 8-year old child to participate in the 'floating peanut task'.[5] In this task, Kofi and the child are confronted with a fixed glass tube. At the bottom of the tube lies a peanut (or a gummy bear in case of the child). Both Kofi and the child try to reach the peanut with their fingers but they fail because the tube is too long and narrow. However, after a number of unsuccessful trials they change their strategy and start filling water into the tube. It does not take long before they can both grab the peanut because with the water level rising the peanut (or the gummy bear) begins to float towards the opening of the tube.

A first, intuitive reaction to this observation might be: Kofi is just as smart as the child! Although they belong to different species they find the same solution to the same problem. Critical defenders of the argument from analogy will certainly hesitate to employ a term such as 'smart' in this context. Still, they would agree that in order to solve the problem Kofi very likely engages in a similar, if not the same, kind of cognitive process as the 8-year old. To this claim one could immediately object that one must not fall into the trap of *anthropomorphism*. That is, one must not ascribe humanlike cognitive powers to nonhuman beings only because they show humanlike behaviours.[6] Otherwise, one would also need to say that a calculator solves a mathematical problem by the same kind of process in which a human being engages when telling you that 2 + 2 is 4. Indeed, there are people who think that machines can be just as intelligent as human beings or, vice versa, that human brains are not very different from cleverly constructed computer hardware. Nevertheless, those who employ the argument from analogy in the explanation of animal behaviour have a serious advantage over the defenders of something like strong artificial intelligence: they can always point to the fact that a calculator's physiological make-up is rather different from the physiology of humans. While a calculator is made of metal wires and cards, a human brain is an organic substance consisting of various kinds of cells, such as nerve cells, glial cells, and blood cells. This is something it has in common with a chimpanzee's brain. Of course, chimp brains and human brains are not physiologically identical, but they are definitely more similar than brains and computers. This is supported by the fact that chimp brains and human brains share an evolutionary history as they seem to have evolved from the same common ancestor. Because of this commonality it is quite plausible to think that they also have a similar mental life. Thus, the *principle of psychological continuity* is inferred from the *principle of evolutionary continuity*.[7]

---

[5] See Hanus et al. (2011) as well as Mendes et al. (2007).

[6] On the problem of anthropomorphism, see Crist (1999); De Waal (1999); Daston and Mitman (2005); Wynne (2007).

[7] See, for instance, Tomasello (2014), 15. For a critical evaluation of this inference, see Sober (2000) and (2005).

With regard to the connection between these two principles, it is hardly surprising that the study of animal minds saw a major boost with the publication of the theory of evolution in the middle of the nineteenth century. In addition to his pivotal treatise on natural selection, the *Origin of Species*, Charles Darwin published a book entitled *The Expression of the Emotions in Man and Animals*. This became one of the first influential scholarly texts on feelings in humans and other animals.[8] A decade later, his younger contemporary, George Romanes, laid the foundation of comparative psychology. He systematically examined differences and similarities in cognition between humans and other animals and he developed one of the first comprehensive theories of animal intelligence.[9] Indeed, both Darwin and Romanes heavily relied on what would now be classified (and possibly rejected) as anecdotal material.[10] Yet, they are the fathers of what is today an established cross-disciplinary subject. When Donald R. Griffin, who coined the term 'cognitive ethology', published his classic *Animal Minds* in 1992, he looked back at several decades of intense and fruitful empirical research that had opened a window not only on chimpanzees' minds but also on the minds of dolphins, pigeons, and honeybees, for example.[11]

However, the problem of unobservability has not been solved by these materials and maybe never will be. As Randolf Menzel and Julia Fischer, two renowned researchers in animal psychology, concede, "we continue to struggle with the question of how to judge the mental life of other species."[12] Still, the refinement of methods and the intensified empirical research have brought us closer to telling what is going on in a head such as Kofi's. This is also the case because the systematic empirical research is accompanied by a wider philosophical debate and reflection over the value and significance of empirical findings. For some, there now even exists a separate philosophical discipline: the *philosophy of animal minds*.[13] In short, we seem to have acquired more knowledge about other animals' mental life than ever before. But one might legitimately ask whether this is true.

Indeed, the modern success story of the study of animal minds easily makes us miss that scholarly interest in animal minds is much older. Already in antiquity, the human-like behaviour of nonhuman animals led to a discussion of animal cognition and other aspects of mental life.[14] It was Aristotle's denial of reason to nonhuman animals, in particular, that produced a controversial debate about the animal/human

---

[8] Darwin (1872).

[9] Romanes (1882) and (1883).

[10] See Wynne (2007).

[11] See the revised and expanded version Griffin (2001). The question Griffin is mainly interested in is not whether animals have mental states at all but rather to what extent and in which sense these states are conscious.

[12] Menzel and Fischer (2011), 1.

[13] See Lurz (2009) and Andrews and Beck (2017). See also Allen and Bekoff (1997); Bekoff et al. (2002); Perler and Wild (2005); Hurley and Nudds (2006); Andrews (2015).

[14] See Dierauer (1977) and the classic by Sorabji (1993) as well as the sourcebook by Newmyer (2011).

boundary.[15] A great many thinkers discussed to what extent humans share certain mental states with other animals and some of them, such as Porphyry and Plutarch, doubted that reason is what sets apart humans from all other animals. In the early modern era, Descartes' famous denial of minds to nonhuman animals further stimulated this discussion. Ironically, it created a relatively strong backlash with thinkers as Michel de Montaigne and David Hume rejecting the Cartesian theory and arguing for a more positive stance towards nonhuman animals' mental life.[16] Montaigne and Hume are amongst those thinkers in the history of philosophy who clearly express and defend the argument from analogy.[17] The philosophy of animal minds is thus far from being a modern invention.

Despite numerous publications on animal minds in the history of (Western) philosophy, the historical reconstruction of this discussion is still incomplete.[18] While the views of ancient and early modern philosophers have been studied to a great deal, the views of medieval thinkers have yet to attract as much attention as they might. There are various reasons for the lack of attention. A general reason is that the study of medieval philosophy still leads a relatively shadowy existence in comparison to other periods in the history of philosophy. Over the last decades much scholarly effort has been put into showing that the Middle Ages are not the 'dark ages' as which they have been characterised since the Renaissance. Still, for many the millennium between the fifth and the fifteenth century seems not as worth studying as the centuries before and after that time.

Besides this general reason there are at least two specific reasons which might explain why the medieval debate about animal minds has not yet been scrutinised. First, there is the biblical doctrine of the 'imago Dei'. According to this doctrine, the most prominent version of which is found in Genesis 1:27, humans have been created in the image of God. Many scholars interpreted this passage as follows: that humans have been created in the image of God means that they are the only earthly creatures with a rational and immortal soul (see Chap. 2). This explanation undoubtedly drove a wedge between humans and other animals, both at a metaphysical and a cognitive level: metaphysically, because they differ regarding the nature of their souls (mortal/immortal); cognitively, since the nature of the soul determines the set of cognitive capacities an individual possesses (rational/non-rational). Second, the theological idea that human souls are rational and immortal was combined with Aristotle's denial of an immaterial intellect to nonhuman animals.[19] In the Latin tradition, this immaterial, immortal, and rational faculty was commonly known as 'intellectus' or 'ratio', but many people also referred to it as 'mens', that is, as mind.

[15] See, for instance, Aristotle, *De anima* II.3, 414b18f. and 415a7f.; *De partibus animalium* I.1., 641b7f.; *Politica* VII.13, 1332b3f. For a complete list, see Sorabji (1993), 12n30.
[16] See Wild (2006); Cheung (2010); Muratori (2013); Buchenau and Lo Presti (2017).
[17] Both Montaigne and Hume defend the argument from analogy but the ways in which they spell it out differ slightly; see Wild (2006), 248.
[18] On the following, see also Oelze (2018a), xi and 3.
[19] The *locus classicus* for the immateriality of the intellect is Aristotle, *De anima* III.4, 429a19–28. On some of the Islamic, Jewish, and Christian theories of the intellect, see Black (2009).

So, in the original and strict sense of the term a medieval philosophy of animal minds does not exist, because 'by the mind alone our soul differs from the soul of nonhuman animals', as Thomas Aquinas put it.[20] Hence, in the eyes of medieval thinkers, nonhuman animals seem to be mindless creatures.

As this sourcebook aims to show, there is still a medieval version of our modern philosophy of animal minds to be discovered. In a broader sense of the term 'mind', medieval thinkers did indeed discuss the mental life of other animals, namely, insofar as they scrutinised their cognition, emotions, and volitions. Although many of them started from the assumption that the souls of nonhuman animals are material, non-rational, and mortal, they wondered about the implications of this definition of the animal/human boundary. Which cognitive skills do humans share with other animals? Which kinds of cognition do other animals lack? Do they feel anger, joy, or hope? And if they do, are their feelings different from ours? Can nonhuman animals freely will something and can they somehow control their desires? These are just some of the questions that medieval thinkers used to ask and, as the texts selected for this volume make clear, they gave a whole range of answers. In many cases, they certainly approached the mental life of animals with a different motivation and from a different perspective than we do (see the next section below). However, in particular with regard to the fundamental philosophical problems sketched above, there is also much continuity between the modern and the medieval debate, and by looking at the medieval views we can definitely learn a lot about our own fascination with the minds of other animals.

## Animals and Minds in Medieval Philosophy

Although the texts in this volume show that medieval thinkers were interested in animals' mental life it would be wrong to suggest that there existed something like the contemporary philosophy of animal minds. In the medieval period, one reason for this is the role of animals, another is the role of philosophy. As far as animals are concerned, they certainly had a different position in medieval society since they were not only companions and suppliers of various raw materials but also served as means of transport in ordinary life and as indispensable means of production in agriculture.[21] The omnipresence and daily contact undoubtedly shaped the views medieval people had of animals, but these views were not directly transmitted into scholarly interest and attention. The main reason for this is the way in which medieval universities worked.[22] In general, they were designed to grant people two kinds of degrees: first, a bachelor's degree and then, consecutively, a master's degree in

---

[20] Thomas Aquinas, *Summa theologiae* III, q. 5, a. 4, co., Editio Leonina XI (1903), 92.

[21] See Salisbury (2011), 10–60; Resl (2007).

[22] See, for instance, Van Engen (2000); Wöller (2016), 39–44.

either theology, medicine, or law. However, to obtain any of these degrees one had first to study philosophy at the faculty of arts. The name derives from the seven liberal arts (*artes liberales*) that were taught there: arithmetic, geometry, astronomy and music (the so-called '*quadrivium*') plus logic, grammar, and rhetorics (the so-called '*trivium*'). Simply speaking, philosophy was a preparatory class for studying at any of the higher faculties. Yet philosophy did not stop at the entrance gates to these faculties. In particular, it entered the faculty of theology because, on the one hand, theologians discussed various problems that can be categorised as philosophical. On the other hand, they employed philosophical methods in order to solve theological problems.

There was a variety of forms in which and techniques by which these problems were tackled. A major place of debate were the commentaries that almost every medieval philosopher and theologian at a (late-)medieval university had to produce. Usually, these included commentaries on the Bible, the church fathers, and the writings of Aristotle. In philosophy of mind, many of them drew on texts from the Arabic tradition in psychology, most importantly, Avicenna and Averroes.[23] Consequently, within the medieval academic curriculum, there were only few places in which animals and their mental life could be treated as a subject in its own right. In other words, animals seldom were the *explanandum*, that is, the scholarly object that is to be explained (seldom, because there were exceptions to that rule such as the commentaries on Aristotle's zoological writings). Instead, they mainly functioned as an *explanans*, that is, the factor by which something else is explained. Therefore, they became a topic whenever a discussion in metaphysics, ethics, theology, or any other subject seemed to benefit from a look at the minds of nonhuman animals.[24]

One might wonder how any of these discussions would benefit from looking at animal minds. The answer lies in the heuristic function animals fulfilled. It was largely based on certain metaphysical and psychological assumptions. One of these assumptions is the *imago-Dei* doctrine mentioned in the previous section. It says that humans have been created 'in the image of God'. However, this expression from Genesis 1:27 is not self-explanatory. The most popular interpretation was that humans have been created in the image of God insofar as they have been created as rational beings or, differently speaking, as creatures endowed with an immaterial, immortal, rational soul.[25] This particular kind of soul makes them similar to God and the angels, and sets them apart from animals and plants. Psychologically, it entails that they possess a particular set of capacities that other creatures lack, including primarily the abilities of (1) concept-formation, (2) judging, and (3)

---

[23] On the different types of medieval philosophical literature, see Kenny and Pinborg (1982).

[24] On animals in medieval philosophy, see De Leemans and Klemm (2007); Oelze (2018a), esp. 21–27; Toivanen (2018). On animals as analytical tools in thirteenth-century theology, see Wei (2020). On the zoological commentary tradition, see de Asúa (1991), (1997), (1999). The most comprehensive overview is provided by Köhler (2000), (2008), (2014).

[25] An alternative interpretation was, for instance, that Christ is the image of God.

reasoning or thinking. In other words, only they have a *mental* life, because the narrow concept of mind is co-extensional with the rational (part of the) soul.

If one takes a closer look at the history of the concept of mind and at the definitions that shaped the medieval debate about animal minds in the Latin West, in particular, one comes across three main traditions: (a) Augustinianism, (b) Aristotelianism, and (c) Arabic psychology, particularly Avicenna. However, this list needs further explanation, first of all, because it is incomplete. At least, one must add Neoplatonism and the Galenic tradition. Second, because, at first glance, the order of the enumeration might seem implausible: Why would Augustine, an early medieval thinker, stand before the ancient philosopher Aristotle? The answer to this question is relatively simple but it is crucial for understanding why most of the texts translated in this volume were written not before but *after* the turn from the twelfth to the thirteenth century (to illustrate this point: only two out of twenty-four texts are from the period pre-1200; for more information on the selection of texts see the section "Note on the texts and translations"). The reason is that before the thirteenth century most of Aristotle's writings were not available in Latin. Translations from Greek and Arabic slowly began to spread around the middle of the twelfth century and the translation movement continued well into the second half of the thirteenth century. It took a while until the texts had been disseminated and incorporated in the syllabi of Western universities.[26] Therefore, during the period from the fifth to the twelfth century and also beyond, it was Augustine's (or some sort of Augustinian) concept of mind that most thinkers employed when writing on animals.

## *Augustine*

Briefly speaking, Augustine considers the mind (*mens*) to be the highest part of the soul.[27] This part is divided into three powers: understanding (*intelligentia*), will (*voluntas*), and memory (*memoria*). The tripartition of the mind is no coincidence. Augustine aims to show that the mind is genuinely the part because of which humans are said to have been created 'in the image of God'. Consequently, he needs to find an equivalent to the divine trinity of Father, Son, and Holy Spirit.[28] This equivalent is the trinity of understanding, will, and memory, and just as Father, Son, and Holy Spirit form one divinity, understanding, will, and memory, constitute one mind. By this analogy, Augustine has proven that there can be unity in trinity and vice versa.[29]

Since the mind has such a peculiar character and since it is the mind that gives humans some sort of share in the divine nature it is evidently missing in other

---

[26] See Dod (1982) and Lohr (1982).

[27] On Augustine's philosophy and concept of mind, see O'Daly (1987) and Brachtendorf (2010).

[28] See Augustine, *De trinitate* XIV.8.11, ed. Mountain (1968), 436; *De quantitate animae* II.3, ed. Hörmann (1986), 133f.

[29] See Augustine, *De trinitate* X.11.18, ed. Mountain (1968), 330f.

animals. Nevertheless, Augustine ascribes to them the lower part of the soul which he calls 'sensation' (*sensus*). It includes at least the five external senses of sight, hearing, smell, taste, and touch. In addition, there is what Augustine calls the 'internal sense' (*sensus interior*).[30] This sense basically enables a being (1) to *integrate* the sensory input delivered by the external senses, (2) to *evaluate* this input in terms of triggering a reaction such as pursuit or avoidance, and (3) to *sense* the status of sensation.[31] To give an example of the latter function: Whenever your eyes are closed, you do not see anything. The eyes themselves, however, are incapable of sensing whether they see something or not. Therefore, Augustine argues, an additional and superior sense is required which provides information on the status of the external sense powers. This sense is the so-called internal sense.

The problem with the internal sense in particular as well as with the distinction between mind and sensation in general is that the boundary between the mind and the rest of the soul is not as clear as it might seem to be at first glance.[32] This is illustrated by the passage from Augustine's *De quantitate animae* that has been translated for this volume (see Chap. 2). There Augustine's interlocutor Evodius repeatedly refers to the cognitive capacities of nonhuman animals. Among other things, he suggests that they seem to possess knowledge (*scientia*).[33] The example he gives is the famous case of Argos, the dog of Odysseus, which is said to have recognised its master even after twenty years of absence. This example leads to an elaborate discussion of the definition of knowledge. In the end, both dialogue partners agree that one needs to find an alternative explanation for the capacities of Odysseus's dog and other animals rather than ascribing knowledge to them. What the discussion shows is that any kind of clear-cut distinction between the mind and other powers immediately provokes the question of whether it is plausible and coherent, and nonhuman animals which lack a mind, according to Augustine, were a most welcome litmus test. This also applies to Aristotle's model of the soul.

## *Aristotle*

As said, Aristotle's model was not available to the Latin West before the majority of his writings, including his treatise on the soul (*De anima*), had been translated in the twelfth and thirteenth centuries. However, it did not take long for it to spread, and its popularity grew quite rapidly. One reason for its successful reception was that it

---

[30] Augustine prominently introduces this sense in *De libero arbitrio* II.5.11.43f., ed. Green (1970), 244. Some scholars argue that he even invented it; see, for instance, Heller-Roazen (2007), 131.

[31] On all of these functions, see Augustine, *De libero arbitrio* II.3.8–4.10, ed. Green (1970), 241–243.

[32] There is a lively discussion, for example, on whether the internal sense also amounts to certain forms of higher-level cognition, such as self-awareness and the cognition of other souls; see Clark (1998); Matthews (1999); Brittain (2002); Toivanen (2013); Silva (2016).

[33] See Augustine, *De quantitate animae* XXVI.50, ed. Hörmann (1986), 194f.

is compatible with both the biblical doctrine of the '*imago Dei*' and the Augustinian model of the soul in which the mind ranks highest.[34] According to Aristotle, the soul is the principle of life or, to put it in Aristotelian terms, the form of a living thing. This means that any living being, including plants, is an ensouled being. This idea might sound strange to modern ears but becomes plausible if one looks at the three different kinds (or – depending on the reading – parts) of (the) soul that Aristotle distinguishes: (1) the *vegetative*, (2) the *sensory*, and (3) the *rational* soul.[35] Each of these souls has a particular function and range. The vegetative soul is responsible for nutrition, growth, and reproduction, and is shared by plants, nonhuman animals, and humans. The sensory soul is the one by which a being can perceive as well as engage with its environment in terms of locomotion. It is not found in plants, but only in nonhuman and human animals (because Aristotle claims that plants can neither sense their environment nor move from one place to another). By the way, this type of soul is the reason why the expressions 'humans and other animals' or 'human and nonhuman animals' are not anachronistic at all. The Latin term '*animal*' is employed for any living being endowed with sensory powers, and since humans share the vegetative and the sensory soul with dogs, apes, bees, and so forth, they are animals. However, they are animals of a particular kind because, according to the Aristotelian model, only they possess the third type of soul, the rational soul, which is responsible for thinking (alternative descriptions of its operations include reasoning, the generation of knowledge, and understanding). This rational soul was commonly identified with the mind. Thus, as in Augustine's psychology, nonhuman animals are by definition excluded from the realm of the mental.

The denial of a mind to nonhuman animals, however, leads to a number of questions which were partly raised by Aristotle himself, partly by his medieval readers and commentators. They all centre on those cases in which nonhuman animals show certain behaviours, mostly complex ones, that are not easily explained without referring to rational, intellectual, or, generally speaking, mental activity. These examples did not, of course, originate from empirical testing as in the floating peanut task described above (see section "A day at the zoo or a contemporary point of view"). Still, some of them did indeed derive from personal observation as, for instance, the case of Roger Bacon's cat (see Chap. 10).[36] Bacon claims to have observed a cat facing the following problem: it aims to catch a fish swimming in a large stone container. Yet, the fish always escapes the cat's claws. Therefore, it finally pulls the stopper, waits until the fish is lying on the dry ground, and then grabs it with ease.[37] As Bacon admits, this behaviour seems to have all the ingredients it takes for thoughtful, rational action: First, the cat analyses the situation. Second, it comes up with a solution, presumably by mentally representing the solution. Third, it acts according to this representation. To be clear, Bacon himself does not speak of mental representations nor does he think that this process is rational in the strict (medieval) sense of the term. Nevertheless, he argues that a behaviour like

---

[34] On the synthesis of Augustine's and Aristotle's psychology, see Kuksewicz (1982).

[35] See Aristotle, *De anima* II.2, 413b11–414a3 and II.3, 414a29–414b19.

[36] Further examples of personal observation are found in Chaps. 8 and 20.

[37] See Roger Bacon, *Perspectiva*, p. II, d. 3, ch. 9, ed. Lindberg (1996), 248.

this challenges the Aristotelian model of the soul, insofar as it seems to run counter to the clear distinction between the sensory and the rational soul.

Other examples which occur in many of the texts involve the skills of bees that build hexagonal combs (see Chap. 10), of monkeys which communicate in human-like ways (see Chap. 8), and of dogs which seem to reason (see Chaps. 13 and 24). However, contrary to Bacon's cat, most of them were not derived from personal observations but from a variety of sources, such as Aristotle's writings (in particular, his texts on natural philosophy), Bible commentaries, encyclopedias, so-called bestiaries (that is, books blending encyclopedic content with animal lore), and travel reports. In many cases it is impossible (or very difficult, at least) to trace back the history of particular examples. However, there is one famous exception to this rule and this is the example of the sheep that perceives a wolf and flees. Admittedly, this is not a very spectacular example nor does it seem to illustrate a complex form of animal behaviour. Nevertheless, it quickly became one of the most popular examples in medieval philosophy of animal minds and it was employed in many different ways and discussions. Originally, it was introduced by Avicenna in his book on the soul (*Liber de anima*) (see Chaps. 4 and 5). This leads to the third tradition that was influential for discussions of animal minds in medieval Latin philosophy: the tradition of Arabic psychology, particularly Avicenna.

## *Avicenna*

The influence of Avicenna's psychology must not be underestimated, particularly, for what it added to the Augustinian and Aristotelian models of the soul: the so-called theory of inner or internal senses. It is exactly this context in which Avicenna comes up with the famous example of the sheep and the wolf (see Chaps. 4 and 5). A sheep, he says, primarily perceives a wolf through its external senses.[38] It sees its colour and its shape, it smells its scent, or hears its howling. However, these perceptions are insufficient for triggering a reaction such as flight, Avicenna argues. Instead, a peculiar internal sense is needed which is called 'estimative power' (*vis aestimativa*) or 'estimation' (*aestimatio*). Its name is descriptive insofar as it illustrates its function: while the external senses perceive the forms (*formae*) of an object, such as the wolf's colour or its smell, estimation evaluates these forms by so-called 'intentions' (*intentiones*), such as the wolf's hostility. Although it is tempting, one must not confuse the medieval meaning of this term with its modern meaning. The idea is not that by the estimative power the sheep perceives the wolf's intention or aim to eat it. Rather, an intention, in the medieval sense of term, is a cognitive vehicle transporting the information that the wolf is hostile towards the sheep.[39]

---

[38] See Avicenna Latinus, *Liber de anima seu sextus de naturalibus*, b. I, ch. 5, ed. van Riet (1972), 86–89, and b. IV, ch. 3, ed. van Riet (1968), 34–40. For a discussion of this example and for a more detailed history of its reception in the Latin West, see Piro (2005); Perler (2006) and (2012).

[39] See Crane (1998), esp. 816, and Amerini (2011), esp. 558f.

Regarding the theory of internal senses in general and the role of estimation and intentions in particular, three points need to be noted. First, this theory is not a unified theory in the sense that Avicenna invented it from scratch. Instead, he took various elements from ancient and late ancient Greek thinkers.[40] Even though his version became quite influential, it was constantly modified by Arabic and Latin authors (see, for instance, the text in Chap. 12, in which Thomas Aquinas explains why he does not entirely embrace Avicenna's theory). Second, although the power of estimation is undoubtedly "the most successful addition to Aristotle's faculty theory",[41] as Dag Hasse put it, one must not ignore Aristotle's own contribution. Contrary to Augustine – and this is one of the advantages of his model of the soul, one might say –, he presents a more fine-grained account of the sensory part of the soul. Admittedly, Augustine also mentions that nonhuman animals might possess powers such as memory, but Aristotle is comparatively explicit in this regard and grants them common sense, imagination, and memory, from which arise capacities such as learning and prudence (see Chaps. 7, 8, and 13). Still, it remains doubtful whether his account of these senses would have been as successful as it was without the assistance of Arabic psychology, particularly the theory of estimation and intentions.

A third point about this theory that is worth noting is that Avicenna somehow leaves it to the reader to decide whether an intention, such as the wolf's hostility, is simply *received* by the estimative power of the sheep or whether it is *generated* by estimation. The first reading emphasises the *passivity* of estimation, whereas the second interprets it as an *active* power.[42] Regardless of whether the first or the second reading is correct, Avicenna's account of estimation and intentions was successful insofar as it stimulated a whole range of debates in the medieval West. One of these debates concerns the question of whether an intention is some sort of general concept. This seems plausible since a sheep does not only flee one particular wolf but wolves in general. Yet, if the estimative power is capable of forming concepts or, to put it in medieval terms, of cognising universals, universal cognition is no longer a unique feature of the intellect. Hence, by ascribing this capacity to sensory powers one would shift the traditional boundary of rationality.

As various texts in this volume show, medieval thinkers employed different strategies in order to tackle this problem. While John Blund claims that the estimative power does not apprehend universals (see Chap. 6), Pseudo-Peter of Spain argues that one can legitimately call the kind of cognition estimation provides 'universal cognition' because it apprehends what he calls 'elevated intentions' (see Chap. 9). Albert the Great analyses the role of estimation in the communication of monkeys and apes (see Chap. 8). Even though he does not think that they abstract universals from particulars he suggests that their estimative power enables them to produce some sort of speech (*loquela*) and to engage in low-level types of reasoning. Thus,

---

[40] On the history of this theory, see (the partly outdated) Wolfson (1935) and Mousavian and Fink (2020).

[41] Hasse (2010), 314. See also Hasse (2000), esp. 127–153.

[42] On this difference, see Oelze (2018a), 65f.

Avicenna's version of the theory of internal senses opened up new fields of discussion, particularly with regard to animal cognition. But why did this peculiar theory become so successful in this context?

There are three aspects that might help to explain the success of this theory. First, it provides a convincing explanation of animal behaviour by differentiating between the apprehension of forms and intentions. Imagine the sheep would only perceive the forms of the wolf – its shape, its colour, its smell etc. – through its external senses. It is certainly possible that this perception of forms immediately triggers a reaction such as flight. In contemporary theories of animal behaviour, this is called the *stimulus-response model*. According to this model, an animal (e.g. a sheep) shows a particular reaction (e.g. flight) every time a certain stimulus (e.g. a wolf) occurs. The strength of this model is that it is parsimonious. It does not introduce any cognitive powers and vehicles beyond external senses and sensible forms.[43] However, it has difficulties explaining why a sheep runs away from a wolf, whereas a wolf does not. The sensible forms received by a sheep and a wolf must be the same unless the sense organs of sheep and wolves significantly differ. But despite the sameness of the stimulus, the response is different. This could certainly be explained by referring to natural instinct: a sheep simply comes with another set of instinctual reactions than a wolf. Yet, such an explanation appears incomplete. It does not explain what instinct is and how it works. Avicenna's theory, by contrast, provides a comparatively detailed explanation. As mentioned before, this theory has its own weaknesses. Nevertheless, it explains why similar stimuli produce different responses in different species: it is because amongst the internal senses there is a distinct faculty – estimation – that is capable of evaluating sensory input in terms of intentions.[44] The evaluative process may differ from one species to another. It can even take different forms within one and the same individual, as Avicenna himself notes, because besides innate responses to certain stimuli there might also be learned reactions, such as a dog's reaction of flight to the perception of a stick with which it has been beaten before (see Chap. 5).[45] In short, Avicenna's theory of estimation turned out to be a helpful addition to traditional accounts of animal behaviour.

A second reason for its success is that the faculty of estimation had been introduced within a particular context but could easily be transferred into other contexts. Albert the Great, for instance, employs it in order to account for the cognitive capacities of highly developed nonhuman animals, such as monkeys and apes, or a peculiar species of apes, more precisely, which he calls 'pygmies' (see Chap. 8). These animals, he states, "have a brighter estimative power than all other animals" to such an extent that "they seem to have something similar to reason".[46] Interestingly, Albert does not explain their behaviour by ascribing rational faculties to them. In

---

[43] For this reason, John Duns Scotus, for instance, favoured it over Avicenna's model; see Perler (2012), 38f.

[44] Kaukua (2014), 106, calls this feature "the subject-specificity of estimation."

[45] See Avicenna Latinus, *Liber de anima*, b. IV, ch. 3, ed. van Riet (1968), 39. For a detailed analysis and discussion of this example, see Oelze (2018a), 63–67.

[46] Albert the Great, *De animalibus*, b. XXI, tr. 1, ch. 3, ed. Stadler (1920), 1332.

other words, he does not downgrade the faculties of intellect and reason. Instead, he upgrades the internal senses, particularly the power of estimation. The same strategy was also chosen by some early modern authors, for instance, Marin Cureau de la Chambre, who argues that nonhuman animals are capable of judging and practical reasoning by virtue of their internal sensory powers.[47] In conclusion, one of the strengths of Avicenna's theory of internal senses was that it was flexible enough to be employed outside its original context. It provided a powerful alternative to redefining the traditional animal/human boundary which was an option most, if not all, medieval thinkers were keen to avoid.

A third reason for its success presumably was that Avicenna's theory was highly compatible with other prevailing models of the soul. As said, both Aristotle's and Augustine's models contain rudiments of what later became the theory (or theories) of internal senses. Yet, there is also another pivotal point with respect to compatibility: like Aristotle and Augustine, Avicenna does not ascribe a mind to nonhuman animals. There is no passage in his writings in which he explicitly considers the possibility that sheep, wolves, or dogs possess rational faculties. However, this does not mean that his theory is detrimental to the idea of a medieval philosophy of animal minds. For as long as this idea draws on a broad concept of mind, Avicenna's theory, which shines through most of the texts selected for this volume, significantly improves any attempts of picturing the mental life of animals.

## The Life of the Mind: Cognition, Emotion, and Volition

If one compares Avicenna's example of the sheep and the wolf with the contemporary example of Kofi, the chimpanzee (see section "A day at the zoo or a contemporary point of view"), it seems that Kofi has a much richer mental life than Avicenna's sheep. While the sheep only seems to have *cognition* of the wolf's features, Kofi also has *emotions* and *volitions*, because in addition to perceiving the twig, the chock block, and the raisins, there are good reasons to assume that he does, for instance, enjoy extracting raisins and willingly engages in this operation. Yet, this comparison ignores various elements of the picture medieval thinkers used to draw of the sheep's (and other animals') psychological activities. Table 1.1 might help to illustrate this.[48]

**Table 1.1** Parts of the soul and psychological activities

|  | Sensitive part | Intellective part |
|---|---|---|
| Apprehensive part | Cognition (sensory) | Cognition (intellectual) |
| Appetitive part | Emotion | Volition |

[47] Marin Cureau de la Chambre, *Traité de la connoissance des animaux* (Paris 1648), 5. On his position, see also Wild (2006), 19–21; Oelze (2018a), 232f.

[48] It is largely based on King (2012), 212.

On the one hand (i.e. on the horizontal level), there is the classical distinction between the *sensitive* and *intellective* part of the soul. The former includes external and internal senses, the latter reason, intellect, and will. On the other hand (i.e. on the vertical level), there is the distinction between an *apprehensive* and an *appetitive* part.[49] This means that the soul not only apprehends the world in various ways but also engages with it by desiring or rejecting what it perceives. Thus, apprehension is identical with *cognition*; the appetitive part generates *emotion* and *volition*. Usually, this multidimensional picture of the soul was used both as a psychological and a biological classification: while humans and nonhuman animals were said to share sensitive powers, the latter were taken to lack the intellective part of the soul. Consequently, the sheep has cognition of the wolf (e.g. of its colours and its hostility) and it develops certain *feelings* about it (e.g. fear), but it does not seem to have a *will* in this situation (e.g. the will to flee). However, this classification is exactly where medieval philosophy of animal minds begins. As mentioned in the section "A day at the zoo or a contemporary point of view", they often functioned as heuristic tools. That is, they were, for instance, employed to show that a certain capacity belongs to the sensitive part of the soul. What is interesting to see now is that this led to discussions of the classification itself. In many cases, this debate did not concern the distinction between the sensitive and the intellective part as such. Rather, it focused on the question of which psychological activities belong to which part, and in this context nonhuman animals provided some kind of litmus test: if a capacity C is exhibited by a nonhuman animal A it must belong to the sensitive soul S and not the intellective soul I, or so the argument runs. But what if a capacity C that is usually attributed to I is shown by A? Obviously, such a case puts the classification to the test and, unsurprisingly, it is this kind of case on which many of the texts in this volume centre. In short, medieval philosophy of animal minds is less about showing *that* animals have all aspects of mental life, but rather about enquiring *whether* they have them.

## *Cognition*

Cognition certainly is the least controversial of the three aspects or parts of mental life. No serious participant in the medieval discussion denied cognition to nonhuman animals. The very definition of 'animal' requires that a living being possesses sensory faculties because sensation is the feature by which animals differ from plants (see the section "Animals and minds in medieval philosophy").[50] Therefore, if there was controversy it did not arise from the boundary between plants and animals but from the boundary between nonhuman and human animals. The question

---

[49] On this division in particular, see King (2008), esp. 53–55.

[50] Consequently, also humans were classified as animals; see Toivanen (2017).

was where sensory cognition or perception ends and intellective cognition begins.[51] Theoretically, the dividing line was relatively clear: intellect and reason are responsible for complex operations such as reasoning and thinking, whereas the external and internal senses produce a number of activities from sight to memory. As regards the external senses, many ancient and medieval thinkers, on the one hand, acknowledged the qualitative superiority of nonhuman animals: "eagles and lynxes see much clearer, vultures smell more sharply, the monkey has a finer sense of taste, the spider a faster sense of touch; the mole and the wild boar hear much clearer," as a common proverb put it.[52] On the other hand, they were aware of certain differences in quantity: not all animals possess each of the five external senses and some of them, such as oysters, have only the most basic sense, touch, which is why they only slightly exceed plants.[53]

The differentiation regarding the quality and the quantity of the senses does not only apply to the external but also to the internal senses. Flies, for instance, lack the faculty of memory, as Albert the Great remarks (see Chaps. 7 and 8). This is clear from the fact that they keep coming back after they have been driven away (the idea here is that they would not do this unless they were incapable of remembering the pain of the blow).[54] Bees and cranes, by contrast, are particularly strong with respect to memory as they often travel over long distances without losing memory of their home, according to Albert (see Chap. 7).[55] Whether an animal possesses good memory, bad memory, or no memory at all is a question of physiology, Albert argues. More precisely, it depends on its bodily mixture or composition. If the sense organs are particularly cold and watery or earthen, they cannot transport and retain the forms of what has been perceived.[56] Yet, a perfect animal, that is, an animal which has all external and internal senses has the following cognitive capacities. The sheep, for instance, can see, hear, and smell the wolf, and although this is unlikely to happen it could potentially also taste and touch it. Furthermore, by virtue of its internal senses (common sense, imagination, estimation, and memory) it can bundle all the information from the external senses to what was called a 'phantasm' (*phantasma*), store it, and evaluate it (see Chap. 12). Thus, it possesses cognition also in the modern sense of the term since cognitive capacities are commonly defined as "mechanisms by which animals acquire, process, store, and act on information from the environment".[57]

---

[51] A number of medieval answers to this question is summarised by Toivanen (2019).

[52] Thomas of Cantimpré, *Liber de natura rerum* IV.1, ed. Boese (1973), 106. On ancient versions, see Sorabji (1993), 15f.

[53] See Thomas Aquinas, *Summa contra gentiles*, b. II, ch. 68, ed. Leonina XIII (1918), 440. On touch as sense that is common to animals, see also Chap. 20.

[54] See Albert the Great, *Metaphysica*, b. I, tr. 1, ch. 6, ed. Geyer (1960), 8f.; *De animalibus*, b. XXI, tr. 1, ch. 1, §9, ed. Stadler (1920), 1326.

[55] See Albert the Great, *Metaphysica*, b. I, tr. 1, ch. 6, ed. Geyer (1960), 9.

[56] Ibid., 8. The background of this argument is the Aristotelian theory of elements (fire, air, earth, water) and qualities (dry, wet, hot, cold); see also Chap. 12.

[57] Shettleworth (2010), 4.

With regard to the medieval definition of cognition, the decisive question, however, is whether the acquisition and processing of information also involve more complex operations: Do animals learn? Can they generalise, categorise, and conceptualise? Do they know to plan for the future? Do they judge and deliberate? Can they communicate by language? Are they capable of reasoning and thinking? Since many of these processes were taken to require an immaterial soul, the straightforward medieval answer seems to be no. Yet, as the texts on cognition in this volume show, this answer was not given by everybody. Instead, many thinkers set out to scrutinise the range of nonhuman animal cognition. So, even though it was rather undisputed *whether* such animals have any cognition at all, the question of *how far* their cognition goes remained – and despite empirical testing still remains – a matter of debate.[58]

## Emotion

As human beings we are used to having not only a cognitive but also an emotional life. For instance, when we encounter a wolf in the wild chances are high that we run away. And when we are asked why we ran away we will possibly answer that it was because of our fear of the wolf. In other words, we do not simply perceive our environment but also evaluate our cognitive contents in an emotional way, and in many situations our emotions drive our behaviour. When this behaviour resembles the behaviour of a nonhuman animal in a similar situation the question arises of whether that animal is driven by an emotion, as well. Does the sheep also flee because it is afraid of the wolf? In contemporary science, this question can be answered by measuring the level of certain hormones such as cortisol.[59] In humans, the cortisol level is high whenever they experience stress. By the argument from analogy and the principle of evolutionary continuity (see the section "A day at the zoo or a contemporary point of view") contemporary researchers conclude that this is the same in many nonhuman animals.[60] But what about the views of medieval thinkers on this subject? They did not have the means of investigating hormone levels, for example, and so one might think that they refrained from ascribing emotions to other animals. However, a closer look reveals that the opposite is true.

In medieval psychology, emotions – or '*passiones*', as they are called in Latin – were seen as an activity integral to the sensitive-appetitive part of the soul (see Table 1.1).[61] Since nonhuman animals were taken to possess sensation and appetitive powers medieval thinkers did not hesitate to grant them a variety of

---

[58] On the spectrum of the contemporary debate, see the references in note 13.

[59] On this method, see, for instance, Paul et al. (2005).

[60] See Bekoff (2007), esp. 36f; Watanabe and Kuczaj (2013).

[61] For an overview of emotions in medieval psychology, see Knuuttila (2002) and (2004); Perler (2018). The articles in Landweer and Renz (2008) also cover other periods.

emotions – from fear (see Chap. 16) to enjoyment or pleasure (see Chaps. 18 and 20). In the thirteenth century, in particular, they began to systematise the spectrum of emotions (see Chap. 17).[62] This systematisation led to a more critical approach to animal emotions, particularly with regard to two questions. The first question concerns the possibility of rational control.[63] Imagine, once again, that you encounter a wolf in the wild. As said before, your first reaction is likely to be flight. Yet, if an expert for wolves tells you that wolves are much more afraid of humans than the other way around it might happen that you begin to change your attitude towards wolves. The next time you see a wolf the rate of your heartbeat might still increase and you might still be fearful but you might not necessarily show the immediate reaction of flight since you have learned to rationally control your emotions. The knowledge of the harmlessness of wolves for humans causes a change in your behaviour. The same occurs when people see a wolf in the zoo. They will not run away frightened because they know that the wolf cannot escape its compound and harm them. But is this option of rationally controlling emotions also available to a sheep?[64] If rational control requires the faculty of reason and if the sheep lacks this faculty it seems that it is also incapable of controlling its emotions. Hence, even if human and nonhuman animals share certain feelings, such as fear, it is possible that there is a difference with respect to the exposure to such feelings.

A second question is whether nonhuman animals possess the entire range of human emotions. This question becomes particularly relevant with regard to feelings that might require cognitive operations on a higher level. For Thomas Aquinas hope is an emotion of this kind (see Chap. 19). On the one hand, nonhuman animals seem to be capable of hoping for something. A hound, for instance, would not chase a hare unless it had the hope of catching it, Aquinas argues.[65] On the other hand, hope is a complex emotion insofar as it involves the cognition of future states. The successful catch of the hare is something that lies in the future. Therefore, the hope for this event to occur seems to require foresight and some notion of the future and whether nonhuman animals possess these cognitive capacities was controversial in the Middle Ages (see, for instance, Chap. 11). In any case, it is interesting to see that medieval thinkers were aware of what could be called the dual nature of emotions. They are evidently somatic because they usually come along with bodily changes, such as a quickened pulse, horripilation, or transpiration. In addition, they are mental in the two senses described above: in some cases one can try to mentally penetrate emotions; in other cases emotions might require mental representations of events. The problem with this ambiguous character is that it seems to be incompatible with the classification of emotions as belonging to the sensitive part of the soul. But that is the reason why animal emotions were such an interesting case to discuss for medieval thinkers: they helped to determine *whether* there is something specifically human in the emotional experience of the world, and if so, *what* it is.

---

[62] On the systematisation of the passions, see Lagerlund (2019).

[63] See Perler (2017) and (2018), esp. 64f.

[64] On some medieval answers, see Perler (2012).

[65] See Thomas Aquinas, *Summa theologiae* I-II, q. 13, a. 2, Editio Leonina VI (1891), 267.

## *Volition*

In comparison to cognition and emotion, volition is the most controversial aspect. With regard to the medieval classification of psychological activities (see Table 1.1), it clearly belongs to the intellective part of the soul. As long as one denies intellective powers to nonhuman animals one cannot coherently grant them a will without making substantial changes to the psychological taxonomy. Traditionally, the faculty of the will was taken to be rational since what is done wilfully seems to originate from deliberation. Whenever we really will something, we have literally made up our minds, and in most cases we can give reasons for why we wanted this rather than that. This is not to say that our reasons are always good reasons or that there is only one influence instead of a variety of influences (intellectual, emotional etc.) on our decision-making. However, in order to be wilful it is crucial for a behaviour to not simply derive from natural impulse or instinct. This is why discussions of the will are naturally intertwined with debates over the freedom of the will and the freedom of choice.[66] (If one wonders why the *freedom* of will and choice matter, the most straightforward philosophical answer is that one can only be morally responsible for one's actions, hence praiseworthy or blameworthy, if one *freely* engaged in them.[67])

Now since natural instinct – which is the opposite of free will and deliberation (see Chap. 23) – plays a pivotal role in medieval explanations of animal behaviour and since the will is evidently classified as rational, one might assume that medieval psychology leaves no room for animal volition. Yet, as most texts on the topic in this volume show, this assumption falls short of covering the entire discussion. Although it is correct that the faculty of the will was commonly denied to nonhuman animals one must not ignore that there was a lively debate over whether it is plausible to claim that nonhuman animal behaviour is neither free nor wilful.[68] In the later Middle Ages, this debate was stimulated by a number of factors, two of which are particularly relevant for the texts translated in this volume.

First, in his *Nicomachean Ethics*, Aristotle says that "children and brutes participate in the voluntary," as Thomas Aquinas puts it (see Chap. 25).[69] This statement requires careful exegesis because it needs to be spelled out what the voluntary (*voluntarium*) is and how it relates to the will (*voluntas*) and free choice (*liberum arbitrium*). Aquinas argues that behaviour can be voluntary without being wilful and free. Declaredly, this looks like a typical scholastic play of words, but what Aquinas

---

[66] The history of this debate is almost impossible to cover. For a brief overview of the medieval discussion, see Korolec (1982). On the contemporary debate, see Kane (2002).

[67] The question of whether nonhuman animals can be moral agents is highly relevant in the field of animal ethics, which is not specifically addressed in this volume. For an overview of some medieval positions, see Oelze (2018b). Chap. 2 also touches the issue.

[68] See, for instance, Nitschke (1967) and Frampton (2008).

[69] Thomas Aquinas, *Quaestiones disputatae de veritate*, q. 24, a. 2, Editio Leonina XXII.3.1 (1973), 684. His question refers to Aristotle, *Ethica Nicomachea* III.4, 1111b8f.

has in mind is the necessity of distinguishing between humans and nonhuman animals, on the one hand, and between animals and 'non-animals' (i.e. plants and non-living beings), on the other hand. A stone, for instance, can move from one place to another. However, it seems absurd to claim that stones move because they *want* to move. Rather, a stone is moved, for example, by the current in a stream or by a hand that throws it. In other words, the motion of a non-living being such as a stone is no *self*-motion. Animals, by contrast, obviously move themselves and they cannot always be moved only by the force or the will of something or somebody else (as pet owners know). Still, the question is *what* sets them in motion. Is it really the will or some sort of will?[70]

This question leads to the second factor that motivated medieval thinkers to address the topic of animal volition, namely, the observation that animal behaviour often looks as if it were intentional and wilful. In his *Sentences* commentary (see Chap. 22), Bonaventure refers to the example of the sheep. Its reaction of flight from the wolf shows that it is capable of rejecting what is bad and of choosing what is good for it, he argues.[71] In his view, this is exactly what the freedom of the will is about: the decision for the good rather than the bad (since this is, apparently, the most rational option).[72] One could object that even though the sheep does something good by fleeing the wolf it does not do this wilfully. Its reaction of flight is an instinctual response and thus it could not *not* run away when perceiving a wolf. This is a powerful objection indeed, but Bonaventure points out that there are also more complex cases of animal behaviour in which animals show different reactions to like stimuli (he does not give an example but one could imagine a horse that sometimes comes and sometimes does not come when we stand at the gate).[73] This kind of behaviour seems to suggest that the animal is not necessarily (or not always) subject to natural impulses but sometimes (if not always) *free* to do what it wants.

The freedom of the will, however, consists in the ability to freely decide what one wants to do, which is why medieval thinkers used to discuss animal volition in conjunction with the freedom of the will and the freedom of choice. While the former was seen as a faculty separate from intellect and reason, the latter was taken to be a capacity arising from the cooperation of these faculties (see Chaps. 21 and 22). The obvious difficulty now was to account for the behaviour of animals without jeopardising the rational nature of the will. As the texts show, the most common strategy for handling this difficulty was to deny free will and free choice to nonhuman animals.[74] Since the will and the faculties of intellect and reason are synonymous with the mind in the strict sense of the term, the medieval answer to the

---

[70] On Aristotle's answer which was adopted by various medieval thinkers, see Corcilius (2008).

[71] See Bonaventure, *Commentaria in quatuor libros sententiarum magistri Petri Lombardi. In secundum librum sententiarum*, d. 25, un. ar., q. 1, (1885), 592.

[72] Since antiquity there was also a debate about those cases in which people obviously choose a bad option; see the comprehensive study by Müller (2009).

[73] See ibid.

[74] It is important to note, however, that not all of them denied the faculty of will to nonhuman animals; see, for instance, Chap. 3.

question of whether nonhuman animals possess minds would have been a resonant no. But does this mean that medieval philosophers were mindless of the mental life of other animals? To this question the answer is also no because they clearly acknowledged that humans and other animals share a variety of psychological activities which, nowadays, are the subject of the philosophy of animal minds. Therefore, the texts in this volume can be read as a medieval contribution to this discipline.

## Note on the Texts and Translations

This book presents twenty-four texts on animal cognition, emotion, and volition. The order of the texts within each section is chronological. This arrangement might be particularly insightful for those interested in the historical continuities and discontinuities as well as in the history of ideas and concepts. To give an example: the idea that animals have a so-called estimative power, by virtue of which they can evaluate the meaning of an object, was introduced to the Latin West by the translations of Arabic texts on psychology (see the section "Animals and minds in medieval philosophy"). It can be interesting to see how this idea shaped the views of Latin authors working roughly after the turn from the twelfth to the thirteenth century, especially when one compares them with texts from earlier periods (e.g. the texts in Chaps. 2 and 3). However, all of the texts can also be read on their own and without paying peculiar attention to the historical developments. Readers who are unfamiliar with the life and works of the authors, the historical context, and the terminology of (medieval) philosophy might find it helpful to take a look at the introductions to and annotations of each text.[75] In addition, a glossary at the end of the volume explains a number of philosophical and psychological terms that frequently occur in most of the texts.

The selection of texts covers only part of the spectrum of contributions to the field. Yet, the main problem with picking texts for a sourcebook on medieval philosophy of animal minds is that this discipline was not a discipline in its own right. For this reason, there is not a single treatise on the subject. Instead, one has to browse various texts on different topics and identify those passages concerning the cognitive, emotional, or volitional life of nonhuman animals. In many cases, these passages only consist of a few phrases and require considerable knowledge of the context. But since the aim of this sourcebook is to make medieval philosophy of animal minds accessible to both experts and non-specialists, a crucial criterion of selection was that texts are neither too short nor too esoteric.[76] Readers who have never studied any medieval and/or philosophical text before will certainly find that

---

[75] Note that information on the life and work of an author is only found in the *first* text of that author in the volume.

[76] Shortness is the main reason why certain major figures such as William Ockham and John Buridan are missing in this volume. Quite often their remarks on animal minds cover only less than a paragraph. However, their positions are portrayed by Oelze (2018a).

many texts do not meet the latter criterion. However, they will hopefully profit from reading the introductions, the annotations, and the glossary as well as the bibliography that comes with each text. It contains the relevant secondary literature plus some material that might help readers to grasp the meaning of specific concepts. Readers who want to compare the English translation to the Latin text find the necessary references in the bibliographical information before each text. The majority of texts is available in modern critical editions. However, there are two exceptions to this rule, namely, the texts in Chaps. 9 and 20. So far, they only exist in medieval manuscripts and/or early prints. Therefore, transcriptions of the Latin have been included in this volume.

The medieval philosophical terminology is undoubtedly challenging for readers. But it is also a challenge for translators. Anyone trying to translate medieval Latin terms into modern English faces the dilemma of presenting a version of the text that, in comparison to the original, is either too anachronistic or too literal. One might argue that finding a way out of this dilemma is the very task of translators. This is certainly true. Nevertheless, the dilemma remains, and every translator has to take up a stance on this problem. I myself have decided to favour a more literal translation over a translation that is closer to modern language, both in syntax and semantics. I am fully aware of the objections that can be raised against this kind of translation. If the worst comes to the worst one might say that the translator has missed his vocation. However, I have done so for a reason: philosophical texts are a special type of texts. In most cases they cannot be read without thoroughly discussing the terms they contain. Quite often, this discussion quickly turns from a *philosophical* into a *philological* debate, which is why it is hardly surprising that some have claimed that problems of philosophy are essentially problems of language. Be that as it may, I found it more constructive to translate the medieval texts in such a way that they do not sound more familiar in the end than they actually are. Unfortunately, this decision increases the number of terms and phrases that are in need of explanation. However, the search for explanations might create a fruitful starting point for identifying differences and similarities between the medieval views and our very own – and this is the main aim of this book.

# Bibliography

## *Primary Sources*

Albert the Great. (1916–1920). *De animalibus libri XXVI* (H. Stadler, Ed.). 2 vols. Münster: Aschendorff.
Albert the Great. (1960). *Metaphysica: Libri quinque priores* (B. Geyer, Ed.) (*Opera omnia* 16/1). Münster: Aschendorff.
Aristotle. (1894). *Ethica Nicomachea* (I. Bywater, Ed.). Oxford: Clarendon Press.
Aristotle. (1957). *Politica* (W. D. Ross, Ed.). Oxford: Clarendon Press.
Aristotle. (1961). *De anima* (W. D. Ross, Ed.). Oxford: Clarendon Press.

Aristotle. (1968). *Parts of animals* (A. L. Peck, Ed. and Trans.). Cambridge, MA/London: Harvard University Press.

Augustine. (1968). *De trinitate libri XV (Libri I–XII)* (*Opera* 16/1 = CCSL 50) (W. J. Mountain, Ed.). Turnhout: Brepols.

Augustine. (1970). *De libero arbitrio* (*Opera* II.2 = CCSL 29) (W. Green, Ed.). Turnhout: Brepols.

Augustine. (1986). *De quantitate animae* (*Opera omnia* I.IV = CSEL 89) (W. Hörmann, Ed.). Wien: Hoelder-Pichler-Tempsky.

Avicenna Latinus. (1968). *Liber de anima seu sextus de naturalibus IV-V* (S. van Riet, Ed.). Louvain: Peeters/Leiden: Brill.

Avicenna Latinus. (1972). *Liber de anima seu sextus de naturalibus I-II-III* (S. van Riet, Ed.). Louvain: Peeters/Leiden: Brill.

Bonaventure. (1885). *Commentaria in quatuor libros Sententiarum magistri Petri Lombardi: In secundum librum Sententiarum* (*Opera omnia* 2). Quaracchi: Collegium S. Bonaventurae.

Marin Cureau de la Chambre. (1648). *Traité de la connoissance des animaux, où tout ce qui a esté dict pour & contre le raisonnement des betes est examiné.* Paris 1648.

Peter of Spain. (2015). *Questiones super libro 'De Animalibus' Aristotelis: Critical edition with introduction* (F. Navarro Sánchez, Ed.). London/New York: Routledge.

Pseudo-Peter of Spain. *Commentum super libros de animalibus* (Venetian redaction). Venice, Biblioteca Nazionale Marciana, Lat. VI, 234, fol. 1ra-303vb.

Roger Bacon. (1996). *Roger Bacon and the origins of* Perspectiva *in the middle ages: A critical edition and English translation of Bacon's* Perspectiva *with introduction and notes* (D. C. Lindberg, Ed. and Trans.). Oxford: Clarendon Press.

Thomas Aquinas. (1891). *Prima secundae Summae theologiae, qq. 1–70* (*Opera omnia* 6). Rome.

Thomas Aquinas. (1903). *Tertia pars Summae theologiae, qq. 1–59* (*Opera omnia* 11). Rome.

Thomas Aquinas. (1918). *Summa contra gentiles, lib. I–II* (*Opera omnia* 13). Rome.

Thomas Aquinas. (1973). *Quaestiones disputatae de veritate, qq. 21–29* (*Opera omnia* 22.3.1). Rome.

Thomas of Cantimpré. (1973). *Liber de natura rerum* (H. Boese, Ed.). Berlin: Walter de Gruyter.

## Secondary Sources

Allen, C., & Bekoff, M. (1997). *Species of mind: The philosophy and biology of cognitive ethology.* Cambridge, MA: MIT Press.

Amerini, F. (2011). Intentionality. In H. Lagerlund (Ed.), *Encyclopedia of medieval philosophy: Philosophy between 500 and 1500* (Vol. 1, pp. 558–564). Springer, Dordrecht et al.

Andrews, K. (2015). *The animal mind: An introduction to the philosophy of animal cognition.* Abingdon/New York: Routledge.

Andrews, K., & Beck, J. (2017). *The Routledge handbook of philosophy of animal minds.* Abingdon/New York: Routledge.

Bekoff, M. (2007). *The emotional lives of animals: A leading scientist explores animal joy, sorrow, and empathy – and why they matter.* Novato: New World Library.

Bekoff, M., Allen, C., & Burghardt, G. M. (Eds.). (2002). *The cognitive animal: Empirical and theoretical perspectives on animal cognition.* Cambridge, MA/London: MIT Press.

Black, D. L. (2009). The nature of intellect. In R. Pasnau (Ed.), *The Cambridge history of medieval philosophy* (Vol. 1, pp. 320–333). Cambridge: Cambridge University Press.

Brachtendorf, J. (2010). Mens. In C. Mayer (Ed.), *Augustinus-Lexikon* (Vol. 3, Fasc. 7/8, pp. 1270–1280). Basel: Schwabe.

Brittain, C. (2002). Non-rational perception in the Stoics and Augustine. *Oxford Studies in Ancient Philosophy, XXII,* 253–308.

Buchenau, S., & Lo Presti, R. (Eds.). (2017). *Human and animal cognition in early modern philosophy and medicine.* Pittsburgh: University of Pittsburgh Press.

Cheung, T. (Ed.). (2010). *Transitions and borders between animals, humans and machines 1600–1800.* Leiden: Brill.

Clark, G. (1998). The fathers and the animals: The rule of reason? In A. Linzey & D. Yamamoto (Eds.), *Animals on the agenda: Questions about animals for theology and ethics* (pp. 67–79). London: SCM Press.

Corcilius, K. (2008). *Streben und Bewegen: Aristoteles' Theorie der animalischen Ortsbewegung.* Berlin: Walter de Gruyter.

Crane, T. (1998). Intentionality. In E. Craig (Ed.), *Routledge encyclopedia of philosophy* (Vol. 4, pp. 816–821). London: Routledge.

Crist, E. (1999). *Images of animals: Anthropomorphism and animal mind.* Philadelphia: Temple University Press.

Darwin, C. R. (1872). *The expression of the emotions in man and animals.* London: Murray.

Daston, L., & Mitman, G. (Eds.). (2005). *Thinking with animals: New perspectives on anthropomorphism.* New York: Columbia University Press.

de Asúa, M. (1991). *The organization of discourse on animals in the thirteenth century: Peter of Spain, Albert the Great, and the commentaries on* 'De animalibus'. PhD Diss. Notre Dame, Ann Arbor.

de Asúa, M. (1997). Peter of Spain, Albert the Great, and the *Quaestiones de animalibus. Physis, 34,* 1–30.

de Asúa, M. (1999). Medicine and philosophy in Peter of Spain's commentary on *De animalibus.* In C. G. Steel, G. Guldentops, & P. Beullens (Eds.), *Aristotle's animals in the middle ages and renaissance* (pp. 189–211). Leuven: Leuven University Press.

De Leemans, P., & Klemm, M. (2007). Animals and anthropology in medieval philosophy. In B. Resl (Ed.), *A cultural history of animals in the medieval age* (pp. 153–177). Oxford/New York: Berg.

De Waal, F. B. M. (1999). Anthropomorphism and anthropodenial: Consistency in our thinking about humans and other animals. *Philosophical Topics, 27*(1), 255–280.

Dierauer, U. (1977). *Tier und Mensch im Denken der Antike: Studien zur Tierpsychologie, Anthropologie und Ethik.* Amsterdam: Grüner.

Dod, B. G. (1982). Aristoteles Latinus. In N. Kretzmann, A. Kenny, & J. Pinborg (Eds.), *The Cambridge history of later medieval philosophy: From the rediscovery of Aristotle to the disintegration of scholasticism 1100–1600* (pp. 43–79). Cambridge: Cambridge University Press.

Frampton, M. (2008). *Embodiments of will: Anatomical and physiological theories of voluntary animal motion from Greek antiquity to the Latin middle ages, 400 B.C.–A.D. 1300.* Saarbrücken: VDM Verlag Dr. Müller.

Griffin, D. R. (2001). *Animal minds: Beyond cognition to consciousness.* Chicago/London: University of Chicago Press.

Hanus, D., Mendes, N., Tennie, C., & Call, J. (2011). Comparing the performances of apes (*Gorilla gorilla, Pan troglodytes, Pongo pygmaeus*) and human children (*Homo sapiens*) in the floating peanut task. *PLoS One, 6*(6), 1–13.

Hasse, D. N. (2000). *Avicenna's De anima in the Latin west: The formation of a Peripatetic philosophy of the soul 1160–1300.* London/Turin: The Warburg Institute-Nino Aragno Editore.

Hasse, D. N. (2010). The soul's faculties. In R. Pasnau (Ed.), *The Cambridge history of medieval philosophy* (Vol. 1, pp. 305–319). Cambridge: Cambridge University Press.

Heller-Roazen, D. (2007). *The inner touch: Archaeology of a sensation.* New York: Zone Books.

Hurley, S. L., & Nudds, M. (Eds.). (2006). *Rational animals?* Oxford: Oxford University Press.

Kane, R. (2002). Introduction: The contours of contemporary free will debates. In id. (Ed.), *The Oxford handbook of free will* (pp. 3–41). Oxford/New York: Oxford University Press.

Kaukua, J. (2014). Avicenna on the soul's activity in perception. In J. F. Silva & M. Yrjönsuuri (Eds.), *Active perception in the history of philosophy* (pp. 99–116). Cham et al.: Springer.

Kenny, A., & Pinborg, J. (1982). Medieval philosophical literature. In N. Kretzmann, A. Kenny, & J. Pinborg (Eds.), *The Cambridge history of later medieval philosophy: From the rediscovery of Aristotle to the disintegration of scholasticism 1100–1600* (pp. 9–42). Cambridge: Cambridge University Press.

King, P. (2008). The inner cathedral: Mental architecture in high scholasticism. *Vivarium, 46*(3), 253–274.

King, P. (2012). Emotions. In B. Davies & E. Stump (Eds.), *The Oxford handbook to Aquinas* (pp. 209–226). Oxford: Oxford University Press.

Knuuttila, S. (2002). Medieval theories of the passions of the soul. In H. Lagerlund & M. Yrjönsuuri (Eds.), *Emotions and choice from Boethius to Descartes* (pp. 49–83). Dordrecht/Boston/London: Kluwer Academic Publishers.

Knuuttila, S. (2004). *Emotions in ancient and medieval philosophy*. Oxford: Clarendon Press.

Köhler, T. W. (2000). *Grundlagen des philosophisch-anthropologischen Diskurses im dreizehnten Jahrhundert: Die Erkenntnisbemühung um den Menschen im zeitgenössischen Verständnis.* Leiden/Boston/Köln: Brill.

Köhler, T. W. (2008). *Homo animal nobilissimum: Konturen des spezifisch Menschlichen in der naturphilosophischen Aristoteleskommentierung des dreizehnten Jahrhunderts. Teilband 1.* Leiden/Boston: Brill.

Köhler, T. W. (2014). *Homo animal nobilissimum: Konturen des spezifisch Menschlichen in der naturphilosophischen Aristoteleskommentierung des dreizehnten Jahrhunderts. Teilband 2.1 und 2.2.* 2 vols. Leiden/Boston: Brill.

Korolec, J. B. (1982). Free will and free choice. In A. Kenny, E. Stump, J. Pinborg, & N. Kretzmann (Eds.), *The Cambridge history of later medieval philosophy: From the rediscovery of Aristotle to the disintegration of scholasticism 1100–1600* (pp. 629–641).

Kuksewicz, Z. (1982). Criticisms of Aristotelian psychology and the Augustinian–Aristotelian synthesis. In N. Kretzmann, A. Kenny, & J. Pinborg (Eds.), *The Cambridge history of later medieval philosophy: From the rediscovery of Aristotle to the disintegration of scholasticism 1100–1600* (pp. 623–641). Cambridge: Cambridge University Press.

Lagerlund, H. (2019). The systematization of the passions in the thirteenth century. In M. Cameron (Ed.), *Philosophy of mind in the early and high middle ages* (pp. 157–177). London/New York: Routledge.

Landweer, H., & Renz, U. (Eds.). (2008). *Klassische Emotionstheorien der Philosophiegeschichte.* Berlin: Walter de Gruyter.

Lohr, C. H. (1982). The medieval interpretation of Aristotle. In N. Kretzmann, A. Kenny, & J. Pinborg (Eds.), *The Cambridge history of later medieval philosophy: From the rediscovery of Aristotle to the disintegration of scholasticism 1100–1600* (pp. 80–98). Cambridge: Cambridge University Press.

Lurz, R. W. (Ed.). (2009). *The philosophy of animal minds.* Cambridge: Cambridge University Press.

Matthews, G. B. (1999). Augustine and Descartes on the souls of animals. In M. J. C. Crabbe (Ed.), *From soul to self* (pp. 89–107). London: Routledge.

Mendes, N., Hanus, D., & Call, J. (2007). Raising the level: Orangutans use water as a tool. *Biology Letters, 3*(5), 453–455.

Menzel, R., & Fischer, J. (2011). Animal thinking: An introduction. In idd. (Eds.), *Animal thinking: Contemporary issues in comparative cognition* (pp. 1–6). Cambridge, MA: MIT Press.

Mousavian, S. N., & Fink, J. L. (Eds.). (2020). *The internal senses in the Aristotelian tradition.* Cham et al.: Springer.

Müller, J. (2009). *Willensschwäche in Antike und Mittelalter: Eine Problemgeschichte von Sokrates bis Johannes Duns Scotus.* Leuven: Leuven University Press.

Muratori, C. (Ed.). (2013). *The animal soul and the human mind: Renaissance debates.* Pisa/Rome: Serra.

Newmyer, S. T. (2011). *Animals in Greek and Roman thought: A sourcebook.* Abingdon/New York: Routledge.

Nitschke, A. (1967). Verhalten und Bewegung der Tiere nach frühen christlichen Lehren. *Studium Generale. Zeitschrift für interdisziplinäre Studien, 4*(20), 235–262.

O'Daly, G. J. P. (1987). *Augustine's philosophy of mind.* Berkeley/Los Angeles: University of California Press.

Oelze, A. (2018a). *Animal rationality: Later medieval theories 1250–1350.* Leiden/Boston: Brill.

Oelze, A. (2018b). Geschichte der Tierethik: Mittelalter. In J. S. Ach & D. Borchers (Eds.), *Handbuch Tierethik. Grundlagen – Kontexte –Perspektiven* (pp. 9–13). Stuttgart: Metzler.

Overgaard, S. (2015). The unobservability thesis. *Synthese, 194*(3), 1–18.

Paul, E. S., Harding, E. J., & Mendl, M. (2005). Measuring emotional processes in animals: The utility of a cognitive approach. *Neuroscience & Biobehavioral Reviews, 29*(3), 469–491.

Perler, D. (2006). Intentionality and action: Medieval discussions on the cognitive capacities of animals. In M. C. Pacheco & J. F. Meirinhos (Eds.), *Intellect et imagination dans la Philosophie Médiévale* (Vol. 1, pp. 72–98). Turnhout: Brepols.

Perler, D. (2012). Why is the sheep afraid of the wolf? Medieval debates on animal passions. In M. Pickavé & L. Shapiro (Eds.), *Emotion and cognitive life in medieval and early modern philosophy* (pp. 32–52). Oxford: Oxford University Press.

Perler, D. (2017). Emotions and rational control: Two medieval perspectives. In A. Cohen & R. Stern (Eds.), *Thinking about the emotions: A philosophical history* (pp. 60–82). Oxford: Oxford University Press.

Perler, D. (2018). *Feelings transformed: Philosophical theories of the emotions, 1270–1670* (T. Crawford, Trans.). Oxford/New York: Oxford University Press.

Perler, D., & Wild, M. (Eds.). (2005). *Der Geist der Tiere: Philosophische Texte zu einer aktuellen Diskussion*. Suhrkamp: Frankfurt am Main.

Piro, F. (2005). Animalité et connaissance animale: Notes sur la doctrine de l'estimative et sur ses interprétations en Occident. In T. Gontier (Ed.), *Animal et animalité dans la philosophie de la Renaissance et de l'Âge Classique* (pp. 131–151). Leuven: Peeters.

Resl, B. (Ed.). (2007). *A cultural history of animals in the medieval age*. Oxford/New York: Berg.

Romanes, G. J. (1882). *Animal intelligence*. London: Kegan Paul, Trench, & Co.

Romanes, G. J. (1883). *Mental evolution in animals*. London: Kegan Paul, Trench, & Co.

Salisbury, J. E. (2011). *The beast within: Animals in the middle ages* (2nd ed.). New York/London: Routledge.

Shettleworth, S. J. (2010). *Cognition, evolution, and behavior* (2nd ed.). Oxford University Press.

Silva, J. F. (2016). Self-awareness and perception in late medieval epistemology. In J. Kaukua & T. Ekenberg (Eds.), *Subjectivity and selfhood in medieval and early modern philosophy* (pp. 157–179). Dordrecht: Springer.

Sober, E. (2000). Evolution and the problem of other minds. *The Journal of Philosophy, 97*(7), 365–386.

Sober, E. (2005). Comparative psychology meets evolutionary biology: Morgan's Canon and cladistic parsimony. In G. Mitman & L. Daston (Eds.), *Thinking with animals: New perspectives on anthropomorphism* (pp. 85–99). New York: Columbia University Press.

Sorabji, R. (1993). *Animal minds and human morals: The origins of the western debate*. London: Duckworth.

Toivanen, J. (2013). Perceptual self-awareness in Seneca, Augustine, and Olivi. *Journal of the History of Philosophy, 51*(3), 355–382.

Toivanen, J. (2017). Entre la raison et la perception: La psychologie animale médiévale et la relation entre les humains et les animaux. In M. Cutino, I. Iribarren, & F. Vinel (Eds.), *La restauration de la création* (pp. 275–297). Leiden/Boston: Brill.

Toivanen, J. (2018). Marking the boundaries: Animals in medieval Latin philosophy. In G. F. Edwards & P. Adamson (Eds.), *Animals: A history* (pp. 121–150). Oxford: Oxford University Press.

Toivanen, J. (2019). Perceptual experience: Assembling a medieval puzzle. In M. Cameron (Ed.), *Philosophy of mind in the early and high middle ages* (pp. 134–156). London/New York: Routledge.

Tomasello, M. (2014). *A natural history of human thinking*. Cambridge, MA/London: Harvard University Press.

Van Engen, J. H. (2000). *Learning institutionalized: Teaching in the medieval university*. Notre Dame: University of Notre Dame Press.

Wasserman, E. A., & Zentall, T. R. (2006). Comparative cognition: A natural science approach to the study of animal intelligence. In idd. (Eds.), *Comparative cognition: Experimental explorations of animal intelligence* (pp. 3–11). Oxford/New York: Oxford University Press.

Watanabe, S., & Kuczaj, S. A. (Eds.). (2013). *Emotions of animals and humans: Comparative perspectives*. Tokyo: Springer.

Wei, I. P. (2020). *Thinking about animals in thirteenth-century Paris: Theologians on the boundary between humans and animals*. Cambridge: Cambridge University Press.

Wild, M. (2006). *Die anthropologische Differenz: Der Geist der Tiere in der frühen Neuzeit bei Montaigne, Descartes und Hume*. Berlin: Walter de Gruyter.

Wild, M. (2013). *Tierphilosophie zur Einführung* (3rd corr. Ed.). Hamburg: Junius.

Wolfson, H. A. (1935). The internal senses in Latin, Arabic, and Hebrew philosophic texts. *The Harvard Theological Review, 28*(2), 69–133.

Wöller, F. (2016). Doing theology at the medieval university. *Ghana Bulletin of Theology. New Series*, 37–52.

Wynne, C. D. L. (2007). What are animals? Why anthropomorphism is still not a scientific approach to behavior. *Comparative Cognition & Behavior Reviews, 2*, 125–135.

# Part I
# Cognition

# Chapter 2
# Perception, Knowledge, Reason, and Mind (Augustine, *De quantitate animae*, Chapters 25–28)

**Abstract** In *On the Magnitude of the Soul*, written around AD 388, Augustine and his interlocutor Evodius discuss the nature of the soul. At a certain point they try to come up with a definition of sensory perception (*sensus*). However, they realise that in order to arrive at a consistent definition a number of qualifications need to be made. One of these qualifications concerns the relation between sensory perception and knowledge (*scientia*). On the one hand, various examples seem to show that animals have knowledge. On the other hand, knowledge seems to require reason (*ratio*), that is, a mental power usually reserved for rational beings such as humans or angels. Therefore, Augustine and Evodius engage in a lively discussion of human and animal cognition and finally agree on a number of points that were to remain influential throughout the entire medieval debate.

## Introduction

Augustine, or Aurelius Augustinus Hipponensis, as he is known in Latin, is certainly one of the most famous and influential medieval thinkers. Born in AD 354 in Thagaste, a small town in today's Algeria (which then belonged to Roman Africa), he went to the city of Carthage in what is now Tunisia to study rhetorics at the age of seventeen.[1] After that he taught this subject in Carthage, Rome, and Milan. Although his mother was a devoted Christian, Augustine followed the religious movement of the Manichaeans for many years and converted to Christianity only at the age of thirty-one. The conversion marks the beginning of his career as a successful cleric, on the one hand (he was Bishop of Hippo from 396 until his death in 430), and as a prolific writer on theology and philosophy, on the other (he produced more than hundred works many of which, such as the *Confessions*, *On the Trinity*, or *The City of God*, are amongst the most important writings in the history of Christianity).

---

[1] On his life, see, for instance, Brown (2000) and O'Donnell (2005).

© The Author(s), under exclusive license to Springer Nature
Switzerland AG 2021
A. Oelze, *Animal Minds in Medieval Latin Philosophy*, Studies in the History of
Philosophy of Mind 27, https://doi.org/10.1007/978-3-030-67012-2_2

In several of his works, the concept of mind plays a crucial role.[2] For instance, with regard to the problem of the trinity, Augustine argues that the divine persons – Father, Son, and Holy Spirit – are one God just as the three faculties of the soul – memory (*memoria*), understanding (*intelligentia*), and will (*voluntas*) – are one mind (*mens* or *animus*).[3] The mind thus functions as an analogy and illustration of how there can be division in unity. At the same time, the mind itself is the very part of the soul that brings about this kind of illustration, and so it is the power by which humans may actually understand something about the trinity. In other words, the mind creates knowledge (*scientia*) by virtue of reason (*ratio*). For Augustine, under-standing, knowledge, and reason set humans apart from animals. This is not to say that they do not share various powers, such as the external senses, a kind of memory, and something that he calls the 'internal sense' (*sensus interior*), that is, a sense which controls and judges the external senses. Nevertheless, Augustine thinks that only humans can engage in all sorts of mental activities.[4] The absence or presence of a mind thus marks the animal/human boundary.

Despite this clear distinguishing feature, Augustine frequently notes that the lines between human and animal cognition seem to be blurred in some cases. One of these cases is illustrated by the passage from *On the Magnitude of the Soul* (*De quantitate animae*) translated in the following. In this treatise, written around AD 388, Augustine and his interlocutor Evodius discuss the nature of the soul. At a certain point they try to come up with a definition of sensory perception (*sensus*). However, they realise that in order to arrive at a consistent definition a number of qualifications need to be made. One of these qualifications concerns the relation between sensory perception and knowledge (*scientia*). On the one hand, various examples seem to show that animals have knowledge. On the other hand, knowl-edge seems to require reason (*ratio*), that is, a power of the mind (*mind*) usually reserved for rational beings such as humans or angels. Therefore, Augustine and Evodius engage in a lively discussion of human and animal cognition and finally agree on a number of points that were to remain influential throughout the entire medieval debate.

## Bibliographical Note

The English translation is based on the following critical edition of the Latin text: Augustine. (1986). *De quantitate animae* (*Opera omnia* I.IV = CSEL 89) (W. Hörmann, Ed.) (pp. 190–202). Wien: Hoelder-Pichler-Tempsky. An alternative English translation can be found in Augustine. (1947). *The magnitude of the soul* (J. J. McMahon, Trans.) (pp. 112–122). Washington, D.C.: The Catholic University of America Press.

---

[2] See O'Daly (1987).

[3] See Augustine, *De trinitate*, X.XI.18, ed. Mountain (1968), 330.

[4] On Augustine's account of animal psychology, see Clark (1998); Matthews (1999); Brittain (2002).

# Translation

XXV. (47) Augustine: […] A definition should contain neither more nor less than what it aims to explain; otherwise it is entirely flawed. Whether it is free of such flaws can be found out by conversion. This will become clear to you by the following examples.

If you asked me 'What is a human being?', and if I defined it as follows: 'A human being is a mortal animal'; then you should not continue with it only because it says something that is true, but you should also test this definition by adding a small word, namely, 'every'. Then you convert it and examine whether the converted version is true as well, that is, whether 'Every mortal animal is a human being' is just as true as 'Every human being is a mortal animal'. Now that this is found to be wrong, you should reject the definition because it contains something that does not belong to it. For not only a human being is a mortal animal but also any beast.[5]

This definition of human being is usually improved if one adds 'rational' to 'mortal' because a human being is a mortal rational animal; and just as every human being is a rational, mortal animal, every rational, mortal animal is a human being.[6]

So the former definition was flawed because it contained more; for, besides human beings, it also included beasts. The latter is perfect because it contains every human being and nothing more than human beings.

But if it contains less it is flawed as well, for instance, when you add 'linguistic'.[7] For although every mortal, rational, linguistic animal is a human being there are still many humans who are not linguists and not included in this definition. Therefore, it is false in its first version; but when converted, it is true, because while 'Every human being is a rational, mortal, linguistic animal' is false, it is true that 'every rational, mortal, linguistic animal is a human being'. However, if what is expressed is neither true in the first version nor in its conversion, it is definitely more flawed than particular statements such as, 'A human being is a white animal', or, 'A human being is a four-legged animal'. For if you said that 'every human being is a white animal' or a 'four-legged animal' you would say something that is false and remained false even if you converted it. Yet, these two differ insofar as some humans at least fall into the first one, because most humans are white, whereas nobody falls in the second, since no human being is a quadruped.

---

[5] Augustine here employs the term '*bestia*' for any kind of nonhuman animal although it specifically refers to wild animals; see Resl (2007), 10. As Clark (1998), 68, points out, Augustine rarely applies more general and neutral terms such as '*animal*' but prefers "words for animals as seen by humans".

[6] This is the classical definition of 'human being' as found in Porphyry, *Isagoge* 4.29–34, ed. Minio-Paluello (1966), 10.

[7] What Augustine has in mind here is a person who is linguistic (*grammaticum*) in the sense that this person is a trained linguist or grammarian (*grammaticus*).

For the time being take this as a lesson on how to test definitions and on how to judge a statement and its conversion. There are many other things to be taught on this subject – full of words and obscurities – which, little by little, I shall explain to you whenever it is convenient, so that you learn them.

(48) Now turn your attention to our definition[8] and correct it more competently, now that you have discussed it. For we found out that what was supposed to be a definition of sensory perception included something else that was not sensory perception, hence it was not true when converted. Perhaps it is true that 'every sensory perception is a change of the body that does not remain hidden from the soul' just as it is true that 'every human being is a mortal animal'. And so, just as it is false that 'every mortal animal is a human being,' since beasts are mortal too, it is false that 'every change of the body that does not remain hidden from the soul is a sensory perception,' because our fingernails grow now and this does not remain hidden from the soul – for we know it – and still we do not sense it but rather recognise it by conjecturing.

So, don't you think that just as the definition of human being, in order to be completed needed the addition of the term 'rational,' by which beasts that were included before are excluded, and nothing but humans and each and every human are included in this definition, something else must be added here as well in order to make sure that it does not contain what does not belong to it, but includes only sensory perception and each and every sensory perception?

Evodius: I think so, but I do not know what can be added.

A: Every sensory perception certainly is a change of the body that does not remain hidden from the soul. However, this phrase cannot be converted because of that kind of bodily change by which it grows or decreases and which is known to us, that is, which does not remain hidden from the soul.

E: Indeed.

A: What? Does this change remain unhidden from the soul because of itself or because of something else?

E: Obviously, because of something else. For to see longer fingernails is something else than to know that they grow.

A: So, if growth itself is a change which we do not perceive by any sense, but by the size that we sense, which is produced by the change, is not a change itself, then it is clear that we cannot know such a change by itself but [only] by something else. For if it would not remain hidden from the soul because of something else would it not be sensed rather than assumed?

E: I understand.

A: So, why are you uncertain about what needs to be added to that definition?

---

[8] This does not refer to the definition of human being but to the definition of sensory perception as 'that which changes the body and does not remain hidden from the soul' (*non latere animam quod patitur corpus*) in ch. XXIII (41) of the treatise.

E: Now I see that the definition needs to be as follows: sensory perception is 'a change of the body which by itself does not remain hidden from the soul'. For I think that every sensory perception is like this, and everything like this is a sensory perception.

(49) A: If that is the case, I admit that the definition is perfect. But if you don't mind, let us test if it is not unhinged by the second flaw, just as the definition of human being, to which 'linguistic' was added. You surely remember that a human being was said to be a rational, mortal, linguistic animal, and that the problem with this definition was that it was true in its conversion but false in its original version. It is wrong that 'every human being is a rational, mortal, linguistic animal,' whereas it is true that 'every rational, mortal, linguistic animal is a human being'.

Thus, this definition is flawed because it does not embrace anything but humans, and yet not every human, and perhaps that is also the case with the one we already praised as perfect. For even though every change of the body which by itself does not remain hidden from the soul might be a sensory perception, not every sensory perception is like that. In order to understand this, look at the following: beasts certainly sense and usually are quite strong with regard to all five senses, depending on how many of them nature has given to them. Or would you deny this?

E: Not at all.

XXVI. A: What? Don't you admit that knowledge is nothing else but having perceived and recognised a thing by solid reason?
E: I admit this.
A: But a beast does not use reason.
E: I also concede that.
A: So, knowledge cannot be granted to a beast. Yet if something does not remain hidden from it, it surely knows something. Thus, beasts do not sense anything if every sensory perception is a change of the body which by itself does not remain hidden from the soul. However, they do sense, as has been admitted just now. So, why do we hesitate to reject that definition which can barely comprise every sensory perception if the sensory perception of beasts is excluded?

(50) E: I must admit that I have been mistaken when I agreed with you that knowledge exists, whenever something is perceived by solid reason. For what I had in mind, when you asked me, were only humans. Indeed, I cannot say that beasts use reason. But I cannot deny them knowledge either. For instance, I think that the dog knew its master, whom it is said to have recognised after twenty years,[9] not to mention many other examples.
A: Please be so kind to tell me the following: if two things are offered to you, one of which is something you are aiming at, the other one being something by virtue

---

[9] This refers to Argos, the dog of Odysseus, in Homer, *Odysseae*, book 17, ed. Allen (1908), ll. 292–294. Its capacity to recognise its master after many years of absence became a famous example of nonhuman animal cognition.

of which you can achieve this aim – to which one would you give more weight, or which one do you prefer to which?

E: Who would doubt that what one is aiming at is more important?

A: Now, if these two things were knowledge and reason, do we achieve reason by knowledge or knowledge by reason?

E: I would say that both things are so intertwined with each other that one can get from one to the other and vice versa. For we would not get to reason itself if we did not know that we have to get there. Thus, knowledge comes first, insofar as we get to reason by knowledge.

A: What? Does one get to this knowledge, of which you say that it comes first, without reason?

E: I would never say this because this would be the greatest rashness.

A: So by reason [we get to knowledge]?

E: No, that is not the case.

A: By rashness, instead?

E: Who would say that?

A: Well, then by what?

E: By nothing, because knowledge is innate to us.[10]

(51) A: It seems to me that you have forgotten what we agreed upon before, when I asked you whether you think that knowledge means to perceive something by solid reason. I think you replied that for you this seems to be human knowledge. But now you say that humans can also have a certain knowledge when something is not perceived by reason. But who would fail to see that nothing can be more opposed than these two, namely, that knowledge is nothing else but perceiving something by solid reason, and that there is also knowledge of a thing that has not been perceived by reason at all. Therefore, I wish to know which one of these you choose, because it cannot be the case that both of them are true.

E: I choose what I have said shortly before because I admit that I came up with the former rather hastily. For if we search between us for something that is true by reason – and this happens by asking and replying – how can we reach the top by making rational conclusions if we do not grant anything else before? But how [could we] grant something correctly without knowing it? So, if this [faculty of] reason could not find something in me that has already been cognised, and which it uses when leading to what has not yet been cognised, I would not learn anything from it; I would not even call it 'reason'.

Therefore, it is to no avail if you do not agree with me that prior to reason there needs to be some knowledge in us based on which reason itself can begin with its work.

A: Let me gratify you and, as I have decided, allow you to make corrections, whenever you have come up with something that you feel uncomfortable with.

---

[10] This might refer to Plato's theory of knowledge, according to which knowledge is innate but forgotten, and hence has to be restored by recollection (*anamnesis*).

However, I ask you not to abuse this permission and not to listen carelessly when I ask you something, so that such bad concessions do not force you to cast doubt on those things that are rightly admitted.

E: You better move on to the rest, because even though I will increase my attention wherever I can – for it embarrasses me to abandon my opinion that often –, I will not stop to fight against this kind of embarrassment and such faults, especially when you give me a hand in correcting them. So, this is not about being obstinate, but about showing constancy.

XXVII. (52) A: May such constancy be entirely with you as soon as possible. You have presented an opinion that I like. However, now turn decidedly to what I want. I ask you to tell me what for you seems to be the difference between reason and reasoning.

E: I am not yet capable of distinguishing them.

A: Now, consider whether you think that there is always reason in humans, both old and young or – to avoid any ambiguity – wise, as long as their mind is healthy and their body is in good shape, that is, as long as it does not have diseases or injuries; or whether reason is sometimes present and sometimes absent just as humans sometimes walk, sometimes sit, and sometimes talk.

E: I believe that reason is always in a healthy mind.

A: In which sense? Does it not seem to you that we, or any other sage, always bring ourselves to the cognition of something by those things which have been conceded or which are obvious, or which have been found by asking others or by connecting them with other things?

E: Not always. I think that humans or sages do not always look for something when they discuss something with themselves or with somebody else. For who is looking for something, has not yet found it; and so, who always searches never finds anything. However, I must say that sages have already found wisdom itself, which is what they, when they were still ignorant, aimed to find by means of discussion or by something else.

A: You are right to say this. And that is why I want you to understand that reason isn't that by which we are led to something yet unknown based on what we have already conceded or recognised. For this, as we agreed, is not always in a healthy mind, whereas reason is always there.

(53) E: I understand but what is the point of this?

A: Well, shortly before, you said that I have to admit that we have knowledge before we have reason, since reason relies on what is already known when leading us to the unknown. But now we found out that what is happening there cannot be called reason, because a healthy mind does not always do this and still always has reason. Yet, perhaps it is rightly called reasoning insofar as reason is a certain glance[11] of the mind, whereas reasoning is an enquiry by reason, that is, the

---

[11] Augustine coined the term '*aspectus mentis*' as an analogy to physical vision. The idea is that just as we perceive things through the eyes our mind sees things through what Augustine calls the 'eye of the mind' (*oculus mentis*), that is, reason (*ratio*); see Van Fleteren (1999).

motion of that glance towards those things at which it needs to glance. And so, this work is required for searching, that one for seeing. Consequently, when that glance of the mind we call 'reason' focuses on a thing and sees it, it is called knowledge. But when the mind does not see anything, even though it looks at something, we call this 'lack of knowledge' or 'ignorance'. For not everybody who looks at something with the bodily eyes sees it, which is something we can most easily experience in the dark. And so, I think it is clear that the glance is one thing, and vision another. With regard to the mind, we call both of them 'reason' and 'knowledge' unless there is something that makes you go in another direction, or unless you think that they have not yet been distinguished clearly enough.

E: This distinction pleases me and I gladly agree with it.

A: Now, see whether you believe that we look at something in order to see, or see in order to look at something.

E: As far as this question is concerned, not even a blind person would doubt that glance exists for the sake of seeing rather than vision for the sake of glancing.

A: So, instead of giving weight to glance, we should rather rely on vision.

E: We should totally rely on that.

A: That is, on knowledge more than on reason.

E: I see that this is what follows.

A: So, it pleases you that beasts are better and happier than humans?

E: May God hold off such terrible madness!

A: You are rightly shocked. However, this is what your statement forces us to claim because you said that they have knowledge and lack reason. But humans are endowed with reason by which they gain knowledge only with difficulty. But even if I would admit that we can easily gain knowledge: how would reason help us feel superior to beasts if they have knowledge, and if one discovers that this is more valuable than reason?

XXVIII. (54) E: I am totally forced either not to grant beasts knowledge, or not to deny that they are deservedly put before me. However, I ask you to explain what kind of a thing that is which I recalled about the dog of Odysseus.[12] For it seems that I was so touched by the admiration of this that I have been barking groundlessly.

A: What else, do you think, it should be, instead of the power to know, than the power to sense? Since with regard to sensory perception many beasts excel humans, although this is not the right place to discuss what might be the reason for this.[13] Regarding mind, reason, and knowledge, however, God put us before them. Still, that sensory power can discern whatever pleases the kind of souls

---

[12] See note 9.

[13] The superiority of nonhuman animals with regard to sensory perception was a commonplace among ancient and medieval thinkers; see Sorabji (1993), 15f.; Köhler (2014), 248–266.

they have, an important power of which is habituation;[14] and it can do this even much more easily because the soul of animals[15] is closely joined to the body. To the body belong the senses which the soul uses in order to find food or to experience pleasure, which takes hold of that body. The human soul, by contrast, itself soars above the body as much as it can by virtue of reason and knowledge, about which we have talked before and which go way beyond the senses; rather, it takes delight in those things that are in itself. The more it declines towards the senses the more it assimilates humans to animals.[16]

That is why also human infants discern much easier by sensory perception the more they are removed from reason, for instance, between the contact and connection with the person who feeds them, and other people whose smell they cannot stand if they are not used to them.

[...]

(56) But let us now return to the main point. And hence see whether you think that it has already been shown that animals[17] do not have knowledge, and that all those capacities that we took to be knowledge and that we admired rely on the power of sensing.

E: It has been sufficiently shown. And if there is anything regarding this matter that needs to be investigated more thoroughly, I will go after it some other time.

# Bibliography

## *Primary Sources*

Augustine. (1947). *The magnitude of the soul* (J. J. McMahon, Trans.). Washington, DC: The Catholic University of America Press.

Augustine. (1968). *De trinitate libri XV: Libri I–XII (Opera* 16.1) (W. J. Mountain, Ed.). Turnhout: Brepols.

Augustine. (1986). *De quantitate animae (Opera omnia* I.IV) (W. Hörmann, Ed.). Wien: Hoelder-Pichler-Tempsky.

Homer. (1908). *Odysseae libros XIII–XXIV (Opera* 4) (T. W. Allen, Ed.). Oxford: Clarendon Press.

Porphyry. (1966). *Isagoge translatio Boethii (Aristoteles Latinus* I.6–7) (L. Minio-Paluello, Ed.). Bruges/Paris: Desclée de Brouwer.

---

[14] Augustine does not have an elaborate theory of habituation or conditioning. But what he has in mind here is basically the kind of learning that today is explained by a stimulus-response model.

[15] In most cases, the term *'belua'* was employed for larger wild animals such as lions. On this terminology see note 5.

[16] The term *'pecus'* was usually applied for cattle.

[17] Once more Augustine employs a term for 'animal' *(fera)* that was usually applied for wild animals.

## Secondary Sources

Brown, P. (2000). *Augustine of Hippo: A biography*. Berkeley/Los Angeles: University of California Press.

Brittain, C. (2002). *Non-rational perception in the Stoics and Augustine* (pp. 253–308). XXII: Oxford Studies in Ancient Philosophy.

Clark, G. (1998). The fathers and the animals: The rule of reason? In A. Linzey & D. Yamamoto (Eds.), *Animals on the agenda: Questions about animals for theology and ethics* (pp. 67–79). London: SCM Press.

Köhler, T. W. (2014). *Homo animal nobilissimum: Konturen des spezifisch Menschlichen in der naturphilosophischen Aristoteleskommentierung des dreizehnten Jahrhunderts, Teilband 2.1 und 2.2*. 2 vols. Leiden/Boston: Brill.

Matthews, G. B. (1999). Augustine and Descartes on the souls of animals. In M. J. C. Crabbe (Ed.), *From soul to self* (pp. 89–107). London: Routledge.

O'Daly, G. J. P. (1987). *Augustine's philosophy of mind*. Berkeley/Los Angeles: University of California Press.

O'Donnell, J. J. (2005). *Augustine: A new biography*. New York: Harper Perennial.

Resl, B. (2007). Animals in culture, ca. 1000-ca. 1400. In id. (Ed.), *A cultural history of animals in the medieval age* (pp. 1–26). Oxford/New York: Berg.

Sorabji, R. (1993). *Animal minds and human morals: The origins of the Western debate*. London: Duckworth.

Van Fleteren, F. (1999). Acies mentis. In A. D. Fitzgerald (Ed.), *Augustine through the ages: An encyclopedia* (pp. 5–6). William B. Eerdmans: Grand Rapids/Cambridge.

# Chapter 3
# Intellect, Reason, and Immortality (Ralph of Battle, *De nesciente et sciente*, Book I, Chapter 4)

**Abstract** This dialogue discusses a number of examples which seem to show that in various situations also nonhuman animals behave quite rationally. Although many of these examples are anecdotes of animal behaviour taken from the theological and philosophical literature of the time, Ralph of Battle uses them to introduce an original and unusual terminological distinction: instead of denying intellect (*intellectus*) and reason (*ratio*) to animals, he – or his protagonist, the sage, more precisely – claims that they have an 'irrational intellect' (*intellectus irrationalis*). This needs to be distinguished from the immortal, human 'rational intellect' (*intellectus rationalis*), which is the power providing understanding of what is good or bad, and hence is a necessary prerequisite for moral responsibility. Not only because of these terminological innovations Ralph's dialogue is an interesting contribution to the early medieval debate over animal minds before the Latin reception of Aristotle's writings on zoology and psychology.

## Introduction

Ralph of Battle is not as well-known as his teacher Anselm, the famous Archbishop of Canterbury. Nevertheless, he definitely deserves more attention than he has yet attracted. Ralph was born in Normandy in 1040, and seems to have studied at the convent school of Bec Abbey where Anselm worked as a teacher.[1] He then held different offices, for instance, as chaplain and prior, until he was elected fourth abbot of Battle Abbey in Battle, a small town in what is now the county of East Sussex, England. There he worked until his death on August 29 in 1124. All of Ralph's theological works we know of seem to have been written before he became abbot of Battle Abbey. They consist of various meditations and prayers, but also of a number of short treatises and dialogues, many of which were inspired by Anselm.[2]

---

[1] On Ralph's life and works, see Goebel (2015), 11–16.

[2] On Ralph's treatises, see Niskanen (2016).

A. Oelze, *Animal Minds in Medieval Latin Philosophy*, Studies in the History of Philosophy of Mind 27, https://doi.org/10.1007/978-3-030-67012-2_3

The dialogue *De nesciente et sciente*, from which the passage translated in the following has been taken, adopts and further develops Anselm's idea of providing a rational foundation to Christian faith. It presents a discussion between a faithful Christian – 'the sage' or 'the one who knows' (*sciens*) – and an atheist – 'the ignorant' or 'the one who does not know' (*nesciens*).[3] One of the main aims of the believer is to show that humans are special creatures as they are endowed with intellect and reason. Therefore, they should use these powers for the correct conduct of life. However, the ascription of these powers to humans leads to the question of how special they really are. At some point, both partners of the dialogue start to discuss a number of examples which seem to show that in various situations also nonhuman animals behave quite rationally. Although many of these examples are anecdotes of animal behaviour taken from the theological and philosophical literature of the time, Ralph uses them to introduce an original and unusual terminological distinction: instead of denying intellect (*intellectus*) and reason (*ratio*) to animals, he – or his protagonist, the sage, more precisely – claims that they have an 'irrational intellect' (*intellectus irrationalis*). This needs to be distinguished from the human 'rational intellect' (*intellectus rationalis*), which is the power providing understanding of what is good or bad, and hence is a necessary prerequisite for moral responsibility. The human intellect's connection with reason is also what finally guarantees the immortality of the human soul, as both interlocutors agree. Interestingly, they point out that the main reason for holding this view is the doctrine of the church, and they obviously struggle with the question of whether the soul of animals is mortal and non-rational. It is this struggle which, apart from the terminological innovations mentioned before, makes Ralph's dialogue an interesting contribution to the early medieval debate over animal minds before the Latin reception of Aristotle's writings on zoology and psychology.[4]

## Bibliographical Note

The English translation is based on the following critical edition of the Latin text (including a German translation) of Ralph's dialogues on philosophical theology: Ralph of Battle. (2015). *Dialoge zur philosophischen Theologie* (S. Niskanen & B. Goebel, Eds. & Trans.) (pp. 258–275). Freiburg/Basel/Wien: Herder.

---

[3] On this dialogue in particular, see Goebel (2015), 28–71.

[4] Another contribution which has received more attention than Ralph of Battle's text is Adelard of Bath, *Quaestiones naturales*, ch. 13–14, ed. and tr. Burnett (1998), 110–119.

## Translation

37. *The ignorant.* Since I have said before,[5] when I was talking about the beast of burden,[6] that it has a soul just as a human being, I ask you to teach me what is different between its soul and the soul of a human being. For, as I have said before, I see that it uses the senses of the body in accordance with its will,[7] just as a human being; and so, if it differs, I wonder, what is different between the soul of a beast of burden and the soul of a human being. Moreover, I want you to tell me if the soul of a beast of burden has an intellect and, if it does have an intellect, what kind of intellect it has.

38. *The sage.* It is clear that there are many differences between the soul of a human being and the soul of a beast of burden, and if you would properly think about this you could easily understand by yourself and from yourself what is different between them. For even though the beast of burden has a soul by virtue of which it lives, like a human being, and in accordance with its will moves its limbs here and there, it still lacks reason and it cannot tell who created it or how [the creator] controls what has been created.

39. For this reason, we do not ascribe the blame for a sin to it, when the beast of burden, or any other animal of this kind, does by chance something which we call 'bad,' exactly because it does not have a rational intellect by which it knows to discern good and bad. Therefore, when it does at some point kill a human being, it will not be sentenced for having committed homicide by those who rightly consider the case, just as a human being, when killing it, must not be found guilty of having committed a sin, as long as there is no other reason apart from killing it. However, an ox or any other animal of this kind, that serve our purposes and whose labour we use as a help to run the businesses from which we live, do not think of our benefits when they work. The reason is that their nature is such that they desire those things that caress them and avoid those things that cause annoyance, as much as they can; and since they do not have the rational sensation[8] by which they would know to discern what is good and what is bad, one does not hold them responsible for any good or bad.

40. And so, it happens that quite often such animals do many things in front of us, according to their nature, which seem indecent to us, but they do not feel any shame; and they do not feel it because their creator has not forbidden that they do such things. Yet, whenever some highly disgraceful humans dare to do something like this shamelessly, they are not called 'rational,' but 'beasts' and 'irrational' by

---

[5] This refers to book I, ch. 2, §28, where the ignorant had asked the sage in which sense beasts of burden differ from humans.

[6] The Latin term '*iumentum*' specifically refers to animals used for hard labour, e.g. horses or asses.

[7] It is interesting to see that Ralph ascribes a will (*voluntas*) to nonhuman animals, because this was usually taken to be a rational faculty; see Part III in this volume.

[8] Instead of translating '*sensus*' with 'sensation,' one could render it more generally as 'perception'.

those who are rational, for the fact that they imitate the customs of beasts contrary to nature and the order of reason.

41. And so, even though, as we have said, animals live, sense, and move towards those things to which the will guides them, they nevertheless lack the rational sensation by virtue of which they would know to discern who created them, why they have been created, or whether they should live forever or die at some point; still, some animals do many things which human beings seriously admire.

42. For instance, a horse, which, in comparison with other animals, seems to be a relatively stupid animal, can sometimes be trained by a trainer such that it immediately collapses as if it died, when the one who trained it lightly touches its head or says something into its ear. Those who stand around it think that it is dead; but when they come closer, it suddenly hits them by kicking out in all directions with its feet as if it were full of anger. This it does until its trainer tells it to calm down, and then the horse returns into the previous position.

43. Similarly, we see dogs doing many things for which they are seriously admired by us and by those who see them, because after they have been trained they quickly carry out the admirable things which their trainers have taught them to do as if they had a great deal of intellect and are in no way willing to bear any delay when they do it. I also heard someone say that in the house of a certain man there lived a dog which used to put a tiny piece of the bread aside that was given to it every day; and as if it was distributing its alms it used to give that piece to another dog that used to come to it every day for this purpose; and so, even though the dog itself would not rationally understand what piety is, it nevertheless piously brought bread to the dog that needed it by taking it away from itself every day.

44. Many people also referred to another dog whose master, when he was traveling alone with the dog, was killed on the way and hastily buried by a bandit.[9] It then returned to the house of the family [of its master] and somehow showed them that he has been killed, and the dog itself led them to the place where he had been killed and buried. After some time had passed, during which many people had already tried very hard to find the one who had done the killing, luck would have it that the dog itself caught sight of the one who had killed its master, when he was standing together with some other men. When it saw him, it immediately attacked only him, leaving anybody else aside, and did not want to desist from him, even when many pushed it away. Since what the dog did was truly admired by some of those who were standing around, they caught the man and asked him what he had done to the dog which was raging as if it wanted to eat him. At first he wanted to deny [what he had done], but since the dog did not in any way stop its attack he saw no way in which he could escape from the dog's rage, and so he eventually confessed to have killed its master.

---

[9]This story is found in various medieval bestiaries; see, for instance, White (2002), 65 f. The church fathers Basil of Caesarea and Ambrose of Milan, whose writings Ralph certainly knew, also mention that dogs are known for taking revenge on the murderers of their masters; see Basil of Caesarea, *Homiliae IX in Hexaemeron* IX.4, ed. Migne (1886), 198D; Ambrose of Milan, *Hexaemeron*, lib. VI, c. 4, §23, ed. Migne (1882), 266B.

45. Similarly, some people say about the stork that, when its body has lost its plumes and feathers because of age, its children and its offspring, which has sprung from it, come to it and cover it and make a pit with their wings and plumes until it has regained its former strength or passes away because of its old age.[10] I could refer to many more stories about animals like these if I would not be afraid of tiring those who read this.

46. *The ignorant.* Thus, you say that certain animals have sensation to such a degree that they seem to have an intellect just as humans, so that they do many things which have been taught to them by their trainers. I ask you to tell me, what is different between their intellect and the intellect of a human being.

47. *The sage.* The Blessed Augustine says[11] that animals do not have an intellect; but even if we call the sense that they see them to have, 'intellect,' there is still a huge difference between their intellect and the intellect of humans, because the intellect of a human being is rational, that is, it brings about those things that belong to reason. The intellect of animals, however, is irrational, because it does not understand at all what should be done in accordance with reason and what should not be done.

48. Humans are also said to be similar to beasts when they do something irrationally and, as the Psalmist[12] says, when they dishonour themselves, that is, when they follow a course of life that is not in accordance with reason, they are compared to foolish beasts of burden and are put on a par with them. Therefore, in another passage, the very same Psalmist warns humans by saying: "Do not become like the horse or the mule which do not have an intellect,"[13] that is, a rational intellect by virtue of which they know to discern between good and bad.

49. For we cannot deny that certain animals almost understand[14] a little bit, because we see them doing those admirable things that they have been taught, and there is no way in which they could be taught to do them if they did not almost understand [them] a little bit. Therefore, they understand a little bit; but, as I have said, they do not understand what is good or bad or by whom they have been created. Therefore, if something has been taught to them but they do not do it, we do not blame them for disobedience, because they do not understand what a great evil disobedience is.

50. Humans, however, who have a rational intellect, rationally understand by whom they have been created and that they must always obey their creator from whom they originate, no matter who they are. When they, at some point, disdain to obey, they are rightly sentenced by all wise people for being arrogant and disobedient because they rationally understand what they should do, but swollen and puffed

---

[10] The love of storks for their family members is also a recurrent theme in Patristic literature where it serves as an example of so-called 'natural virtues'; see, for instance, Basil of Caesarea, *Homiliae IX in Hexaemeron* VIII.5, ed. Migne (1886), 175C.

[11] Augustine, *De quantitate animae* XXVI.49, ed. Hörmann (1986), 194. See Chap. 2 in this volume.

[12] See Psalm 49:13 and 21.

[13] Psalm 32:9.

[14] The expression '*quasi intellegere*' could also be rendered 'as if they understand'. This would imply that animals seem to have intellectual understanding but actually do not have it.

up with arrogance refuse to do what they should do and do what they should not do. See! As I have promised before, I have tried to explain to you, to the best of my abilities, what is different between the intellect of a human being and the intellect of an irrational animal [...].[15]

57. *The ignorant.* To the best of my abilities, I will try to remember this and the other things that you have said. But even though you have told me many things about beasts I still want you to explain to me more clearly how their soul is in them. I am not asking whether it is invisible (because I know that it is invisible), but I wish to know how their soul uses the senses that these beasts have.

58. *The sage.* It is clear that beasts have corporeal senses which their soul uses according to the impulse of their will. With regard to these senses, there is not much of a difference between beasts and humans, because they see, hear, and do many other things according to these senses that they have in common with humans. But since they are irrational, they themselves cannot rationally discern this. For even though they do of course see through the eyes and hear through the ears, they do not understand that it is the proper task of the eyes to see or of the ears to hear, because if they would understand this by the discernment of reason, they would certainly have a rational intellect. And although beasts have a sense for avoiding those things that harm them and for seeking those instead that suit them, they still do this by natural appetite rather than by rational intellect.

59. *The ignorant.* And how do you know that beasts do not have a rational intellect?

60. *The sage.* I know it from the fact that if they had a rational intellect, they would know to avoid evil. But since they do not know to discern between what is decent and what is indecent, ugly and beautiful, useful and useless, they indiscriminately do indecent and decent, useful and useless, ugly and beautiful things. From this fact it is clear that they do not in any way have a rational intellect. For they do not know to do anything that does not properly pertain to the care of their own body or their own benefit. And so, when we put a leash on them, so that they do our work from which we and they must live, we see that they come to it both reluctantly and against their will; quite often they even fight tooth and tail as much as they can against being forced to work, and run away, so that we hurt them with awful lashes.

61. Finally, when the Psalmist says to those humans who use reason, "Do not become like the horse and the mule which have no intellect,"[16] he forbids them to desist from living in accordance with the rational intellect and to live according to the irrational appetite which they have, and according to which beasts live, because then they would be put on a par with the latter and imitate the beasts by subordinating reason to pleasure and lust.

62. The very same Psalmist also says in another place: "Although humans were in an honourable position, they did not understand."[17] The honour of humans is to

---

[15] The paragraphs omitted digress into the difference between the human heart and the human soul.
[16] See note 12.
[17] Psalm 49:21.

have a rational intellect by which they differ from beasts, but if they do not care about living in accordance with it they do not understand (that is, they neglect to understand what it means to live in accordance with reason). Therefore, they are compared to foolish beasts of burden (that is, to those beings that lack reason), and they are put on a par with them, not by the [human] condition, but by imitation.

63. *The ignorant.* I think enough has been said about the way in which the soul of beasts uses its senses, about the fact that they do not have a rational intellect, and about the way in which humans are put on a par with beasts. However, I ask you to answer the question of whether the soul of beasts itself is immortal or perishes together with its body. And, if you say that it perishes with its body, show me for which reason you claim this.

64. *The sage.* I do not believe that the soul of beasts is immortal, but perishes with its body and returns to nought, because this is what the Holy Church believes, and the divine law is such that neither I nor any other Christian person can believe in anything else. Regarding the reason that you asked me to give [for this view], that is, how the soul of a beast dies when the body of the beast itself perishes, I can tell you, what, to me, seems to be the case. But no matter what I say, I do not move away from the ready belief of the Holy Church, through the confirmation of which every faithful Christian moves firmly and safely. If, however, somebody wants to have a different discussion about this than the one that is in accordance with the custom and authority of the Holy Church, I do not want to hear it, because I believe in the opinions and views of the Holy Fathers rather than in the wordy disputations of those people who talk emptily, "no matter what they talk about nor what they affirm"[18] rightly knowing it.

65. Still, I will add what I understand of this based on the safe faith about which I have been talking; and if it is true or comes close to the truth, it will be heard; if not, it will be rejected. Yet we do not move away from the firm foundation of faith.

66. For I am sure that the soul of beasts does not have a rational intellect as we have shown in many ways before. So, since the soul of beasts with its intellect does not adhere to reason, because reason is an imperishable thing and God, from whom every rational intellect [originates], is the highest reason, it seems to be more in line with reason that, since the soul of beasts itself is not enlightened by the brightness of the rational intellect, it perishes with its body, returns to nought as its body, together with which it has basically followed nothing but the pleasures and arbitrary appetites of this very body, as long as it lived. So, naturally the soul of beasts perishes with the body, because, as long as it has been in it, it has not naturally understood what else it should do than to follow the pleasures of the flesh and those things that pertain to the care of the belly; and so, it has naturally satisfied those appetites of the body in all kinds of ways as much as it could and as long as it stayed with it. And since that is the case it seems not to be in line with reason that the soul of beasts lives after the decay [of the body], [the very same soul] that was not animated by a

---

[18] 1 Tim. 1:7.

rational life as long as it was in the body, by which it was brought to life, just as it gave life to the body in which it was.

67. For no soul will live after the decay of its body except for the one that, as long as it was in the body, had a rational intellect as well as its life by which it was brought to life and truly understood itself to be alive; because just as the soul helps the body with [the matters of] life, as long as it is in it, the rational intellect brings life to the soul that it enlightens. Moreover (as I have said just before), since reason is an eternal thing, and since God, who is eternal, is the highest reason, the soul that always stuck to reason together with its body, as long as it was with the body, does not die.

68. *The ignorant.* I think, you have satisfyingly answered the questions I had about the soul of beasts; and you have clearly shown that it does not live after death, since it is devoid of reason as long as it stays in the body, and so it cannot have any life after the decay of its body.

# Bibliography

## *Primary Sources*

Adelard of Bath. (1998). *Conversations with his nephew: On the same and the different, Questions on natural science and On birds* (C. Burnett, Ed. & Trans.). Cambridge: Cambridge University Press.

Ambrose of Milan. (1882). *Hexaemeron libri sex* (J.-P. Migne. Ed.) (PL 14, 133–288). Paris.

Augustine. (1986). *De quantitate animae* (*Opera omnia* I.IV) (W. Hörmann, Ed.). Wien: Hoelder-Pichler-Tempsky.

Basil of Caesarea. (1886). *Homiliae IX in Hexaemeron* (J.-P. Migne. Ed.) (PG 29, 1–208). Paris.

Ralph of Battle. (2015). *Dialoge zur philosophischen Theologie* (S. Niskanen & B. Goebel, Eds. & Trans.). Freiburg/Basel/Wien: Herder.

## *Secondary Sources*

Goebel, B. (2015). Einleitung. In Ralph of Battle, *Dialoge zur philosophischen Theologie* (S. Niskanen & B. Goebel, Eds. & Trans.) (pp. 11–77). Freiburg/Basel/Wien: Herder.

Niskanen, S. (2016). The treatises of Ralph of Battle. *The Journal of Medieval Latin, 26,* 199–225.

White, T. H. (2002). *The book of beasts: Being a translation from a Latin bestiary of the twelfth century.* Madison: Parallel Press.

# Chapter 4
# The Animal Soul and Its Powers (Avicenna Latinus, *Liber de anima*, Book I, Chapter 5)

**Abstract** Once Avicenna's psychological works had been translated into Latin during the second half of the twelfth century, Latin thinkers' accounts of animal cognition significantly changed. This change mainly revolved around the so-called theory of internal senses. It postulates that, in addition to the five external senses, animals usually have a certain number of internal senses. These include, for instance, imagination and memory, but also, and most notably, a sense called 'estimation' or 'estimative power'. By this power, a sheep, for example, perceives features such as the harmfulness of a wolf. Even though this example is embedded in a relatively technical text containing a great deal of physiological terminology, it rapidly became the prime example in Latin discussions of animal minds.

## Introduction

It might not be self-evident to include an Islamic thinker from the Arab world in a collection of texts by medieval Christian authors from the Latin West. However, Ibn Sīnā, or Avicenna (as his name was latinised), is an excellent case in point for the fact that one must not ignore the various, fruitful connections that existed between medieval Islam and Christianity. Avicenna was born in 980, in a small village close to Bukhara in what is today Uzbekistan.[1] Apparently gifted, he received early training in Islamic theology and Arabic literature, but also in arithmetic, Greek philosophy, law, and medicine. Given this comprehensive education – which, in many parts, was self-education rather than ordinary academic training – it is hardly surprising that he is often referred to as polymath. In his early twenties, he had already brought it to some fame and, after he had been delving into books of all kinds since his childhood, began to produce his own writings. Around the same time, he had to leave his home and began what has rightly been called his life's "odyssey".[2] It

---

[1] On his life, see, for instance, McGinnis (2010), esp. 17–26.

[2] McGinnis (2010), 3.

A. Oelze, *Animal Minds in Medieval Latin Philosophy*, Studies in the History of Philosophy of Mind 27, https://doi.org/10.1007/978-3-030-67012-2_4

finally led him to modern Iran where he stayed, interrupted by numerous more or less voluntary travels, until the end of his life in 1037.

Nevertheless, his fame outlasted his death. It became even bigger when some of his writings were translated into Latin, at a time when most of Aristotle's works were transmitted to Western Europe, sparking a whole new way of academic learning, teaching, and discussion.[3] Therefore, the Latin Avicenna is intimately linked to the Latin Aristotle (the same applies to other Islamic thinkers, such as Averroes, for example). One of the fields in which this connection is particularly relevant and obvious, is the study of animal cognition. In this regard, one could even say that Avicenna is a watershed, because once one of his psychological works had been translated into Latin as the book on the soul (*Liber de anima*) during the second half of the twelfth century, Latin thinkers' accounts of animal cognition significantly changed.[4] This change mainly revolved around the so-called theory of internal senses. It postulates that, in addition to the five external senses of sight, hearing, smell, taste, and touch, animals usually have a certain number of internal senses.[5] These include, for instance, imagination and memory, but also, and most notably, a sense called 'estimation' or 'estimative power' (*aestimatio/estimatio*, or *vis/virtus aestimativa/estimativa* in Latin).[6] As the passage from book I, chapter 5, of the *Liber de anima*, translated in this chapter, shows, Avicenna claims that estimation apprehends so-called 'intentions' (*intentiones*). These features are different from forms, such as shape, size, or colour, and hence cannot be grasped by any of the external senses.[7] The example he gives in this context is the hostility or harmfulness of a wolf perceived by a sheep. Even though this example is embedded in a relatively technical text containing a great deal of physiological terminology, it rapidly became the prime example in Latin discussions of animal minds (see Chaps. 6, 9, 12, 15, 16, 17, 22, and 25 as well as the section "Animals and minds in medieval philosophy" in Chap. 1 to this volume).[8] In other words, by this text (and by some others, such as the text in Chap. 5) Avicenna decisively shaped how Latin thinkers looked at the cognitive capacities of nonhuman animals. This is the reason why, despite its different background and origin, it forms an indispensable part of a sourcebook on animal minds in medieval Latin philosophy.

---

[3] On the transmission of Aristotle's works, see Dod (1982) and Lohr (1982). On the Latin Avicenna, see Janssen (2011).

[4] On the reception of the *Liber de anima* in the Latin West, see Hasse (2000).

[5] It is important to note that various versions of this theory already existed long before Avicenna; see Wolfson (1935). Some even claim that it can be traced back to Aristotle; see some of the articles in Mousavian & Fink (2020). On Islamic versions, in particular, see Di Martino (2016).

[6] For an analysis, see Black (1993) and (2000).

[7] On intentions in medieval Arabic philosophy, see Di Martino (2006) and Black (2010).

[8] For a philosophical analysis, see Perler (2012).

## Bibliographical Note

The English translation is based on the following critical edition of the Latin text: Avicenna Latinus. (1972). *Liber de anima seu sextus de naturalibus I-II-III* (S. van Riet, Ed.) (pp. 82–90). Louvain: Peeters/Leiden: Brill. To date, the Latin text has not been translated into English. However, there are translations from Arabic into English and French: Avicenna. (1952). *Avicenna's psychology: An English translation of* Kitāb al-Najāt, *book II, chapter VI with historico-philosophical notes and textual improvements on the Cairo edition* (F. Rahman, Trans.) (pp. 25–31). Oxford University Press: London; Avicenna. (1956). *Psychologie d'ibn Sīnā (Avicenne) d'après son œvre As-Šifā', vol. 2* (J. Bakoš, Ed. & Trans.) (pp. 28–31). Prague: Éditions de l'Académie Tchécoslovaque des sciences.

## Translation

The animal[9] soul, however, has two powers in the first instance, namely, a motive and an apprehending one.

But the motive one is of two kinds: for either it is motive for the reason that it orders a movement; or it is motive for the reason that it brings about a movement. Motive, however, insofar as it orders a movement, is the appetitive and desiring power. This power commands another moving power to move, when the form[10] of what is desired or rejected is imagined in the imagination. Of this we will speak later. This [appetitive power] has two parts: one that is called 'concupiscible power', which is the power commanding to move, so that those things which are considered necessary or useful, that is, things pleasing the appetite, are approached; [and] another one that is called 'irascible,' which is the power commanding to push away what is considered hurtful or harmful, that is, things repelling the appetite. The motive power, however, insofar as it brings about [a movement], is the power inhering in the nerves and muscles, contracting the tendons and ligaments, that are in the limbs, toward the origin,[11] or the other way around, relaxing, stretching, and turning the tendons and ligaments away from the origin.

The apprehending power, however, is split: for one is the power which apprehends from outside; another one which apprehends from inside.

---

[9] I translate the Latin term '*vitalis*' as '*animal*' in this context, because in the Aristotelian tradition, to which Avicenna belongs, the distinctive feature of this soul is that it enables a being to perceive rather than simply to *live* (which is what '*vitalis*' means in the most basic sense).

[10] The meaning of this term is explained more below.

[11] I.e. the point where tendons and ligaments are actually connected to muscles and/or bones.

Apprehending from outside, however, are the five or eight[12] senses. Among them is sight, which is a power located in the optic nerve for apprehending the form of what is formed in the crystalline humour[13] out of the likenesses of coloured bodies that effectively come through radial particles to the surfaces of even bodies.[14] Also among them is hearing, which is the power located in the nerve extending to the surface of the optic[15] nerve for apprehending the form of what comes to it through the motion of the air, which is compressed between a striking thing and a thing being struck that resists the contraction that occurs and from which comes a sound. And this motion [of the air outside] reaches the air that is lying at rest in the cavity of the optic[16] nerve, causing a motion similar to its own, and the extensions of this movement touch the nerve. Also among them is smell,[17] which is the power located in two little pieces of flesh in the anterior part of the brain, that are similar to nipples, for apprehending what the inhaled air brings of the odour that is in a vapour mixed with the air, or of the odour that is impressed on it by an alteration of a thing spreading odour. Also among them is taste, which is the power located in the nerve that extends to the body of the tongue, for apprehending the flavours that have been released from the bodies containing them, when they are mixed with the viscous liquids[18] of the tongue in a mixing together that alters it. Also among them is touch, which is the power located in the nerves of the skin of the entire body and its flesh, for apprehending what touches it and, by an altering opposition, affects the constitution and state of its composition. To some, however, it seems that this power is not a most specific species,[19] but a genus of four, or even more, powers that are evenly distributed over the whole body. One of them discerns the opposition that exists between hot and cold; another one discerns the opposition that exists between humid and dry; the third discerns the opposition that exists between hard and soft; the fourth, however, discerns the opposition that exists between rough and smooth. But since they exist altogether in one organ, they are considered to be essentially one.

Yet, of the powers apprehending from inside, some apprehend sensible forms, others apprehend sensible intentions. Some of the apprehending powers, however, apprehend and act at the same time, others apprehend and do not act; some apprehend primarily and others secondarily.

---

[12] As Avicenna explains more below, some people claim that smell is only an umbrella term for four distinct species of senses perceiving different tangible qualities.

[13] I.e. the lens.

[14] On Avicenna's so-called 'intromissionist' theory of vision, see, for instance, Lindbergh (1976), 43–52, and Smith (2015), 159–166.

[15] The English translation of the Arabic original has "ear-hole" instead of 'optic nerve'; see Avicenna (1952), 26. This term makes more sense in this context although the Latin text has '*nervus opticus*'. See also Avicenna Latinus (1972), 84n64.

[16] See note 15.

[17] On medieval theories of smell, see Robinson (2019).

[18] I.e. the saliva.

[19] I.e. a species to which there are no subspecies.

The difference between apprehending a form and apprehending an intention[20] is this: a form is what both the internal and the external sense apprehend. But the external sense apprehends it first and then passes it on to the internal sense, as, for instance, a sheep apprehends the form of a wolf, that is, its shape, its physique, and its colour. But the sheep's external senses apprehend it first and the internal sense thereafter. An intention, however, is what the soul apprehends from the sensible things although the external sense does not previously apprehend it, as, for instance, a sheep apprehends the intention that it has from the wolf, which certainly is the reason why it must fear it and flee, although the [external] sense does not in any way apprehend this. That, however, what the external sense apprehends first from the wolf, and [what] the internal sense [apprehends] thereafter, is here called 'form' in the proper sense of the term. That, however, which the hidden powers apprehend without the [external] sense is, at this point, called 'intention' in the proper sense of the term.

Yet, the difference that exists between apprehending with acting[21] and apprehending without acting is this: one of the tasks of the internal senses is to combine some of the forms and intentions that have been grasped with others, or to separate them from others. Thus, apprehending and acting both take place in this [power] that apprehends. But apprehending without acting is, when the form or intention is only recorded by the power in such a way that it cannot act upon it at all.

Yet, the difference between apprehending primarily and apprehending secondarily is this: apprehending primarily is when the form is acquired in a mode of acquisition that belongs to the thing as such. Apprehending secondarily, however, is when the acquisition of the thing comes from something else that has been brought to it.

The first of the hidden apprehending powers of the animal [soul] is fantasy, which is the common sense. This is the power located in the first cavity[22] of the brain, which receives by itself all the forms that are imprinted[23] on the [external] senses and passed on to it. Behind it is the imagination or the forming [power], which is also a power located in the outermost part of the fore cavity of the brain, retaining what the common sense receives from the five [external] senses. This remains in it, even when the sensibles have been removed. However, you must know that [the capacity of] receiving something comes from one power, and this is distinct from another power from which comes [the capacity of] retaining something. Take water, for example: it has the power of receiving carvings,

---

[20] For secondary literature on this concept, see note 7.

[21] For a detailed discussion of activity in perception, according to Avicenna, see Kaukua (2014).

[22] Avicenna's division of the brain into cavities or ventricles is inspired by Galen, see Hall (2004), esp. 73–81. On his medical account of internal senses, see also Pormann (2013). For medieval illustrations of brain functions, see Clarke and Dewhurst (1996), 8–41.

[23] The Aristotelian notion literally was that objects, or certain features of objects, more precisely, are 'imprinted' on the sense organs. Hence the term 'sense impression'.

delineations, and any kind of shapes, but it does not have the power of retaining [them], even though we shall establish the truth of this only later. But if you want to know the difference between the task of the external sense, the task of the common sense, and the task of the forming [power], pay attention to the state of a single raindrop that is falling, and you will see a straight line. Or pay attention to the state of a line, one end of which is rotated, and you will see a circle. However, it is impossible that you apprehend a thing or a line or a circle unless you have often looked at it. But it is impossible that the external sense sees it twice; it sees it only where it is.[24] When it is, however, recorded by the common sense and removed before the form disappeared from the common sense, the external sense apprehends it where it is, and the common sense apprehends it as if it still were where it was, and as if it were where it is, and [so] it sees a circular or straight extent. The external sense, however, can in no way match this, but the forming [power] apprehends these two [states] and forms it[25] even though the thing that is already gone is destroyed.

Behind this [power] is a power that is called 'imaginative' (in connection with the animal soul) or 'cogitating' (in connection with the human soul). This is the power located in the middle cavity of the brain where the worm[26] is. It usually combines something that is in the imagination with something else, or separates something from something else, just as it likes. Next to it is the power of estimation, which is the power located in the upper middle cavity of the brain, that apprehends the non-sensed[27] intentions that are in the single sensible things, as, for instance, the power that is in the sheep and that judges[28] that this wolf must be fled and that this lamb must be nursed. This power also seems to play a role in the composition and division of imagined items. Behind it is the memorative and[29] recollective power, which is the power located in the rear part of the brain, that retains what the estimative power apprehends from the non-sensed intentions of the single sensible things. However, the relation of the power of memory to the power of estimation is the same as the relation of the power that is called 'imagination' to the [external] sense, and this power's relation to the intentions is as that power's relation to the sensible forms. These are the powers of the animal or sensory soul.

---

[24] In other words, when you see a raindrop, you see a dot, not a line.

[25] I.e. the perception of a circle or a straight line.

[26] Avicenna also adopts the idea that there is a particular, worm-like brain structure from Galen; see Hall (2004), esp. 77–80.

[27] Intentions are non-sensed insofar as they are not perceived by the external senses.

[28] In what sense a power like estimation can judge, is discussed by Oelze (2018), 100–129.

[29] One must not confuse memory and recollection as they perform very different tasks; see texts 4, 6, and 7.

# Bibliography

## *Primary Sources*

Avicenna. (1952). *Avicenna's psychology: An English translation of* Kitāb al-Najāt, *book II, chapter VI with historico-philosophical notes and textual improvements on the Cairo edition* (F. Rahman, Trans.). Oxford University Press: London.

Avicenna. (1956). *Psychologie d'ibn Sīnā (Avicenne) d'après son œvre Aš-Šifā', vol. 2* (J. Bakoš, Ed. and trans.). Prague: Éditions de l'Académie Tchécoslovaque des sciences.

Avicenna Latinus. (1972). *Liber de anima seu sextus de naturalibus I-II-III* (S. van Riet, Ed.). Louvain: Peeters/Leiden: Brill.

## *Secondary Sources*

Black, D. L. (1993). Estimation (wahm) in Avicenna: The logical and psychological dimensions. *Dialogue, 32*(2), 219–258.

Black, D. L. (2000). Imagination and estimation: Arabic paradigms and western transformations. *Topoi, 19*(1), 59–75.

Black, D. L. (2010). Intentionality in medieval arabic philosophy. *Quaestio, 10*(1), 65–81.

Clarke, E., & Dewhurst, K. (1996). *An illustrated history of brain function: Imaging the brain from antiquity to the present* (2nd ed.). San Francisco: Norman Publishing.

Di Martino, C. (2006). Ma'ānī / intentiones et sensibilité par accident. In M. C. Pacheco & J. F. Meirinhos (Eds.), *Intellect et imagination dans la philosophie médiévale* (Vol. 1, pp. 507–521). Brepols: Turnhout.

Di Martino, C. (2016). External and internal human senses. In R. C. Taylor & L. X. López-Farjeat (Eds.), *The Routledge companion to Islamic philosophy* (pp. 263–272). New York/Oxford: Routledge.

Dod, B. G. (1982). Aristoteles Latinus. In N. Kretzmann, A. Kenny, & J. Pinborg (Eds.), *The Cambridge history of later medieval philosophy: From the rediscovery of Aristotle to the disintegration of scholasticism 1100–1600* (pp. 43–79). Cambridge: Cambridge University Press.

Hall, R. E. (2004). Intellect, soul and body in Ibn Sīnā: Systematic synthesis and development of the Aristotelian, Neoplatonic and Galenic theories. In J. McGinnis (Ed.), *Interpreting Avicenna: Science and philosophy in medieval islam* (pp. 62–86). Leiden: Brill.

Hasse, D. N. (2000). *Avicenna's De anima in the Latin west: The formation of a Peripatetic philosophy of the soul 1160–1300.* London/Turin: The Warburg Institute – Nino Aragno Editore.

Janssen, J. (2011). Ibn Sīnā (Avicenna), Latin translations of. In H. Lagerlund (Ed.), *Encyclopedia of medieval philosophy: Philosophy between 500 and 1500* (Vol. 2, pp. 522–527). Dordrecht: Springer.

Kaukua, J. (2014). Avicenna on the soul's activity in perception. In J. F. Silva & M. Yrjönsuuri (Eds.), *Active perception in the history of philosophy* (pp. 99–116). Cham: Springer.

Lindberg, D. C. (1976). *Theories of vision from Al-Kindi to Kepler.* Chicago: University of Chicago Press.

Lohr, C. H. (1982). The medieval interpretation of Aristotle. In N. Kretzmann, A. Kenny, & J. Pinborg (Eds.), *The Cambridge history of later medieval philosophy: From the rediscovery of Aristotle to the disintegration of scholasticism 1100–1600* (pp. 80–98). Cambridge: Cambridge University Press.

McGinnis, J. (2010). *Avicenna.* Oxford: Oxford University Press.

Mousavian, S. N., & Fink, J. L. (Eds.). (2020). *The internal senses in the Aristotelian tradition.* Cham: Springer.

Oelze, A. (2018). *Animal rationality: Later medieval theories 1250–1350*. Leiden/Boston: Brill.

Perler, D. (2012). Why is the sheep afraid of the wolf? Medieval debates on animal passions. In M. Pickavé & L. Shapiro (Eds.), *Emotion and cognitive life in medieval and early modern philosophy* (pp. 32–52). Oxford: Oxford University Press.

Pormann, P. E. (2013). Avicenna on medical practice, epistemology, and the physiology of the inner senses. In P. Adamson (Ed.), *Interpreting Avicenna: Critical essays* (pp. 91–108). Cambridge: Cambridge University Press.

Robinson, K. (2019). *The sense of smell in the middle ages: A source of certainty*. London: Routledge.

Smith, A. M. (2015). *From sight to light: The passage from ancient to modern optics*. Chicago: University of Chicago Press.

Wolfson, H. A. (1935). The internal senses in Latin, Arabic, and Hebrew philosophic texts. *The Harvard Theological Review, 28*(2), 69–133.

# Chapter 5
# Modes of Estimation (Avicenna Latinus, *Liber de anima*, Book IV, Chapter 3)

**Abstract** Avicenna's book on the soul decisively shaped Latin thinkers' views of animal minds. One of its most influential elements was the theory of the internal senses, particularly, of the faculty of estimation. Many interpreters used, and still use, to call the reaction triggered by estimation an instinctual response. However, in book IV, chapter 3 of the *Liber de anima*, Avicenna shows that this is but one way or 'mode' (*modus*) in which estimation works. A more basic mode is what he calls a God-given 'caution' (*cautela*), such as the sucking and the blink reflex; a more complex mode is 'by experience' (*per experientiam*). The latter clearly resembles what contemporary psychologists use to term 'associative learning'. The example that Avicenna gives in this context is a dog that learns to fear sticks by associating the perception of its form with the experience of pain. This example was adopted (sometimes with slight modifications) in various Latin texts on animal minds.

## Introduction

Avicenna's book on the soul (*Liber de anima*) decisively shaped Latin thinkers' views of animal minds. One of its most influential elements was the theory of the internal senses, particularly, of the faculty of estimation (see the section "Animals and minds in medieval philosophy" in Chap. 1 to this book as well as the introduction to Chap. 4). In book I, Chap. 5, Avicenna illustrates the nature of this power by referring to a sheep which flees a wolf (see Chap. 4). The sheep, he argues, would not do this unless its estimative power perceived the wolf's harmfulness, that is, a feature that is different from those (physical) properties perceived by the external senses. Now, since sheep seem to be naturally afraid of wolves, interpreters used, and still use, to call this reaction an instinctual response. However, in the passage translated in the following, Avicenna shows that this is but one way or 'mode' (*modus*) in which estimation works. A more basic mode is what he calls a God-given 'caution' (*cautela*), such as the sucking and the blink reflex; a more complex mode is 'by experience' (*per experientiam*). The latter clearly resembles what contemporary psychologists use to term 'associative learning'. The example that

A. Oelze, *Animal Minds in Medieval Latin Philosophy*, Studies in the History of Philosophy of Mind 27, https://doi.org/10.1007/978-3-030-67012-2_5

Avicenna gives in this context, namely, the example of a dog that learns to fear sticks – by associating the perception of its form with the experience of pain – has not become as famous as the sheep and the wolf. Nevertheless, it was adopted (sometimes with slight modifications) in various Latin texts on animal minds (see Chaps. 10, 16, and 25).[1]

## *Bibliographical Note*

The English translation is based on the following critical edition of the Latin text: Avicenna Latinus. (1968). *Liber de anima seu sextus de naturalibus IV-V* (S. van Riet, Ed.) (pp. 34–41). Louvain: Peeters/Leiden: Brill. To date, the Latin has not been translated into English. However, there is a translation from Arabic into French: Avicenna. (1956). *Psychologie d'ibn Sīnā (Avicenne) d'après son œvre Aš-Šifā', vol. 2* (J. Bakoš, Ed. and trans.) (pp. 129–131). Prague: Éditions de l'Académie Tchécoslovaque des sciences.

## *Translation*

Now that we have carefully examined the discussion of the character of the imaginative and forming [power],[2] we must talk about the character of the memorative [power], and what lies between it and the cogitative [power] in the moment of estimating.[3] So, we say that estimation is the most prominent judge[4] in animals which judges by way of a devised imagination,[5] although this [judgment] might not be correct. And this is what happens to a human being who thinks that honey is bitter because it is similar to bile.[6] For estimation judges that this is the case, and the soul follows the estimation although the intellect disproves it. Animals, however, and those humans who are similar to them, do not base their actions on anything but that judgment of estimation which lacks rational discernment but works by way of devising only what is in its mind. However, because of the connection with reason, something is added to the [internal sense] powers of humans, which is why their internal faculties differ from the faculties of animals. Therefore, from the uses of

---

[1] For a philosophical analysis of this example and for further references, see Oelze (2018), 54 f. and 63–68.

[2] See Avicenna Latinus, *Liber de anima* IV.2, ed. van Riet (1968), 12–34.

[3] On the internal senses and their functions, see Chap. 4.

[4] On sensory judgments, see Oelze (2018), 100–129. See also Chaps. 14 and 15.

[5] A less literal translation may be 'by association,' because the idea is that a present sense impression is (erroneously) interpreted in the light of an impression stored in the imagination.

[6] This example is found in Aristotle, *Sophistici elenchii* 5, 167b6–7. According to Tuominen (2014), 58, it is inspired by ancient Greek mothers' custom of putting honey or bile on their nipples in order to encourage or discourage breastfeeding.

combined sounds, colours, odours, combined flavours, and hope and desire, they obtain something which other animals do not get. And their internal imaginative power is such that it is good for [engaging in] sciences and, most of all, their power of memory is very good for sciences, because it brings together experiences for us, which memory retains, particular considerations, and other things of this kind.

But let us return to dealing with what is said about estimation, because it is necessary to examine the cases concerning estimation in which the intellect does not participate in the moment of estimating. It is certain that estimation immediately apprehends intentions which are in the sensibles, just as sense apprehends forms,[7] in such a way that nothing from these intentions is sensed and such that most of them are neither useful nor harmful in this moment.

Thus, we say that estimation itself is brought about in many ways. One of them is the instinct[8] that is found in everything originating from divine mercy, as, for instance, the ability of a baby that, shortly after its birth, sucks at the breasts; or as the ability of an infant that, when it is lifted in order to stand and is about to fall, immediately hurries to stay by someone or to protect itself by something. And when it wants its eyes to stay free from dirt, it immediately shuts them before it understands what happens to it and what it must do in this situation, as if this lies in the nature of its soul and is not done by choice.[9]

Apart from that, animals also have natural instincts.[10] For this reason there are relations that exist between these souls, and the principles of these [relations] are constant guides, contrary to the relations that happen to exist at one time but do to exist at another time, as, for instance, something that is considered with the intellect and something that suddenly comes to mind; for all things come from that place. And by these instincts estimation apprehends intentions that are mixed with the sensibles and concern what is useful or harmful. Therefore, every sheep is afraid of a wolf even if it has never seen it before, or if nothing bad has come from it. Likewise, many animals fear the lion. But also most birds fear birds of prey and flock with others without discernment. And this is one mode.

Another mode, however, is like that [cognition] produced by experience. For when an animal will have experienced pain or pleasures, the usefulness of the sensible thing or the harmfulness of the sensible thing, which are connected with the form of the sensible, will have reached it. And the form of that thing, and the form of that which is connected with it, will have been inscribed in the forming power. And the intention of the comparison of these things, and the judgment about them, will have been inscribed in memory. For there is no doubt that memory naturally apprehends this. Now, when, at a later date, the same form appears outside the imaginative [power], it will be moved by the form, and together with that [form] it will be moved by what has been connected with it from the useful and harmful

---

[7] On the difference between intentions and forms, see Chap. 4.

[8] The literal translation of the Latin term employed here would be 'caution' (*cautela*). However, I follow modern interpreters such as Tellkamp (2012), 630, in translating it as 'instinct'.

[9] I.e. by voluntary decision. On choice, in particular, see Chap. 24.

[10] See note 8.

intentions, and memory will entirely proceed by way of movement and enquiry; this is in the nature of the imaginative power. But estimation will perceive all of this at once and it will see the intention through that form. And this is the mode that happens by experience. For this reason, dogs fear stones and sticks and similar things.[11]

Sometimes, however, other judgments arise from estimation by way of resemblance. For when a thing will have had some form that is connected with an intention of estimation in some sensible thing, but which is not always connected with all of these, its intention will be seen when the form has been seen.

Sometimes, however, animals differ in their judgment that is required for their actions, so that these [actions] comply with the powers. That, however, which is required most is memory and sense. But the form mainly works because of memory and recollection. Memory, however, also exists in other animals. But recollection,[12] which is the ability of recalling what has faded, is found in humans alone, as I think. For cognising something where it has been, and that has disappeared later on, cannot work unless by a rational power. But if there were another power besides the rational, it could be estimation, but only if it is adorned with rationality. For other animals remember only when they remember; but when they do not remember, they do not wish to remember nor do they cogitate for this reason. Rather, this wish and this desire exist only in humans.

# Bibliography

## *Primary Sources*

Aristotle. (1958). *Topica et sophistici elenchii* (W. D. Ross, Ed.). Oxford: Oxford University Press.
Avicenna. (1956). *Psychologie d'ibn Sīnā (Avicenne) d'après son œvre Aš-Šifā', vol. 2* (J. Bakoš, Ed. and trans.). Prague: Éditions de l'Académie Tchécoslovaque des sciences.
Avicenna Latinus. (1968). *Liber de anima seu sextus de naturalibus IV-V* (S. van Riet, Ed.). Louvain: Peeters/Leiden: Brill.

## *Secondary Sources*

Oelze, A. (2018). *Animal rationality: Later medieval theories 1250–1350*. Leiden/Boston: Brill.
Tellkamp, J. A. (2012). *Vis aestimativa* and *vis cogitativa* in Thomas Aquinas's *Commentary on the Sentences*. The Thomist, 76, 611–640.
Tuominen, M. (2014). *The ancient commentators on Plato and Aristotle*. Abingdon/New York: Routledge.

---

[11] On the association of the form of a stick with the form of pain, see also *Liber de anima* IV.2, ed. van Riet (1968), 2.

[12] On the difference between memory and recollection, see Chap. 7.

# Chapter 6
# Estimation and Concept Formation (John Blund, *Tractatus de anima*, Chapter 19)

**Abstract** John Blund, born in England around 1175, is one of the first Latin thinkers to discuss Avicenna's theory of estimation. But even though he adopts this theory he notes that it gives rise to various problems and questions. He wonders, for example, whether intentions are universals, that is, general concepts. They seem to be universal insofar as, for instance, the feature of hostility is found in all wolves. Hence, the question arises whether nonhuman animals such as sheep have access to universals or engage in concept formation by virtue of their estimative power. Does this power conceptualise perceptual contents? Differently speaking, does the sheep see wolves rather than grey furry things? If it does, can it also combine various concepts and form propositions which are true or false? Questions as these puzzled many thirteenth-century thinkers, and John Blund was one of the first to provide an answer to them.

## Introduction

John Blund was born in England around 1175, but not much is known about his life and career.[1] He seems to have studied at the faculty of arts at Oxford and Paris where he then taught liberal arts (which at that time was an undergraduate course in philosophy) between 1200 and 1209. After that he studied and taught theology at Paris, before returning to Oxford in 1229. Besides working as a university teacher, he also seems to have held some ecclesiastical offices up to his death in 1248. Despite the general lack of details regarding his life, it is clear that he made his career at a time which was characterised by various important changes at European universities in general, and in the subjects of philosophy and psychology in particular. One of these changes was the transmission of Aristotle's writings on natural philosophy and psychology (see the section "Animals and minds in medieval philosophy" in Chap. 1 to this book). Many of these works, including the treatise on the

---

[1] For some short remarks on his career, see Dunne (2013), ix–x.

A. Oelze, *Animal Minds in Medieval Latin Philosophy*, Studies in the History of Philosophy of Mind 27, https://doi.org/10.1007/978-3-030-67012-2_6

soul (*De anima*), had been translated from Greek into Arabic in the Islamic world long before they became available in Latin Europe.[2] Therefore, it is hardly surprising that there already existed an Arabic Aristotelianism, so to speak, which, in many cases, was received in combination with the Latin translations of Aristotle's works.

One of the most influential Islamic scholars in this context was Avicenna who, in his book on the soul (*Liber de anima*), developed a famous version of what is usually referred to as the theory of internal senses (see Chaps. 4 and 5). According to this theory, humans and nonhuman animals do not only have several external senses, such as sight or hearing, but also certain internal senses, such as imagination and memory. Avicenna's most original contribution to this theory was an inner sense called 'estimation' (*aestimatio*) or 'estimative power' (*vis* or *virtus aestimativa*) in Latin. By this power, animals perceive certain relational properties of objects that are not grasped by one of the external senses. The most famous illustration of this is a sheep's perception of the feature of hostility in a wolf (see Chap. 4). While the sheep's external senses perceive so-called sensible 'forms' (*formae*), such as the wolf's colour, odour, or sound, its estimative power perceives what Avicenna's Latin translators called 'intentions' (*intentiones*), for example, the wolf's hostility.[3] The perception of intentions was considered to be crucial for an animal's survival as it triggers certain reactions such as the sheep's reaction of flight from the wolf.

John Blund is one of the first (if not *the* first) to discuss this theory, namely, in his treatise on the soul (*Tractatus de anima*).[4] This text, written during the transition from the twelfth to the thirteenth century, is one of the earliest writings on Aristotle's and Avicenna's psychology in the Latin West that we know.[5] Although Blund adopts Avicenna's theory of estimation he notes that it gives rise to various problems and questions. In the chapter on estimation that is translated in the following, he wonders, for example, whether intentions are universals, that is, general concepts. They seem to be universal insofar as, for instance, the feature of hostility is found in all wolves. Hence, the question arises whether nonhuman animals such as sheep have access to universals or engage in concept formation by virtue of their estimative power. Does this power conceptualise perceptual contents? Differently speaking, does the sheep see wolves rather than grey furry things? If it does, can it also combine various concepts and form propositions which are true or false? Questions as these puzzled many thirteenth-century thinkers, and John Blund was one of the first to provide an answer to them.[6]

---

[2] See Dod (1982) and Lohr (1982).

[3] On intentions in medieval Arabic philosophy, see Di Martino (2006) and Black (2010).

[4] Another important text is Thomas Aquinas' *Summa theologiae* I.78.4 (see Chap. 12).

[5] On this text, see Werner (2005) and Dunne (2013). An overview of natural philosophy in the early thirteenth century provides Marrone (2005).

[6] For other texts on universal cognition and concept formation, see Chaps. 8 and 9.

## *Bibliographical Note*

The English translation is based on the following critical edition (also containing a new English translation) of the Latin text: John Blund. (2013). *Treatise on the soul* (D. A. Callus & R. W. Hunt, Eds.; M. W. Dunne, Trans.) (*Auctores Britannici Medii Aevi* 2, New Edition) (pp. 136–142). Oxford: British Academy/Oxford University Press.

## *Translation*

Ch. 19: On estimation.

254. Next comes [a chapter on] estimation. Therefore, it has to be seen what estimation is and what it is for. From Avicenna[7] it has been received that estimation is a power placed in the middle concavity of the brain[8] for apprehending non-sensed intentions which are in singular and sensed things. It judges whether a thing should be fled because of an intention, if that intention is something harmful; or [it judges whether it should be] sought because of an intention, if it is something suitable. This power is, for instance, in a sheep that judges that it must flee from this wolf and that it must take care of this lamb, which is the sheep's own lamb. The commentator[9] calls an intention a singular quality which does not fall into [the range of] sense [and] which is either harmful or suitable to a thing; harmful as, for instance, the property which is in a wolf, because of which the sheep flees from a wolf; suitable as, for instance, that property which is in the sheep, because of which the lamb seeks it out.

255. But it is objected: the imagination apprehends nothing unless according to the image[10] that it receives from the common sense. Similarly, the common sense perceives nothing unless according to the likeness of the external thing which has been formed in itself by [the perception of] the external sense. So, for the same reason nothing will be formed in the organ of the estimation unless by the impression that has been formed in the imagination before, because estimation is the power that is placed behind imagination, and whatever is in the imagination originates from sensory perception. Hence, nothing is grasped by estimation unless it has been apprehended by sense before. Therefore, estimation does not perceive an intention

---

[7] See Avicenna Latinus, *Liber de anima* I.5, ed. van Riet (1972), 89 (see Chap. 4).

[8] The idea that the brain is divided into three cells or ventricles, in which different powers are located, comes from Galen. Latin thinkers knew it mainly through Nemesius of Emesa; see van der Eijk (2008).

[9] Since the middle of the thirteenth century, this expression was usually applied to Averroes who was considered to be the most important commentator of Aristotle. John Blund, however, refers to Avicenna Latinus, *Liber de anima* I.5, ed. van Riet (1972), 86 (see Chap. 4).

[10] What is meant by this is a (mental but not necessarily visual) representation of something.

unless a likeness of the intention has been established in the sense before. Hence, an intention is a thing which falls into [the range of] sense.

256. Moreover, since the wolf is a thing that is separate from the sheep, how can a likeness of the intention existing in the wolf be established in the estimation unless there has, first of all, been a change[11] in the sense of the sheep, produced by the intention existing in the wolf? For the sense is the medium between the thing sensed and the estimation. Indeed, how could a fire that is distant from a human being warm the human being unless the air in between receives the warmth from the heat[12] of the fire?

257. Solution. It must be said that an intention is a thing grasped by the estimation, not falling into [the range of] sense. It is apprehended by the soul through the mediation of sense, so that no other power is required for the apprehension of an intention, nor is its image in the sense or in the imagination. However, an image of the intention is produced by apprehension in the estimation, but its image is not in the sense nor in the imagination. Rather, in the estimation an image of the intention is produced which does not exist by any likeness of the intention in any of those things that are between the organ of estimation and the bearer of the intention, as has been said before[13] with regard to sight, [namely], that the image of the thing seen is in [the sense of] sight. And still, there is no entirely similar image in the air in between. But since, to somebody, this might seem difficult to understand, one can say that a likeness of the intention is produced in the sense and in the imagination. Yet, the soul does not apprehend according to them, because sense and imagination do not conform in nature with the proper bearer of the intention. However, the organ of estimation is of a very similar nature as what is by itself and properly the bearer of the intention. Therefore, the apprehension of an intention takes place according to the estimative power.

258. Furthermore, as has been said before,[14] by estimation sometimes a composition is made, sometimes a division is made. However, nothing can be composed according to estimation unless the extremities of that composition are apprehended first. So, when a sheep according to estimation composes in its soul this, namely, that it must flee from a wolf, it first apprehends this 'to flee', and the thing that is designated by that term 'wolf'. However, this 'to flee' is a universal, and that term 'wolf' signifies a universal. Thus, by estimation universals are apprehended. And so, brute animals can apprehend universals.

259. Moreover, concerning the composition and division of estimation, there is truth or falsity. So, since it is true that the wolf is to be fled by the sheep, it can be perceived by virtue of the power of estimation that this is true; and, for the same reason, that its composition is false. And so, if by the estimative power it can be

---

[11] The idea here is that perception occurs through a bodily change (*immutatio*) in the sense organs.

[12] This refers to heat as one of the four primary qualities (hot, cold, wet, and dry) which, according to Aristotle's cosmology, characterise the four elements (earth, water, air, and fire).

[13] I.e., John Blund, *Tractatus de anima*, c. 18, §252, eds. Callus & Hunt (2013), 136.

[14] See note 13.

determined what is true and what is false, brute animals can discern the true from the false; and so, brute animals can mutually employ arguments.

260. Solution. To the first [argument] it must be said that universals cannot be apprehended by brute animals. For estimation apprehends nothing but singulars. Therefore, by virtue of the estimative power, it is not apprehended that one must flee from a wolf [in general], but that one must flee from this wolf which is present to sense, or was present to sense before. And since, by this term 'this wolf,' a singular is signified, what is further signified by the term 'must flee,' is drawn to the singular by the qualification 'from this wolf'.

261. To the other [argument] it must be said that, even though there is composition or division in the estimative power, and truth and falsity concern them, by the estimative power it cannot be perceived that there is truth and falsity. Rather, [this can be perceived] only by intellect and reason. Therefore, although the thing in which there is truth or falsity is perceived by brute animals, the true, insofar as it is true, or the false, insofar as it is false, is not perceived by them. For they do not apprehend truth or falsity, since they lack intellect and reason.

# Bibliography

## Primary Sources

Avicenna Latinus. (1972). *Liber de anima seu sextus de naturalibus I-II-III* (S. van Riet, Ed.). Louvain: Peeters/Leiden: Brill.

John Blund. (2013). *Treatise on the soul* (D. A. Callus and R. W. Hunt, Eds.; M. W. Dunne, Trans.) (*Auctores Britannici Medii Aevi* 2, New Edition). Oxford: British Academy/Oxford University Press.

## Secondary Sources

Black, D. L. (2010). Intentionality in medieval arabic philosophy. *Quaestio, 10*(1), 65–81.

Di Martino, C. (2006). Ma'ānī / intentiones et sensibilité par accident. In M. C. Pacheco & J. F. Meirinhos (Eds.), *Intellect et imagination dans la philosophie médiévale* (Vol. 1, pp. 507–521). Brepols: Turnhout.

Dod, B. G. (1982). Aristoteles Latinus. In N. Kretzmann, A. Kenny, & J. Pinborg (Eds.), *The Cambridge history of later medieval philosophy: From the rediscovery of Aristotle to the disintegration of scholasticism 1100–1600* (pp. 43–79). Cambridge: Cambridge University Press.

Dunne, M. W. (2013). Introduction to the new edition. In J. Blund (Ed.), *Treatise on the soul* (pp. ix–xxix). Oxford: British Academy/Oxford University Press.

Lohr, C. H. (1982). The medieval interpretation of Aristotle. In N. Kretzmann, A. Kenny, & J. Pinborg (Eds.), *The Cambridge history of later medieval philosophy: From the rediscovery of Aristotle to the disintegration of scholasticism 1100–1600* (pp. 80–98). Cambridge: Cambridge University Press.

Marrone, S. (2005). The philosophy of nature in the early thirteenth century. In L. Honnefelder, R. Wood, M. Dreyer, & M.-A. Aris (Eds.), *Albertus Magnus und die Anfänge der Aristoteles-Rezeption im lateinischen Mittelalter. Von Richardus Rufus bis zu Franciscus de Mayronis* (pp. 115–158). Aschendorff: Münster.

Van der Eijk, P. J. (2008). Nemesius of Emesa and early brain mapping. *The Lancet, 372*(9637), 440–441.

Werner, D. (2005). Einleitung. In J. Blund, *Tractatus de anima. Traktat über die Seele. Lateinisch-Deutsch* (D. Werner, Ed. and Trans.) (pp. 9–94). Freiburg/Basel/Wien: Herder.

# Chapter 7
# Memory, Learning, and Prudence (Albert the Great, *Metaphysica*, Book I, Treatise 1, Chapter 6)

**Abstract** Aristotle's *Metaphysics* gave rise to various discussions of animal cognition in the later Middle Ages, because it starts with a distinction between different kinds of animals based on their cognitive capacities. While all animals can engage in sensory perception (*sensus*), not all of them have memory (*memoria*), and even fewer are capable of receiving instruction (*disciplina*) and of employing prudence (*prudentia*). The latter was usually defined as the capacity to plan for the future based on past experiences. However, it was controversial to what extent nonhuman animals are endowed with this capacity. In Albert's view, certain nonhuman animals can be called prudent, at least in a broader sense of the term. Thus, the sixth chapter of the first part of book I of his *Metaphysics* commentary (written around 1264) is an interesting example of his attempt to combine the interpretation of Aristotle with a satisfactory explanation of animal behaviour.

## Introduction

As the name suggests, Albert the Great (or Albertus Magnus in Latin) was one of the greatest scholastic thinkers, not only in the eyes of modern scholars, but also for his contemporaries. Many of them referred to him as 'universal doctor' (*doctor universalis*).[1] Albert was born in Germany during the transition from the twelfth to the thirteenth century (the exact place and date of birth are controversial). In his youth, he seems to have studied arts at what later became the University of Padua. It might have been during this time that he joined the comparatively young order of the Dominicans. After studying and lecturing theology at Cologne or Bologna, he travelled to different places mostly in Germany, until he was sent to Paris, around 1240, where he taught as a master in theology from around 1244 to 1248. The University of Paris turned out to be crucial for his career. There he met Thomas Aquinas, who became his most famous student, and he also came in contact with

---

[1] A concise introduction to his life and works is Kitchell and Resnick (1999). For a comprehensive collection of essays on his life, his works, and their reception see Zimmermann (1981).

A. Oelze, *Animal Minds in Medieval Latin Philosophy*, Studies in the History of Philosophy of Mind 27, https://doi.org/10.1007/978-3-030-67012-2_7

Aristotle's writings, many of which had just been translated into Latin, and some of which had been banned from the curriculum since they were considered to jeopardise Christian faith. In the following years, Albert accomplished the impressive mission of commenting upon all works of Aristotle. Besides being a productive author, he also played an important role within the Dominican order. After moving from Paris to Cologne he founded the *studium generale* (a precursor of the University of Cologne) and, in 1254, was elected prior provincial of the German branch of the Dominicans which, at that time, stretched across various parts of Western, Central, and Eastern Europe. He remained an active member of the order and a prolific writer on philosophy and theology until his death on November 15 in 1280.

Albert's writings fill numerous volumes and cover almost anything from logic, metaphysics, and natural philosophy to ethics, politics, and theology.[2] He commented on Aristotle, but he also wrote commentaries on Pseudo-Dionysius, Peter Lombard, and the Bible, and so he played a crucial role for the reception of Aristotle in particular as well as for the late-medieval development of philosophy, science, and theology in general.[3] Amongst his writings is one of the few extant commentaries on Aristotle's books *On Animals* (*De animalibus*) in which Albert discusses the physiology and psychology of animals (see Chap. 8). However, he pays attention to the question of animal mentality in other writings, as well.

One of these is his commentary on Aristotle's *Metaphysics* (written around 1264).[4] The *Metaphysics* is a text that gave rise to various discussions of animal cognition in the later Middle Ages, because it starts with a distinction between different kinds of animals based on their cognitive capacities.[5] While all animals can engage in sensory perception (*sensus*), not all of them have memory (*memoria*), and even fewer are capable of receiving instruction (*disciplina*) and of employing prudence (*prudentia*). The latter was usually defined as the capacity to plan for the future based on past experiences, but it was controversial to what extent nonhuman animals are endowed with this capacity. While, for example, John Duns Scotus remained critical towards ascribing prudence to such animals (see Chap. 13), Albert is less hesitant to claim that certain nonhuman animals can be called prudent, at least in a broader sense of the term.[6] Thus, the sixth chapter of the first part of book I of his *Metaphysics* commentary translated below is an interesting example of his

---

[2] The edition by Borgnet (1890–1899) counts 38 volumes many of which contain more than one work. However, some were identified as inauthentic. The more recent *Editio Coloniensis*, which now is the standard critical edition, presents 70 of Albert's works in 41 volumes but is not yet finished.

[3] On Albert's role in thirteenth-century philosophy, science, and theology, see, for instance, the articles in Weisheipl (1980), Senner (2001), and Resnick (2013).

[4] See Anzulewicz (forthcoming).

[5] The Latin reception of the *Metaphysics* was mediated by the commentary of the Arabic philosopher Averroes. On Albert's reception of the *Metaphysics*, see Honnefelder (2011).

[6] An overview of late-medieval positions on animal prudence, including Albert and Scotus, provide Köhler (2014), 136–153, and Oelze (2018), part V. For some remarks on Albert's account of animal prudence, see also Guldentops (1999); Anzulewicz (2009); Roling (2013).

attempt to combine the interpretation of Aristotle with a satisfactory explanation of animal behaviour.

## Bibliographical Note

The English translation is based on the following critical edition of the Latin text: Albert the Great. (1960). *Metaphysica: Libri quinque priores* (B. Geyer, Ed.) (*Opera omnia* 16/1) (pp. 8–10). Münster: Aschendorff. This commentary has not yet been translated into English. However, there is a Spanish translation of the first book: Albert the Great. (2013). *Introducción a la metafísica: Paráfrasis de san Alberto Magno al primer libro de la Metafísica de Aristóteles, Edicion bilingüe* (D. Torrijos Castrillejo, Ed. & Trans.). Madrid: Ediciones Universidad San Dámaso.

## Translation

Ch. 6. On the sources from which knowledge first derives in those who know, which are sensory perception, memory, and reason.

After this,[7] however, those powers by virtue of which knowledge is brought to the one who knows, need to be examined. *Thus,*[8] we say that *animals certainly have been created* or generated *as having sensory perception.* For the actualisation of an animal is the sensory soul. And for those animals which sense, sensing through the powers of the sensory life means to be. However, the first of these actualisations of animals is like sleep, the second like wakefulness. And so, at first, animals having sensory perception are created such that the state of sense is like sleep. Then they [begin to] use sense, because wakefulness indeed corresponds to the reaching out of the senses towards the sensible things. And so, if the first faculty of cognition and the first power with regard to us is for sensing, it is the first [source or power] from which knowledge originates in us. And this first [source or power], which, first of all, consists in having sense and in being able to engage in this kind of cognition, comes from the genus of living beings, not from the constitutive difference[9] of human beings. We ask which sense it is that provides the first faculty and power of knowing. From those things that have been determined in the second book of *On the*

---

[7] In Chap. 5 of his commentary, Albert discussed what Aristotle means by the 'natural longing for knowing' (*naturale sciendi desiderium*) that is attributed to humans in *Metaphysics* I.1, 980a21.

[8] The passages printed in italics are literal quotations from the Latin translation of Aristotle's text.

[9] This difference, also known as 'specific difference' (*differentia specifica*), is the difference by which humans were taken to differ from all other animals. It was usually defined as rationality.

*Soul*[10] and in the book *On Animals*[11] it is clear that this sense is touch; this is the basis of all other senses and it is this [sense] which has a soft mixture and reaches the middle by receding from the excess of the contraries so that it does to some extent resemble heaven because of its mildness and suitable mixture.[12] Therefore, the source is placed in something similar to the mover of the heaven. And so, having the power of knowing, the animal spirit,[13] which carries the forms of cognition, can circulate in it because of the softness. And with respect to these two, the understanding of sensible cognition is completed, as far as grasping [something] is concerned.

Yet, knowing is not completed by one single apprehension of sensible things, but rather by two other [cognitive operations] in conjunction with it. One of them is the [act of] storing similar sensible things that have been grasped. Here the universal is one grasping of the many things that are essentially similar. But the storing of what has been grasped before, together with what has been grasped later, and of these two with what has been grasped third, fourth, and so forth, is done by memory. The single grasp of what is common to all of these, however, is done by reason. And it is these three [operations][14] by which knowledge is brought to the one who knows. Therefore, it is necessary for us to distinguish different kinds of animals, and to see in which of them these three sources of knowing come together.

*Thus*, as we have said, we say that *animals* are generated as *having sensory perception* according to their genus, although some of them use sensory perception only very little regarding the life that is open to sense. *But in some* of the animals *memory does not arise from sensory perception* by virtue of the act [of perception] that has been produced, because they do not retain the sensible things that have been apprehended due to the watery coldness or earthiness of their [bodily] mixture which immobilises the animal spirit that transports the sensible forms.[15] This is evident with regard to the genus of flies: immediately after they have been driven away with a fly flap, they continue bothering, because they do not remember the attack. Furthermore, they do not gather at fixed dwellings nor do they seem to have anything that is similar to memory.[16] And so, any [animals] which are like this do

---

[10] Albertus Magnus, *De anima*, b. II, tr. 3, ch. 30–35, ed. Stroick (1968), 141–148.

[11] The editors of the critical Latin edition refer to the following passage: Albertus Magnus, *De animalibus*, b. XII, tr. 1, ch. 1, §12, ed. Stadler (1916), 802. However, one could also refer to ibid., b. I, tr. 1, ch. 5, §64, 24, where Albert says that 'it is the sense of touch by which an animal is an animal'.

[12] This argument is based on Aristotle's cosmology, according to which each sense has its particular 'mixture' (*complexio*) depending on the mix ratio of the four elements (earth, water, air, and fire).

[13] According to the theory of the Greek physician Galen (AD 129–c. 216), the 'animal spirit' (*spiritus animalis*) is the lightest of the three invisible substances flowing through the nerves. It is stored in the ventricles of the brain and carries sensory impressions or 'forms'.

[14] I.e. sensing, remembering, and forming concepts.

[15] This argument is also based on Aristotle' theory of elements (see note 12) and Galen's concept of animal spirits (see note 13). The idea is that particularly cold and earthy organs are unsuitable for retaining the sensory impressions carried by the animal spirit.

[16] This is also mentioned in Albert the Great, *De animalibus*, b. XXI, tr. 1, ch. 1, §9, ed. Stadler (1920), 1326; see Chap. 8.

not have foresight or prudence. Rather, by sensory perception alone, they seek what is pleasant for their sense, and flee what is unpleasant. *But in some* memory of the sensible things that have been grasped arises from sensory perception by virtue of the act [of perception] that has been produced. Now, memory is not only a store and a heap of the forms of sensible things that have been grasped before, but also of the intentions[17] of what is pleasant or unpleasant, good or bad, friendly or hostile, and other such things that are grasped by estimation together with the sensible things, as we have shown in the book *On memory and recollection.*[18] *Consequently, some* animals *are certainly prudent*, [namely], those which have a conduct of life based on memory. *Yet, others* which are strong only with respect to sensory perception are imprudent. However, to those which are prudent by memory, I do not employ 'prudent' in the strict sense of prudence, which is an active habit with true reason concerning those things that are in us, relevant for life.[19] But those that do not have true reason use memory in place of reason and in some way arrange what is favourable for their life by a certain likeness of civilised behaviour and happiness. This can be seen in bees and cranes and many animals of this kind. But *bees* as well as cranes are strong only with regard to memory. A sign for this is that they return to their proper dwellings and housings from remote places to which they have moved.

However, there is yet another difference in animals, though not with regard to memory and sensory perception (because of which an animal is an animal), but with respect to the two things said before, and also with regard to the sharing in hearing which, in a certain sense, cannot be found in all. As it happens, one can have hearing in two ways: first, insofar as the usefulness of what is gathered in connection with sensory perception [is grasped], and insofar as this sound or voice heard more or less reveals what the feeling[20] is about; like, for instance, when we see birds which have heard sad or happy twittering fly away or flock together. The other kind of sharing in hearing is the kind in which hearing consists in catching the names that signify things. And we see that certain animals have this kind of hearing; and we see that any of those which have this kind of hearing together with memory, which itself requires the sense of the animal nature, are *more trainable* than those which do not have the faculty of remembering such things heard. For those animals keep the *sounds* and names *they hear* in memory, and to similar voices and sounds they do many things that are similar to acts of training. For here I call 'instruction' any kind of doctrine that has been grasped by hearing, and so hearing itself is called the trainable sense.[21] Here we do not pay attention to the special character of instruction or doctrine that is intellectual. Rather, we call instruction a kind of learning that comes about by sensible signs, as when dogs, monkeys, or parrots and the like learn

---

[17] On the concept of intentions that are perceived by estimation see Chaps. 4, 5, and 6.

[18] Albert the Great, *De memoria et reminiscentia*, tr. 1, ch. 1, ed. Donati (2017), 114.

[19] This refers to Aristotle's definition in the *Nicomachean Ethics* VI.5, 1140b4, where prudence (*phronesis*) is defined as "a truth-attaining rational quality, concerned with action in relation to things that are good and bad for human beings" (tr. Rackham 1926, 337).

[20] The term '*affectus*' can also mean 'state of body or mind', 'emotion', 'volition', or 'intention'.

[21] On hearing as sense required for learning see also Chap. 8.

through cues. Since, however, this kind of learning consists in two kinds of art, namely, liberal and mechanical, a great many animals seem to be learned with regard to certain basic liberal arts, such as jumping, acrobatics, dancing, or anything else of this kind, but few with regard to mechanical [arts].[22] For instance, a monkey sometimes imitates a certain mechanical art due to its proximity to a likeness[23] of human beings. However, I call those arts 'liberal' which we want for their own sake and not for something else, such as the art of music and dancing, jumping, fist-fighting, tournament, and anything else of this kind where we enjoy the exercising itself. 'Mechanical', by contrast, I call any kind of those [arts] which we pursue not for their own sake but for some other purpose, as, for instance, forging is not for forging but for [producing] a sword, bootmaking for [producing] shoes; and there are many more of this kind. But these have been thoroughly examined in the *Ethics*.[24]

Yet, there is a difference between prudence and instruction with regard to the things which they concern and with regard to those from which they originate. For, prudence is a certain sagacity that exists with regard to those things profitable for life. [It comes] from memory of the pleasurable things that have been grasped by sensory perception by virtue of a sensory act which has been brought about. Instruction, by contrast, is a sagacity concerning those things by which an art based on the memory of sounds exists, insofar as they are – as names or concepts – signs for things.

And so, some animals are certainly prudent without instruction, and certainly all of them are capable of remembering. Still, they cannot hear the sounds insofar as these are – as names – signs for things. Bees, for instance, even though they hear sounds, cannot hear them in the aforementioned manner, and so [can] no other genus of animals of this kind. For this kind of hearing of sounds is not completed by the sense of hearing alone but also by the power of estimation which in some way brings together what is signified by a name or a sound with the name. But any animals which, besides memory, also have this sense that stores the intentions and notions of things and names, are capable of learning; and certainly they hear in the aforementioned way.

*Thus,* from all the things that have been mentioned, one can draw the conclusion that, with regard to their conduct of life, certain *other* animals *live* from *imaginations and memories* alone. For we have said in the science *Of the Soul*[25] that imagination is the storage of sensible species insofar as they are the images of things. In this sense, imagination is some kind of memory. But memory is a heap of those things that are appropriate or inappropriate for life which one intends to reach by

---

[22] Albert here slightly deviates from the traditional concept of liberal arts which were usually divided into *trivium* (grammar, logic, rhetoric) and *quadrivium* (arithmetic, geometry, music, and astronomy).

[23] The idea that monkeys are likenesses of humans has a long history; see Janson (1952), 73–89.

[24] Albert the Great, *Ethica*, b. I, tr. 3, ch. 8, ed. Borgnet (1891), 40f.

[25] Albert the Great, *De anima*, b. III, tr. 1, ch. 1, ed. Stroick (1968), 166.

movement. Therefore, these things are called 'intentions'[26] by Peripatetic[27] philosophers. And so, whatever these animals grasp from such things for the conduct of life, they do not have experience, because experience has two aspects: one is somehow formal, and this is the grasp of what is similar in many things; the other one is material, and is the memory of what has been gathered. *They do not participate in experience* unless in the sense of the material aspect that is in them. For instance, a bird, as we have said in the science *Of Animals,*[28] which is fighting with a snake and which senses that it has been wounded, treats itself with wild lettuce and returns to the fight. *But the genus of humans*, in all its diversity, is strong in its conduct of life and in the art of producing something, because 'art is a productive habit together with true reason',[29] *and* [the genus of humans] is strong [in acting] on the basis of reasons in practical and theoretical matters. This has already been examined by us in the *Ethics.*[30] For even though the nature of humans is one with regard to the particular species, there still is a whole range [of natures] with regard to the faculties of the soul, the mixtures [of the body], and the places which they inhabit. Yet, across the board and in all regions, [the genus of humans] participates in arts regarding communicative contexts, in rational enquiries regarding the theoretical realm, and in customs with regard to virtue.

And so, in this way the question about the faculties or abilities of nature, by virtue of which the grasping of what can be known is completed, has been settled.

# Bibliography

## *Primary Sources*

Albert the Great. (1891). *Ethica* (A. Borgnet, Ed.) (*Opera omnia* 7). Paris: Vivès.

Albert the Great. (1916–1920). *De animalibus libri XXVI* (2 vols). (H. Stadler, Ed.). Münster: Aschendorff.

Albert the Great. (1960). *Metaphysica: Libri quinque priores* (B. Geyer, Ed.) (*Opera omnia* 16/1). Münster: Aschendorff.

---

[26] Albert here points to the fact that the noun '*intentio*' is related to the verb '*intendere*' which can mean 'to stretch' but also 'to aim at'. However, it is important to note that the Latin term '*intentio*' is a translation of the Arabic term '*ma'na*,' the meaning of which is not equivalent to the modern meaning of 'intention'; see Crane (1998), esp. 816, and Amerini (2011), esp. 558f.

[27] I.e. Aristotelian philosophers.

[28] Albert the Great, *De animalibus*, b. VIII, tr. 2, ch. 2, §47, ed. Stadler (1916), 590. Albert mentions that this example is found in Avicenna's *De animalibus* of which he knew the Latin translation by Michael Scot (see b. IX, ch. 2, Venice c. 1500, fol. 15v-16r). Avicenna seems to have adopted this example (in a slightly modified version) from Aristotle's *Historia animalium* IX.6, 612a24-28. Based on this passage, Albert reports a similar story about a weasel in *De animalibus*, b. XXI, tr. 1, Chap. 2, §11, ed. Stadler (1920), 1327; see Chap. 8.

[29] This definition is based on Aristotle, *Nicomachean Ethics* VI.4, 1140a21.

[30] Albert the Great, *Ethica*, b. VI, tr. 2, ch. 5, ed. Borgnet (1891), 414f.

Albert the Great. (1968). *De anima* (C. Stroick, Ed.) (*Opera omnia* 7/1). Münster: Aschendorff.
Albert the Great. (2013). *Introducción a la metafísica: Paráfrasis de san Alberto Magno al primer libro de la Metafísica de Aristóteles, Edicion bilingüe* (D. Torrijos Castrillejo, Ed. & Trans.). Madrid: Ediciones Universidad San Dámaso.
Albert the Great. (2017). *De sensu et sensato cuius secundus liber est De memoria et reminiscentia* (S. Donati, Ed.) (*Opera omnia* 7/2A). Münster: Aschendorff.
Aristotle. (1894). *Ethica Nicomachea* (I. Bywater, Ed.). Oxford: Clarendon Press.
Aristotle. (1957). *Metaphysica* (W. Jaeger, Ed.). Oxford: Clarendon Press.
Aristotle. (1965–1991). *History of animals*. 3 vols. (A. L. Peck & D. M. Balme, Eds.). Cambridge, Mass./London: Harvard University Press.

## Secondary Sources

Amerini, F. (2011). Intentionality. In H. Lagerlund (Ed.), *Encyclopedia of medieval philosophy: Philosophy between 500 and 1500* (Vol. 1, pp. 558–564). Dordrecht: Springer.
Anzulewicz, H. (2009). Albertus Magnus und die Tiere. In S. Obermaier (Ed.), *Tiere und Fabelwesen im Mittelalter* (pp. 29–54). Berlin/New York: Walter de Gruyter.
Anzulewicz, H. (forthcoming). Der Metaphysik-Kommentar des Albertus Magnus und das Buch Lambda. *Eine Einführung*.
Crane, T. (1998). Intentionality. In E. Craig (Ed.), *Routledge encyclopedia of philosophy* (Vol. 4, pp. 816–821). London: Routledge.
Guldentops, G. (1999). The sagacity of the bees: An Aristotelian topos in thirteenth-century philosophy. In C. G. Steel, G. Guldentops, & P. Beullens (Eds.), *Aristotle's animals in the middle ages and renaissance* (pp. 275–296). Leuven: Leuven University Press.
Janson, H. W. (1952). *Apes and ape lore in the middle ages and the renaissance*. London: Warburg Institute.
Honnefelder, L. (2011). Metaphysik als, Erste Wissenschaft': Die kritische Rezeption der aristotelischen Metaphysik durch Albert den Großen. In id. (Ed.), *Albertus Magnus und der Ursprung der Universitätsidee: Die Begegnung der Wissenschaftskulturen im 13. Jahrhundert und die Entdeckung des Konzepts der Bildung durch Wissenschaft* (pp. 332–353). Berlin: Berlin University Press.
Kitchell, K. F., Jr., & Resnick, I. M. (1999). Introduction: The life and works of Albert the Great. In Albert the Great, *On animals: A medieval Summa zoologica* (K. F. Kitchell & I. M. Resnick, Trans.) (Vol. 1, pp. 1–42). Baltimore: Johns Hopkins University Press.
Köhler, T. W. (2014). *Homo animal nobilissimum: Konturen des spezifisch Menschlichen in der naturphilosophischen Aristoteleskommentierung des dreizehnten Jahrhunderts, Teilband 2.1 und 2.2*. 2 vols. Leiden/Boston: Brill.
Oelze, A. (2018). *Animal rationality: Later medieval theories 1250–1350*. Leiden/Boston: Brill.
Resnick, I. M. (Ed.). (2013). *A companion to Albert the great: Theology, philosophy, and the sciences*. Leiden/Boston: Brill.
Roling, B. (2013). Die Geometrie der Bienenwabe: Albertus Magnus, Karl von Baer und die Debatte über das Vorstellungsvermögen und die Seele der Insekten zwischen Mittelalter und Neuzeit. *Recherches de théologie et philosophie médiévales, 80*(2), 401–504.
Senner, W. (Ed.). (2001). *Albertus Magnus: Zum Gedenken nach 800 Jahren: Neue Zugänge, Aspekte und Perspektiven*. Berlin: Akademie Verlag.
Weisheipl, J. A. (Ed.). (1980). *Albertus Magnus and the sciences: Commemorative essays 1980*. Toronto: Pontifical Institute of Medieval Studies.
Zimmermann, A. (Ed.). (1981). *Albert der Große: Seine Zeit, sein Werk, seine Wirkung*. Berlin/ New York: De Gruyter.

# Chapter 8
# Learning, Language, and Reasoning(Albert the Great, *De animalibus*, Book 21, Treatise 1, Chapters 2–4)

**Abstract** In his commentary on Aristotle's zoological works, Albert the Great notes that there are different degrees of learning. Although many nonhuman animals can be trained to follow the commands of their masters, only humans seem to be capable of learning to the extent that they engage in arts and sciences. Nevertheless, certain nonhuman animals, namely, monkeys and so-called pygmies come very close to humans because of their faculty of estimation and a power which Albert calls 'shadow of reason'. They can engage in basic forms of practical reasoning and produce some sort of language. Although Albert's account is not based on empirical research, unlike modern theories of animal psychology, his commentary shows interesting parallels to contemporary views and it is undoubtedly a substantial and important contribution to medieval zoology.

## Introduction

Amongst the works of Aristotle commented upon by medieval scholars is a comparatively voluminous treatise on animals known as '*De animalibus*'. Strictly speaking, it is a combination of several writings: the 'History of Animals' (*Historia animalium*), 'On the Parts of Animals' (*De partibus animalium*), and 'On the Generation of Animals' (*De generatione animalium*). In many cases, encyclopaedic medieval texts on animals were added to these treatises. Although various medieval thinkers seem to have commented on the *De animalibus* only few commentaries have survived.[1] One of these commentaries has been written by an unknown author, called Pseudo-Peter of Spain (see Chap. 9). Another one comes from Albert the Great.[2]

By and large, Albert's commentary is a paraphrase of Aristotle. In some parts, however, he deviates from Aristotle's text and develops his own and, quite often,

---

[1] See Asúa (1991); Köhler (1999); Van den Abeele (1999); Perfetti (2004).

[2] On Albert's commentary in particular, see Asúa (1994) and Resnick and Kitchell (1999), 34–42. In fact, there is also a second commentary; see text 15.

A. Oelze, *Animal Minds in Medieval Latin Philosophy*, Studies in the History of Philosophy of Mind 27, https://doi.org/10.1007/978-3-030-67012-2_8

original account of animal psychology and physiology. The first chapters of book 21 which have been translated for this volume provide a good example. In these passages, Albert presents a classification of animals which is obviously inspired by the Aristotelian idea of a 'ladder of nature' (*scala naturae*).[3] According to this idea, all beings, from minerals and plants to insects, monkeys, and humans, can be ranked depending on their degree of both physiological and psychological complexity. Yet, Albert is aware of the fact that such a classification is only as good and helpful as the set of criteria on which it is based. With regard to animals, that is, beings which, contrary to plants and non-living bodies, are endowed with various sense organs, he suggests that psychological features or cognitive capacities form good criteria of classification. In particular, he emphasises memory and hearing because they are required for learning.[4]

As Albert notes, there are different degrees of learning or of the capacity of receiving instruction (*disciplinabilitas*).[5] Although many nonhuman animals can be trained to follow the commands of their masters, only humans seem to be capable of learning to the extent that they engage in arts and sciences. Nevertheless, certain nonhuman animals, namely, monkeys and so-called pygmies,[6] come very close to humans with respect to their cognitive capacities. According to Albert, they are 'likenesses of humans' (*similitudines hominum*) because their faculty of estimation. By this power animals judge *how* things are (e.g. harmful or useful, hostile or friendly), and, in some respect, it can be quite similar to human reason. This means that pygmies have what Albert calls a 'shadow of reason' (*umbra rationis*). By this capacity they can engage in basic forms of practical reasoning and produce some sort of language. Although Albert's account is not based on empirical research, unlike modern theories of animal psychology, his commentary shows interesting parallels to contemporary views and it is undoubtedly a substantial and important contribution to medieval zoology.[7]

## Bibliographical Note

The English translation is based on the following critical edition of the Latin text: Albert the Great. (1920). *De animalibus libri XXVI* (H. Stadler, Ed.) (pp. 1325–1335). Münster: Aschendorff. For an alternative English translation, see: Albert the Great.

---

[3] On the idea of a great chain of beings see Lovejoy (1936), esp. 24–98. On the Aristotelian *scala naturae* in particular see Granger (1985) and Coles (1997).

[4] His account is largely based on Aristotle, *Metaphysica* I.1, 980a27f.

[5] I prefer to translate '*disciplinabilitas*' with 'capacity of receiving instruction' rather than with 'learning,' because what Albert seems to have in mind is not the modern and much broader concept of learning but first and foremost animals' capacity to follow certain commands or instructions.

[6] On pygmies, their nature, and their status in the animal kingdom see n5.

[7] On Albert's contribution to medieval zoology and animal psychology, see, for instance, Hünemörder (1980); Köhler (2001); Tkacz (2007) and (2013); Anzulewicz (2009). A careful analysis of book 21 is provided by Wei (2020), 147–165.

(1999). *On animals: A medieval Summa zoologica* (I. M. Resnick & K. F. Kitchell, Jr., Trans.) (Vol. 2, pp. 1414–1425). Baltimore: The Johns Hopkins University Press.


## Translation

Ch. 2: On the modes of perfection of animals, on how many there are in general, and what they are with respect to the soul and with regard to the body, from which the nature of the pygmy can be known.

[8] Theophrastus,[8] however, says that one must speak about the perfection of other animals in two ways. For some of them are more perfect than others with respect to the body, and some are more perfect than others with regard to the powers of the soul. And each of these perfections is twofold, because that concerning the body either concerns the size of the body or the quality[9] of its equality or [bodily] mixture. And that [perfection] which indeed concerns the size of the body is further divided into two [aspects], because the perfection of the size either concerns the size of a continuous quantity[10] or it concerns the number of organs, which is the number of a discrete quantity. For instance, the elephant has a trunk which other animals do not have, and it uses it for many purposes in place of hands.

In addition, that [perfection] which concerns the soul is divided into or made of two aspects. It consists either in participating in several internal powers[11] of the soul or in participating in several external powers[12] amongst a number of senses. And regarding the participation in the internal apprehending powers, there are two kinds [of participation]: one of them concerns the number of powers; the other one concerns the mode and the quality. For some of the animals seem to have few or no internal powers, while others are so strong in these that they even seem to have something similar to reason. Still, amongst those which have these kinds of abilities and powers, some, such as bees, have a certain subtlety in them, which others that are larger in size do not have. And it is necessary for us to specify each mode of perfection or imperfection of animals, because from the mode of their perfection and imperfection a great deal about their nature and works can be known.

[9] Now, let us first speak of the modes of perfection with regard to the soul. While first dealing with the perfection of the soul we will examine the one that concerns the number of powers and abilities of the soul. And let us use the technique

---

[8] Theophrastus (c. 371–287 BC) studied at the academy of Plato before becoming the successor of Aristotle as head of the Peripatetic school in Athens. It is rather unlikely that Albert knew any of his writings directly and it is unclear to which of Theophrastus' statements he refers in this passage.

[9] I.e. the quality of the mix ratio of the four elements (air, water, earth, and fire) which, in Aristotelian cosmology, constitute all living and non-living bodies.

[10] For Aristotelians the 'continuous quantity' is the spatial dimension of a body. It is different from the specific number (e.g. of limbs) or 'discrete quantity'; see Kraus (2016), 147–149.

[11] E.g. imagination, estimation, or memory. On the inner senses, see also Chaps. 4 and 12.

[12] Sight, hearing, taste, smell, and touch.

that Aristotle passed on at the beginning of the First Philosophy,[13] where he says that we see all animals to have some sense and grasp of sensible things.

From [perception by] sense, however, memory is produced in some [animals], but not in others. And that memory is not produced from sensation in some we know from the fact that memory is what makes [someone] return [to something], based on what has been grasped by sense before, even when that thing is [presently] absent. For instance, we see sated vultures flying away from the place of the cadaver and later returning by memory of the place and the cadaver. And in this way flocks return to stables and birds to nests and the like. About those animals, however, which only seek what is presently sensible, and which do not return to a sensible thing that is absent on the basis of what they have grasped before, we know that they do not have any memory of previously grasped things. And this is how flies are which, after they have been driven away, come back, not remembering the blow received before.[14] We also see that they do not keep fixed dwelling-places; and we see that they only seek what is presently sensible.

[10] Moreover, we see certain animals having a certain [kind of] prudence concerning things they gather for themselves. Still, they are incapable of being instructed, as is evident in bees which have a great deal of prudence in gathering things and which, nevertheless, cannot be instructed. The same applies to ants.[15] For it is possible that they take care of their stocks in advance by prudence. But that they do not follow the voices of humans and do not fear their threats nor seem to flee terrifying sounds is a sign [of the fact] that they are not capable of being instructed by the teaching of humans. Therefore, some even say that they do not hear sounds. This, however, has been proven wrong in previous chapters[16] because they seem to hear sounds. Yet, whatever is the case regarding [their sense of] hearing, it is undoubtedly true that they do not hear sounds for instruction so that they could be called by names and instructed as many other animals, such as dogs and monkeys[17] and certain others, are instructed.

Now, hearing is possessed by animals in two ways: By some it is possessed only insofar as it is a sense; by others it is possessed insofar as it is a sense and insofar as it is a sense capable of receiving instruction. Now, this second mode is possessed

---

[13] See Aristotle, *Metaphysica* I.1, 980a27f.

[14] See also Albert the Great, *Metaphysica*, b. I, tr. 1, ch. 6, ed. Geyer (1960), 8f. (see Chap. 7).

[15] On Albert's views on bees and ants, see Guldentops (1999); Anzulewicz (2009); Roling (2013).

[16] The passage to which Albert refers is unclear. However, someone who (in accordance with Aristotle) claimed that bees lack the sense of hearing is Thomas Aquinas, *In duodecim libros Metaphysicorum Aristotelis expositio*, b. 2, lec. 1, n. 12, eds. Cathala & Spiazzi (1964), 8.

[17] The Latin term '*simia*' is not co-extensional with the modern English 'simians'. While the latter includes (New and Old World) monkeys and apes (including humans), the former only refers to nonhuman primates. In most cases in which Albert employs this term it seems that what he has in mind are monkeys rather than (nonhuman great) apes. However, his classification also includes so-called 'pygmies' which he considers to rank between cognitively lowly-developed monkeys and highly-developed humans; see esp. ch. 3, §16 and note 22 below. On apes in the Middle Ages, see Janson (1952).

by animals in two ways, because this sense is capable of receiving instruction insofar as, from sounds and voices, the meaning of the intentions of the one who produces a sound or calls is grasped. For this is the way in which sounds and voices
constitute instruction. This, however, happens in two ways because at some times
sounds and voices produce an indistinct, at other times a distinct sign of an intention. They produce an indistinct sign in brute animals and a distinct sign in humans.
And so, any animals which possess hearing (in terms of a sense that is capable of
receiving instruction) and which, in addition, have memory (by which they keep the
signs of the instruction that they got either distinctly or indistinctly) are capable of
receiving instruction and perceive a distinct or indistinct instruction. Thus, many
animals do many things at the voices of humans: the elephant bends its knee in the
presence of the king at the voice of the one who tells it to do so, and dogs do many
things like this. Yet, bees and other small animals do not in any way perceive sounds
and voices instructively although they are very strong with regard to memory. And
so, this is the reason for the capacity of receiving instruction in some animals. The
lack of this kind of capacity of receiving instruction is most present in very small
animals, such as bees and wasps and achathys[18] and fleas and other vermin of
this kind.

[11] However, some animals seem to participate in something like experience to
a minor degree. Experience arises from many memories, because many memories
of one and the same thing establish the power and faculty of experience. We see that
many animals, apart from humans, have some experiential cognition of particulars.
For instance, a weasel, after it has been hurt by fighting with a snake, applies a leaf
of wild lettuce, which is called 'pig snout'[19] by some, as an antidote. We have mentioned many other things like this that are done by animals in previous passages.[20]
Still, they do not properly participate in experience, because they do not get to the
universal [concept], to art,[21] and reason by experience. Nevertheless, they do to
some degree participate in experience, as we have already said.

Some [animals], however, are so developed with regard to these powers that they
have a certain imitation of art, even though they do not attain art [in the strict sense
of the term]. And we see this happening in animals in two ways. Some seem to be
capable [of receiving instruction] by sight and by hearing because they do what they
see and they retain what they hear (as monkeys, for example). Certain [animals],
however, are so strong in receiving instruction by hearing that they even mutually

---

[18] It is unclear which animal Albert means by 'achathys'. The editor of the Latin text suggests that
it comes from the Greek terms for (male) cicadas (*achétēs*) or spiders (*aráchnē*).

[19] It is not entirely clear which plant is meant by 'pig snout' (*rostrum porcinum*) although Albert
mentions it several times in his treatise on plants (*De vegetabilibus*). In the index of the Latin edition of *De animalibus*, it is identified as common dandelion (*taraxacum officinale*).

[20] E.g. *De animalibus*, b. VIII, tr. 2, ch. 2, §47, ed. Stadler (1916), 590, and *Metaphysica*, b. I, tr. 1,
ch. 6, ed. Geyer (1960), 10. These instances are modified versions of the example in Aristotle,
*Historia animalium* IX.6, 612a24–28.

[21] 'Art' here means any of the liberal and mechanical arts such as arithmetic or architecture.

indicate their intentions as [does] the pygmy[22] which speaks[23] although it is a non-rational[24] animal. Hence, with regard to cognitive[25] powers, the pygmy seems to be the most perfect animal after humans. And it seems that, in comparison to all other animals, it gathers its memories so much more and perceives more of the signs it has heard that it seems to have something imitating reason, although it lacks reason. For reason is the power of the soul for running through experiences that have been acquired from [several] memories. By a topical[26] and syllogistic habit[27] it elicits a universal, and from this it gathers the principles of arts and sciences by similar habits. The pygmy, however, does not do this; and it does not separate what it acquires by hearing from the intentions[28] of sensible things. Yet, given that they are intentions of sensible things it commends them to memory. And, in this way, it gathers by speech and indicates to others what it has gathered.

[12] And so, even though the pygmy speaks it does not engage in discussions nor does it speak about the universals of things. Rather, its vocal expressions concern the particular things about which it speaks. For its speech is produced by a shadow that is reflected from the sinking of reason.[29] Reason has two functions. One of them comes from its reflection on sense and memory, and this is the perception by experience. The second function, however, is what it has insofar as it is raised to the simple intellect.[30] And this is where it is tending to elicit a universal, which is the starting point of art and science. The pygmy, however, has nothing but the former of these functions. Therefore, it has nothing but a shadow of reason because all the light of reason rests in the second function. But I call 'shadow' that which is a reflection darkened by the matter of sensible things and not separated from the attachments of

---

[22] For Albert, pygmies are '*simiae*', that is, a peculiar kind of monkey or ape (see note 17). Yet they come close to humans, both in cognition and physiology. On pygmies in medieval philosophy in general and in Albert in particular, see Koch (1931); Janson (1952), esp. 84–89; Köhler (1992) and (2008), 419–443; Thijssen (1995); Friedrich (2009), 138–141; Roling (2010), 486–498; Salisbury (2011), 122–124.

[23] On the language of pygmies, see Resnick and Kitchell (1996); Tellkamp (2013), 214–217; Köhler (2014), 487f.; Oelze (2018), 73–75; Toivanen (2018), 138f.

[24] This means that they lack the psychological *faculty* of reason. However, they seem to be capable of engaging in basic forms of rational *processes*, as the following paragraphs show.

[25] I translate '*animalis*' with 'cognitive' since cognition is the characteristic feature of all animals.

[26] In (Aristotelian) logic, the Latin term '*localis*' can have the particular meaning of something pertaining to a certain *topos*, that is, a place from which an argument (a syllogism) can be invented.

[27] A technique of reasoning to which one gets used by exercise or habituation. On the many meanings of 'habit' (*habitus*) in medieval philosophy, see Faucher and Roques (2018).

[28] In this case 'intention' means a particular kind of sensory information, namely, information on relational properties, such as the hostility of the wolf that is perceived by the sheep. On intentions in this sense see, for instance, texts 3, 4 and 5.

[29] The metaphor seems to work like this: the 'sun of reason' is shining in human animals. Pygmies, by contrast, only see a shadow since the sun is below their (cognitive) horizon. On the origin and meaning of this concept, see Köhler (2008), 434f., and (2014), 199.

[30] The kind of intellect by which humans acquire knowledge of (scientific) subjects; see Anzulewicz (2013), 332.

matter. Therefore, the pygmy does not in any way perceive anything from the quid-dities[31] of things nor does it ever perceive the forms of arguments. Its speech is like the speech of mentally disabled people who are mentally deficient by nature in the sense that they are insensible to reasons. However, the difference here is that the pygmy faces a lack of reason by nature, whereas a mentally disabled human does not suffer from a lack of reason but rather from a lack of the usage of reason because of melancholy[32] or some other affliction.

[13] This kind of perfection, however, comes right after [the perfection of] humans. For this reason the pygmy does not adhere to perfect civility and laws, but rather follows such things by a natural impulse, just as other brute animals [do], even though it walks upright. And it uses the hand not insofar as the hand is a tool of the intellect and one of those tools or organs that serve a specific purpose; but rather in the way in which certain animals use the forefoot for various purposes as, for instance, most kinds of mice grab food with the forefoot and put it in their mouth. In this way the pygmy also uses its hand in many situations, but not for the works of art. Hence, its hand is not a hand in the full sense of the term. But since it always stands upright its spiritual [organs][33] are much clearer. Therefore, it has a better [power of] apprehension than the rest of the brutes, but it does not attend to shame about something shameful and to honour about something honourable. And this is a sign for the fact that it does not possess the judgment of reason. Therefore, when it speaks, it neither employs rhetorical nor poetic persuasive arguments, which are even less perfect than all [other] forms of reasonings. And, therefore, it always stays in the woods and does indeed not obey any civility. That faculty of the soul, however, which we have called 'shadow of reason' before[34] has somehow remained unnamed by the philosophers. Yet, circumscribing it we know that this faculty adds some power beyond the estimative power. For if the estimative power of brutes judges about the intentions that are grasped together with the sensibles, that [shadow of reason] does even more, because it transmits the thing of this kind of intention to memory, elicits what has been experienced, and later uses that for what it is useful.

[14] However, it must not be omitted here that what is estimated and experienced relates to the universal in two ways. The first way is the theoretical way. There the quiddity of things, that is, the truth of things, is grasped either by itself or in a general sign from what has been experienced, remembered, and received by sense. And in this way the remembered and the experienced are not found in the pygmy. In another way, what has been remembered and experienced is in it, namely, insofar as it adds to attraction and flight. And in this way the experienced and the remembered are acquired by the pygmy. Therefore, we have said above that it participates in experience to a minor degree. For the pygmy does not grasp this unless it relates to

---

[31] The whatnesses, i.e. the essences or essential natures, of things.

[32] Since antiquity melancholy was considered to be a mental disorder caused by an excess of black bile (gr. *mélas kholé*.); see Hirvonen (2014).

[33] I.e. those organs which carry bodily spirits or humours.

[34] See §12 and note 29.

what is useful or harmful in a thing existing in reality. Likewise, other brute animals correlate all intentions which they apprehend with these, and therefore they never separate them from particulars, but rather combine them with such things. For this reason brutes are also called 'mute animals' because with their concepts they can never speak about the truth of things. So, according to what has been said above, the pygmy stands more or less between human beings, who have a divine intellect, and other mute animals, in which no light of the divine [intellect] can be discovered, because it has experiential cognition by virtue of a shadow of reason which it got more than other animals. Nevertheless, by its nature it is closer to brutes than to humans. This is clear from what has been said before, because experience belongs to the universal and [the realm of] theory more than it belongs to the particular and to movement.

Ch. 3: How animals are capable of receiving instruction by a certain participation in the powers of the soul, and how this works in the genera of monkeys[35] in particular.

[15] The [different] genera of the other monkeys, of which there are quite many, seem to participate in the soul in the third grade of the powers of the soul and [its] abilities. For instruction arises in humans, who are the only animals capable of receiving instruction according to their nature, by way of learning and by discovery. That [kind of instruction], however, which works by learning is twofold, namely, intellective and sensory. Monkeys seem to possess sagacity more than other animals. Hence, they are capable of receiving instruction with regard to sensibles. For this reason they are called '*symeae*' (from the Greek term for 'playing'), because they playfully imitate the sensibles to which their attention has been directed much more than other animals.[36] Therefore, some wise people[37] have also passed on [the idea] that these animals have been made for playing, and by this sagacity imitate whatever they see, and by hearing gather the intentions, which have been arranged for games at the level of sensory perception, of those who call [them]. This is the first grade of the capacity of receiving instruction. For, first, it is necessary for the one who is able to receive instruction to pay attention to and gather with care things seen and heard; [second, it is necessary] to gain experience from what has been gathered and stored in memory; and, [third,] to acquire a pure universal from these things, insofar as this is the starting point of science or art or prudence or any other intellectual ability of this kind.

From these three grades, however, monkeys only reach the first; and this they reach only by imagination and memory. They do not further participate in experience and use experience neither to a major nor to a minor degree. In this regard, they are inferior to pygmies.[38] However, imagination works much easier in them insofar

---

[35] See note 17.

[36] This etymology is wrong because the Greek term '*simós*' simply means 'snub-nosed'.

[37] It is unclear to whom Albert refers here.

[38] This shows that Albert differentiates between humans, monkeys, and pygmies; see note 17 and note 22.

as it does not relate the thing sensed or seen to experiential cognition, because what is related to experiential cognition is held back by the gathering of remembered things or by the memory of things grasped. What is not related is, however, immediately applied to a sensible. And from this it comes that monkeys, having the first faculty of receiving instruction, immediately imitate what they see, whereas pygmies and humans do not immediately imitate. As we have said before, monkeys only have the first faculty of receiving instruction. A sign for this is that they do not distinguish between what or who is imitated.

[16] However, besides all the things which have been inferred above, it must be noted that no animal is capable of receiving instruction at all unless by an instinct of nature. Now, by means of instruction humans achieve three things, namely, theoretical sciences, mechanical arts, and moral virtues; and they achieve none of these without reason and intellect. This is self-evident with regard to theoretical science. As to art, it is certain too, because art is a production of the things which it brings about in connection with reason. In [the realm of] virtue, however, the middle[39] is reached, which is a middle that has been determined by reason insofar as a wise person has determined it. For this reason no animal can be instructed in any of these three things at all. But since humans have two senses capable of receiving instruction, namely, sight and hearing, as has been specified in the *Book on Sense and Sensibilia,*[40] sight serves in the discovery of instruction. And since the discovery of it does not happen unless reason gathers the things remembered and sensed, no other animal is capable of being instructed by sight [alone], because it does not possess the faculty of finding out something through the gathering of sensible things. Hearing, however, is a sense capable of receiving instruction from the signs of things and from other things. Hence, certain animals can be instructed by hearing, but none of them [can be instructed] by sight alone. And from this it is known that monkeys have a better [cognitive] power than other animals because they perceive instructions by hearing and an exemplary imitation of the things that are done by sight. No other animal does this, except of humans, pygmies, and monkeys. Therefore, it is clear that these three animals descend by continuous degrees. Humans participate in the sense capable of receiving instruction in every way as well as in memory, experience, reason, science, and art. Pygmies, however, participate in the sense capable of receiving instruction as well as in memory and in experience to a minor degree, but not in reason, science, and art. Monkeys participate in the sense capable of receiving instruction with regard to hearing and insofar as they perceive by sight something that has been arranged for the sake of instruction. That is, they engage in imitation and possess memory of sensible things, but from this they cannot gain any experience at all. Other brutes, however, cannot even grasp any kind of instruction by sight; only by hearing they perceive some instruction.

---

[39] According to Aristotle, one of the main principles of ethics is to find the middle (*mesótēs*) between 'too high' and 'too little'.

[40] Albert the Great, *De sensu et sensato*, tr. I, ch. 2, ed. Donati (2017), 22.

[17] And from what has been established above it is now even clearer that, while there are theoretical forms and moving forms[41] in humans, neither monkeys nor any other animals perceive instructions unless by moving forms. This is why even amongst those animals that are capable of receiving instruction many are so with regard to movements in particular. And so, animals are instructed in walking around, standing, or searching for something, but not in art or science. Hence, none of the animals is instructed at all if they are not set in motion by a desire for things which can be done: and these things are either particulars or, furthermore, things grasped in particulars which such animals can perceive somehow.

However, it seems that the genus of monkeys comes before all other brute animals in estimating – by sense, imagination, and memory – what is harmful or useful. For while others have the capacity to estimate things which are useful for or harmful to themselves, and which they then pursue or flee, a monkey estimates things which are useful both for itself and for other animals. Hence, when seeing a young [monkey], it shows the young the teat, not its own, but its mother's [teat] which nursed it if it is allowed to do so. It shows the young [monkey] the teats of the females if it is allowed to do so; other animals do not do this. From this it is known that monkeys have a better estimation[42] than other animals. But in all these situations they are not moved by anything but a phantasm.[43] Therefore, they frequently err (just as other animals do). And as said before, error frequently occurs where the imagination is not connected to the intellect. And in such animals there is no practical syllogism[44] but an imperfect argumentation.[45]

[18] In the context of theoretical disciplines, the enthymeme[46] and the example[47] are imperfect types of argumentations. However, their imperfection can be eliminated by a reduction to a syllogism. In this way, there are imperfect practical syllogisms in these animals which only possess a phantasm-based estimation of what is operable or desirable; this produces an impulse to do something. But there is a difference with regard to the fact that an enthymeme starts from what falls under a universal insofar as it is something that belongs to several or all [things or individuals]. The phantasm-based estimation, however, works solely on the basis of what is seen. Therefore, it is often deceived, like from a fallacy of accident,[48] because it proceeds from things seen here and now. Similarly, it considers objects to be things that must be fled or pursued because they accidentally have this [feature that made

---

[41] I.e. things setting somebody or something in motion; see Albert the Great, *Liber de principiis motus processivi*, tr. 2, ch. 10, ed. Geyer (1955), 34.

[42] On the faculty of estimation see Chaps. 4, 5, 6, and 12.

[43] A (mental) representation made of sensory information.

[44] A form of reasoning in which the conclusion is an action.

[45] The following passage on the simple forms of reasoning in which pygmies engage is thoroughly discussed by Roling (2011), 229–233; Tellkamp (2016); Oelze (2018), 150–155.

[46] A syllogism with an unstated premise.

[47] A syllogism which contains a concrete, but unproven instance of something.

[48] An argument which is invalid because one term or subject is an accidental exception to a general rule.

them flee or pursue the other things], too, insofar as they are here and now. However, pygmies seem to engage in inductive reasoning[49] in the sense that they have experience to a minor degree in accordance with the formative syllogism (which the Greeks call 'practical'). But they do not perfectly induce something because they do not attain to the grasp of a universal. Moreover, there is no way in which these animals make use of examples, because an example cannot be formed without some gathering by reason.

[19] So, these two genera of animals [i.e. monkeys and pygmies], with respect to all falling under them, are a likeness[50] of humans before all [other] animals, not in the theoretical disciplines, but rather in what concerns movements. Hence, these animals certainly have a brighter estimative power than all other animals. This is why they estimate phantasms better than other animals, and why they elicit the intentions grasped in connection with the phantasms better than some of the other animals, in such a way that they seem to have something similar to reason and, in particular, seem to have something that is similar to the act[51] of reason, which compares the intentions in the sensible objects themselves and in the phantasms grasped and not separated from them. And this is the reason why these genera of animals are called 'likenesses of humans'. A sign for this is that they have round heads as if they were a compressed sphere divided into three ventricles.[52] And, like humans, [they have] semi-circular and immovable ears, hands with long fingers, and a curvature of the arm at the elbow towards the inward facing side of the chest. And, like humans, they use their hands for various purposes although, unlike humans, they do not use them for purposes related to art; like humans, they have a wide but not a deep chest and, like humans, they have a short neck and broad shoulders. Like the females of humans, their females have teats hanging down the breast, and in relation to the size [of their bodies] they have large vulvas located at the end of the belly, so that the vaginal opening runs towards the navel, and so it is placed like the vulva of [human] women. These animals copulate with the female lying on her back and the male on top of her, just as humans copulate. This correspondence regarding the outward appearance also indicates that there is a correspondence with regard to the interior, because, as said, their estimative power is much more similar to reason than the estimative power of any other animals.

And so, in this way and in other similar ways, there are powers of the soul in these animals which, amongst brute animals, come closest to a likeness of humans.

Ch. 4: On the things which can be noted regarding the capacity of receiving instruction of four-legged animals.

---

[49] The inference of a general rule from several particular instances.

[50] Janson (1952), 85, claims that this is "the earliest conception of a 'missing link', the earliest attempt to bridge the chasm between mankind and the rest of the animal world." However, the idea that monkeys have a "likeness of human reason" (*similitudo rationis humanae*) can already be found in the seventh century; see Isidor of Seville, *Etymologiae*, b. 12, ch. 2, ed. André (1986), 115.

[51] The process taking place in reason, e.g. reasoning.

[52] According to the Galenic theory of the brain, the brain is divided into three chambers or ventricles, in each of which resides a particular power such as memory.

[20] Whatever other four-legged animals there are, they seem to have less discernment regarding whatever they do than the aforementioned [animals]. And for all of them three things should be taken into consideration, namely, hearing, estimation, and memory. As we have said in the foregoing [paragraphs], hearing is present in humans with three differences of ability, or according to three modes of sensory ability by hearing. One is the judgment of sounds; and this belongs to all those [animals] which have hearing. In humans, this is even the sense of instruction to the degree that voices are grasped by hearing insofar as they are the signs of concepts or feelings which are in the soul of the one who utters them, and insofar as they refer to things which are signified by names. This [happens] in two ways: in one mode, the theoretical quiddities of things are signified by names; in the other mode, the operable form[53] becomes known by names. Regarding this [form], there is either an effect of the one who utters it, or a thing for which there exists a bestial desire as, for instance, dogs are moved by the voices or sounds of deer. The first of these [modes] belongs to the sense of hearing insofar as it is a particular sense originating from the common sense which is the source[54] of the senses. The second [mode] belongs to the sense of hearing insofar as reason makes it reflect on itself. Therefore, this cannot at all be found in any non-rational animal. The third [mode], however, belongs to the sense [of hearing] insofar as the faculty that says whether something should be fled or pursued or done, which is imagination or estimation, is joined to it. Therefore, certain four-legged as well as two-legged animals perceive sounds in this mode and voices in each of these modes. For most animals perceive voices insofar as they are signs of the one who utters them, and they are moved to pursuing or fleeing it. For instance, a lamb runs away when it hears a wolf, and it follows when it hears the shepherds.

[21] In this mode, however, in which vocal expressions are the signs of emotions or of the will of the one who utters the voices, voices can be perceived in two ways. In one mode, [they are perceived] distinctly; in the other mode indistinctly. Any [animals] which distinctly grasp the goal that is pursued by the one who utters the voices, can be instructed; and these are many, and they can do this only by instruction and not by nature. Those, however, which do not perceive the goal, but perceive a certain anger or benevolence regarding the goal, flee the one who calls, or they approach him. But they cannot be instructed, at least not to a major degree, but only to a very minor [one]. Hence, we see dogs and some other animals learning many things. Horses, mules, and donkeys, however, are found to be more stupid in this matter although we have already seen horses, donkeys, and geese which have learned certain games or imitations. Small animals are less perceptive and capable of receiving instruction than large animals in these matters. Nevertheless, a large mouse, called a 'rat,' has recently been seen which, sitting upright on a table, held a candle.[55]

---

[53] In modern terms, a stimulus which causes a reaction.

[54] Insofar as it reflects on their activities (e.g. by sensing, hearing). On this metaphor, see also Albert the Great, *De anima*, b. 2, tr. 4, ch. 8, ed. Stroick (1968), 159.

[55] In b. VIII, tr. 6, ch. 1, §229, ed. Stadler (1916), 668, Albert mentions that he himself observed a mouse doing this in some part of northern Germany.

[22] In the estimation of animals it is particularly the case that the estimation is formed by the apprehension of the imagination and the striving after an object of desire. And it compares to the sensory soul as choice [compares to the rational soul] in rational animals; and if this [faculty] is very pure and in a good organ, it brings about a good judgment of the intentions of things. By 'pure' I mean, however, that its spirit[56] is pure and clear and hotly tempered and neither slow because of coldness, nor does it confuse [different] operations because of being excessively hot. A 'good organ' is not melancholic[57] and receives the spirits with the same clarity with which they are carried to it. For, in general, those animals can better discern sounds which appear by hearing. This is why terrestrial animals with melancholy, as if they lack an inner light, cannot judge well about the intentions which have been grasped in sensible things. Others, however, about which we have talked [before], are different in this respect. Hence, they judge better. And so, since sounds and voices are both the signs of the emotions of those animals producing them and the signs of things, those animals which have brighter estimations judge by hearing about things as well as about volitions of those producing the sounds. Those [animals] which estimate less well do not judge the things, but only those [animals] producing sounds; and this they do only indistinctly.

[23] Similarly, one should pay close attention to the memories of animals. We see that, in humans, this power has four different abilities. The first of them is to keep well the forms that have been grasped by sense. The second ability is to keep well the intentions which have been elicited from the sensibles by estimation. The third ability is to recall well by recollection the sensibles grasped. The fourth ability is to recall well the intentions elicited from the sensibles. Any animal which participates in memory with all of these abilities is well capable of receiving instruction if it [also] has a sense of hearing that is capable of receiving instruction, and [if it has] a good estimation. Any animal which possesses none of these abilities is not capable of receiving instruction. And any animal which possesses some of them fully, but others not (or all of them, but without fully participating in all of them), is capable of receiving instruction to a moderate degree. These four abilities, which we have said to be in memory, are usually reduced to two powers: the first two occur in a dry and cold environment; the other two occur in a hot and humid environment. Therefore, they are called 'recollection' rather than 'memory'.[58] However, we have discussed these matters in the book *On Memory and Recollection*.[59] And so, quite often it happens that animals having a good memory have a bad [capacity of] recollection and vice versa.

[24] However, animals' capacity of receiving instruction is exerted by recollection rather than by memory, especially in the part which is recollective of intentions.

---

[56] The bodily fluid which transports the sensory forms.

[57] I.e. does not have an excessive amount of black bile; see note 32.

[58] While memory (*memoria*) is the simple recognition of something present, recollection (*recordatio*; *reminiscentia*) is the active (mental) search for something that has been perceived in the past. The latter was usually denied to nonhuman animals; see Oelze (2018), 168–174.

[59] Albert the Great, *De memoria et reminiscentia*, tr. 2, ch. 7, ed. Donati (2017), 135–137.

The sign for this is that animals which have been trained for [playing] games and for [following] the gestures and the commands of their masters, perceive their will and do those things which they have been commanded to do according to the will of their masters. From [the fact] that they sometimes do not do the things which they have been instructed to do, unless by threats or flatteries or some terrifying sign or flattery, it can be inferred that they apprehend, by hearing and recollection, the will and the emotions rather than the concepts of their masters. This is why they do [what they are supposed to do] following the emotions and not the concepts that are signified by the voice of the one who brings it about. Therefore, they do not apprehend the articulation of the voice. Nevertheless, they correctly do what they have been commanded to do, and they are moved by instruction in the way in which nature moves [them] rather than in the way in which the intention of certain things grasped and conceived moves; because being moved by this kind of conceived thing belongs to reason, whereas being moved by a habit in a natural way of moving can be found in any sensory power of brutes.

[25] We see something similar to this in the mechanical arts, the works of which are best performed by those having a habit[60] from habituation without knowing the purpose of their work. They play the harp, play the fiddle, or do something else only by the habit of habituation and without knowing at all the purpose of their activity. The difference between humans and brutes which are moved by the habit of instruction is similar. For brutes are moved as if they paid attention to voices by nature only insofar as they [i.e. the voices] are a sign of the will of the one who calls, but without fully perceiving the articulation of the speech by which the master, who commands them [to do] certain works, addresses them. Humans, by contrast, do what they have been told to do in accordance with the intention of the articulation which lies in the speech of the one who commands.

It has been determined before that animals are sometimes immediately moved towards desirable things by sense itself. Similarly, some of them immediately obey what they have been instructed [to obey] because of an easily working faculty which they have from the habit of instruction. Still, even though every instruction consists in all of the three things that have been mentioned before, the most important of these is the recollection of intentions, because if these are recalled well, all the things commanded are done in such a way that certain animals even seem to have some sort of reason in these matters, although in reality they do not have [it] because they do not separate the intentions by which they are moved from the sensibles that have been grasped by sense.

And so, according to these and similar things, and according to the [different] degrees [of instruction] that exist in this context, the capacity of receiving instruction is found in animals either to a major, a minor, or a moderate degree.

---

[60] I.e. a capacity that has been obtained by exercise or habituation. See also note 27.

# Bibliography

## *Primary Sources*

Albert the Great. (1916–1920). *De animalibus libri XXVI*. 2 vols. (H. Stadler, Ed.). Münster: Aschendorff.
Albert the Great. (1955). *Liber de principiis motus processivi* (B. Geyer, Ed.) (*Opera omnia* 12). Münster: Aschendorff.
Albert the Great. (1960). *Metaphysica: Libri quinque priores* (B. Geyer, Ed.) (*Opera omnia* 16/1). Münster: Aschendorff.
Albert the Great. (1968). *De anima* (C. Stroick, Ed.) (*Opera omnia* 7/1). Münster: Aschendorff.
Albert the Great. (1999). *On animals: A medieval Summa zoologica*. 2 vols. (I. M. Resnick & K. F. Kitchell, Jr., Trans.). Baltimore: The Johns Hopkins University Press.
Albert the Great. (2017). *De sensu et sensato cuius secundus liber est De memoria et reminiscentia* (S. Donati, Ed.) (*Opera omnia* 7/2A). Münster: Aschendorff.
Aristotle. (1957). *Metaphysica* (W. Jaeger, Ed.). Oxford: Clarendon Press.
Aristotle. (1965–91). *History of animals*. 3 vols. (A. L. Peck & D. M. Balme, Eds.). Cambridge, MA/London: Harvard University Press.
Isidor of Seville. (1986). Étymologies *XII. Des animaux* (J. AndrÉ, Ed.). Paris: Belles Lettres.
Thomas Aquinas. (1964). *In duodecim libros Metaphysicorum Aristotelis expositio* (M.-R. Cathala & R. M. Spiazzi, Eds.). Turin/Rome: Marietti.

## *Secondary Sources*

Anzulewicz, H. (2009). Albertus Magnus und die Tiere. In S. Obermaier (Ed.), *Tiere und Fabelwesen im Mittelalter* (pp. 29–54). Berlin/New York: Walter de Gruyter.
Anzulewicz, H. (2013). Anthropology: The concept of man in Albert the Great. In I. M. Resnick (Ed.), *A companion to Albert the Great: Theology, philosophy, and the sciences* (pp. 325–346). Leiden/Boston: Brill.
Asúa, M. de. (1991). *The organization of discourse on animals in the thirteenth century: Peter of Spain, Albert the Great, and the commentaries on 'De animalibus'*. PhD Diss. Notre Dame, Ann Arbor.
Asúa, M. de. (1994). El De animalibus de Alberto Magno y la organización del discurso sobre los animales en el siglo XIII. *Patristica et Mediaevalia, 15*, 3–26.
Coles, A. (1997). Animal and childhood cognition in Aristotle's biology and the scala naturae. In W. Kullmann & S. Föllinger (Eds.), *Aristotelische Biologie: Intentionen, Methoden, Ergebnisse* (pp. 287–323). Stuttgart: Steiner.
Faucher, N., & Roques, M. (Eds.). (2018). *The Ontology, psychology and axiology of habits (habitus) in medieval philosophy*. Cham: Springer.
Friedrich, U. (2009). *Menschentier und Tiermensch: Diskurse der Grenzziehung und Grenzüberschreitung im Mittelalter*. Göttingen: Vandenhoeck & Ruprecht.
Granger, H. (1985). The scala naturae and the continuity of kinds. *Phronesis, 30*(2), 181–200.
Guldentops, G. (1999). The sagacity of the bees: An Aristotelian topos in thirteenth-century philosophy. In C. G. Steel, G. Guldentops, & P. Beullens (Eds.), *Aristotle's animals in the middle ages and renaissance* (pp. 275–296). Leuven: Leuven University Press.
Hirvonen, V. (2014). Mental disturbances: Medieval theories. In S. Knuuttila & J. Sihvola (Eds.), *Sourcebook for the history of the philosophy of mind: Philosophical psychology from Plato to Kant* (pp. 605–613). Dordrecht: Springer.

Hünemörder, C. (1980). Die Zoologie des Albertus Magnus. In G. Meyer & A. Zimmermann (Eds.), *Albertus Magnus: Doctor universalis 1280–1980* (pp. 235–248). Mainz: Matthias-Grünewald-Verlag.

Janson, H. W. (1952). *Apes and ape lore in the middle ages and the renaissance*. London: Warburg Institute.

Koch, J. (1931). Sind die Pygmäen Menschen? Ein Kapitel aus der philosophischen Anthropologie der mittelalterlichen Scholastik. *Archiv für Geschichte der Philosophie, 40*(2), 194–213.

Köhler, T. W. (1992). Anthropologische Erkennungsmerkmale menschlichen Seins: Die Frage der 'Pygmei' in der Hochscholastik. In A. Zimmermann & A. Speer (Eds.), *Mensch und Natur im Mittelalter* (pp. 718–735). Berlin/New York: Walter de Gruyter.

Köhler, T. W. (1999). Die wissenschaftstheoretische und inhaltliche Bedeutung der Rezeption von *De animalibus* für den philosophisch-anthropologischen Diskurs im 13. Jahrhundert. In C. G. Steel, G. Guldentops, & P. Beullens (Eds.), *Aristotle's animals in the middle ages and renaissance* (pp. 249–274). Leuven: Leuven University Press.

Köhler, T. W. (2001). Der Tiervergleich als philosophisch-anthropologisches Schlüsselparadigma – der Beitrag Alberts des Großen. In W. Senner (Ed.), *Albertus Magnus: Zum Gedenken nach 800 Jahren: Neue Zugänge, Aspekte und Perspektiven* (pp. 437–454). Berlin: Akademie Verlag.

Köhler, T. W. (2008). *Homo animal nobilissimum: Konturen des spezifisch Menschlichen in der naturphilosophischen Aristoteleskommentierung des dreizehnten Jahrhunderts. Teilband 1.* Leiden/Boston: Brill.

Köhler, T. W. (2014). *Homo animal nobilissimum: Konturen des spezifisch Menschlichen in der naturphilosophischen Aristoteleskommentierung des dreizehnten Jahrhunderts, Teilband 2.1 und 2.2.* 2 vols. Leiden/Boston: Brill.

Kraus, L. B. (2016). *Ontologie der Grenzen ausgedehnter Gegenstände*. Berlin/Boston: Walter de Gruyter.

Lovejoy, A. O. (1936). *The great chain of being: A study of the history of an idea*. Cambridge, MA/London: Harvard University Press.

Oelze, A. (2018). *Animal rationality: Later medieval theories 1250–1350*. Leiden/Boston: Brill.

Perfetti, S. (2004). I libri De animalibus di Aristotele e i saperi sugli animali nel XIII secolo. In C. Crisciani, R. Lambertini, & R. Martorelli (Eds.), *Parva naturalia. Saperi medievali, natura e vita* (pp. 143–170). Istituti editoriali e poligrafici internazionali: Pisa.

Resnick, I. M., & Kitchell, K. F., Jr. (1996). Albert the Great on the 'language' of animals. *American Catholic. The Philosophical Quarterly, 70*(1), 41–61.

Resnick, I. M., & Kitchell, K. F., Jr. (1999). Introduction: The life and works of Albert the Great. In A. Magnus (Ed.), *On animals: A medieval Summa zoologica* (Vol. 1, pp. 1–42). Baltimore: The Johns Hopkins University Press.

Roling, B. (2010). *Drachen und Sirenen: Die Rationalisierung und Abwicklung der Mythologie an den europäischen Universitäten*. Leiden/Boston: Brill.

Roling, B. (2011). Syllogismus brutorum: Die Diskussion der animalischen Rationalität bei Albertus Magnus und ihre Rezeption im Mittelalter und in der Frühen Neuzeit. *Recherches de théologie et philosophie médiévales, 78*(1), 221–275.

Roling, B. (2013). Die Geometrie der Bienenwabe: Albertus Magnus, Karl von Baer und die Debatte über das Vorstellungsvermögen und die Seele der Insekten zwischen Mittelalter und Neuzeit. *Recherches de théologie et philosophie médiévales, 80*(2), 401–504.

Salisbury, J. E. (2011). *The beast within: Animals in the middle ages*. New York/London: Routledge.

Tellkamp, J. A. (2013). Albert the Great on perception and non-conceptual content. In L. X. López-Farjeat & J. A. Tellkamp (Eds.), *Philosophical psychology in arabic thought and the latin aristotelianism of the 13th century* (pp. 205–221). Paris: Vrin.

Tellkamp, J. A. (2016). Aping logic? Albert the Great on animal mind and action. In J. Kaukua & T. Ekenberg (Eds.), *Subjectivity and selfhood in medieval and early modern philosophy* (pp. 109–123). Dordrecht: Springer.

Thijssen, J. M. M. H. (1995). Reforging the great chain of being: The medieval discussion of the human status of 'pygmies' and its influence on Edward Tyson. In R. Corbey & B. Theunissen (Eds.), *Ape, man, apeman: Changing views since 1600* (pp. 43–59). Leiden: Leiden University.

Tkacz, M. W. (2007). Albert the Great and the revival of Aristotle's zoological research program. *Vivarium, 45*(1), 30–68.

Tkacz, M. W. (2013). Albertus Magnus and the animal histories: A medieval anticipation of recent developments in Aristotle studies. *Proceedings of the American Catholic Philosophical Association, 87*, 103–113.

Toivanen, J. (2018). Marking the boundaries: Animals in medieval latin philosophy. In G. F. Edwards & P. Adamson (Eds.), *Animals: A history* (pp. 121–150). Oxford: Oxford University Press.

Van den Abeele, B. (1999). Le '*De animalibus*' d'Aristote dans le monde latin: modalités de sa reception mediévale. *Frühmittelalterliche Studien, 33*, 287–318.

Wei, I. P. (2020). *Thinking about animals in thirteenth-century Paris: Theologians on the boundary between humans and animals*. Cambridge: Cambridge University Press.

# Chapter 9
# Universal Cognition (Pseudo-Peterof Spain, *Commentum super libros De animalibus* VIII)

**Abstract** The commentary on Aristotle's zoological works by Pseudo-Peter of Spain is one of the few texts in which a late-medieval author develops an innovative account of universal cognition. This capacity was usually taken to be a prerogative of the intellect of humans, angels, and God. However, according to Pseudo-Peter, there are good arguments to claim that nonhuman animals cognise universally insofar as they do, for instance, identify individuals on the basis of what he calls 'common forms' (*formae communes*). Moreover, he argues that the kind of intentions they grasp (e.g. the hostility of a wolf) are some sort of intermediary between individual and universal intentions. For this reason, he suggests calling them 'elevated intentions' (*intentiones elevatas*). Thus, he revises the traditional concept of intentions and broadens the rather narrow concept of universal cognition such that it can accommodate the various cognitive achievements of nonhuman animals. This is something rarely seen in the medieval discussion of animal cognition.

## Introduction

The most extensive and most popular medieval commentary on Aristotle's so-called 'Books on Animals' (*libri de animalibus*) was written by Albert the Great in the middle of the thirteenth century (see Chap. 8). However, there is at least one older commentary, written presumably between 1246 and 1249, by Peter of Spain (1205–1277).[1] Although many aspects of Peter's life and works remain unclear, his commentary on *De animalibus* obviously belongs to the medical tradition.[2] It deals with questions concerning the physiology and anatomy of animals much more than with psychological issues, and so it is less relevant for anyone interested in medieval philosophy of animal minds. Yet, there is another thirteenth-century commentary on the 'Books on Animals', written in Paris at some point before 1260. For a while, it

---

[1] See Asúa (1991), (1997), and (1999). See also briefly De Leemans and Klemm (2007), 164f.

[2] For the latest critical edition, see Peter of Spain, *Questiones super libro 'De Animalibus' Aristotelis*, ed. Navarro Sánchez (2015).

A. Oelze, *Animal Minds in Medieval Latin Philosophy*, Studies in the History of Philosophy of Mind 27, https://doi.org/10.1007/978-3-030-67012-2_9

was also attributed to Peter of Spain. But since this attribution could not be proven, the author is now simply referred to as Pseudo-Peter of Spain.[3]

Amongst the most noteworthy passages of this commentary are the questions on universal cognition translated in the following.[4] Of course, this is not the only text dealing with the question of whether nonhuman animals can engage in universal cognition (see Chaps. 6, 8, 10, and 12). Yet, it is one of the few texts in which a late-medieval author develops an innovative account of what was usually taken to be a prerogative of the intellect of humans, angels, and God. In his opinion, there are good arguments to claim that nonhuman animals cognise universally insofar as they do, for instance, identify individuals on the basis of what he calls 'common forms' (*formae communes*). Moreover, he argues that the kind of intentions they grasp (e.g. the hostility of a wolf) are some sort of intermediary between individual and universal intentions.[5] For this reason, he suggests calling them 'elevated intentions' (*intentiones elevatas*). Thus, he revises the traditional concept of intentions and broadens the rather narrow concept of universal cognition such that it can accommodate the various cognitive achievements of nonhuman animals. This is something rarely seen in the medieval discussion of animal cognition.

## Bibliographical Note

The Latin text is a slightly modified version of T. W. Köhler's transcription of two manuscripts: Venezia, Biblioteca Nazionale Marciana, Lat. VI, 234, fol. 1ra-303vb, and Firenze, Biblioteca Medicea Laurenziana, Plut. LXXXIII 24, fol. 1ra-85vb. The English text is the first translation into a modern language.

## Text

De primo queritur, utrum animalia discernant et cognoscant individuales intentiones rerum et formas, quia in hoc fundantur mores; ut cum canis obedit homini, cognoscat, quod est homo, vel solum cognoscat per accidens; exemplum: Lupus invadit canem et dimittit lupum; queritur, utrum cognoscat speciem eius. Videtur quod sic.

[1] Prima ratio. Sicut dictum est superius, animalibus brutis debetur mutuus aspectus cum rebus aliis, ut ab aliis recipiant iuvamenta et nocumenta. Ista non solum currunt a parte complexionis, sed circa substantiam et speciem. Unde ratione

---

[3] See Köhler (2000), 255; (2008), 24–26; (2014), 361. According to Köhler (2008), 25n64, there are two versions of the text, a Venetian and a Florentine redaction. However, both of them are based on the same questions by the same master. The present selection is taken from the former. A transcription was kindly provided by Theodor W. Köhler.

[4] For a detailed analysis and discussion, see Köhler (2014), 361–364, and Oelze (2018), 78–81.

[5] On the medieval notion of intentions, see texts 3, 4, 5 and 11.

speciei ovis discernit lupum, et sic de aliis. Ergo et cetera. Hoc idem est in medici-
nis, quia operantur a specie.

[2] Ratio secunda talis: Rerum quedam perficiuntur ab anima, quedam a natura.
Sed in illis, que perficiuntur ab anima, regimen discretius est quam in illis, que a
natura. Sed in illis, que discernunt a natura, discernunt speciem discretione naturali,
ut adamans ferrum ab auro. Ergo brutum discernit discretione naturali et habet aliam
supra, que est cognitio. Ergo oportet, quod apprehendat res et cognoscat et non
solum accidentia.

[3] Tertia ratio. Omnis substantia cognitiva, que circumscriptis accidentibus ratione speciei sequitur rem apprehensam et fugit et obedit vel inobediens est ei, appre-
hendit discretam substantiam rei et non solum accidentia. Anima bruti huiusmodi.
Ergo et cetera. Hoc patet, quia anima agne fugit lupum ratione lupi, non fugit canem,
ymo ratione speciei sequitur sociam; ymo ovis obedit homini quia homo, et leo
obedit magistro ratione persone individue. Ergo fit discretio ratione speciei et circa
speciem. H <ec> supra accidentia.

Sed contra. D <ici>t Avicenna et Algazel: Duplex est cognitio. Quedam est rei
per principia vera eius; hec solum debetur intellective anime; per hoc probat intellectum inesse homini. Unde cognoscit speciem non secundum quod stans vel huiusmodi. Alia est cognitio per accidentia; hec est sensitive, ut dicunt, quod cognoscit
aliquem in quantum sedet vel huiusmodi. Sed cognitio bruti sensitiva est. Ergo
solum cognoscit accidentia et non substantiam.

Dicendum, quod bruta cognoscunt species rerum et substantias. Unde asinus
cognoscit hominem et speciem eius cognitione naturali. Similiter dico de aliis.

Ad rationem. Solvit Averroes: Cognitio substantie est duplex. Una est, que cadit
super quidditates rerum universales, que intentiones universales ab omnibus indi-
viduis separate sunt et ab omnibus dependitiis accidentium. Hec intellective. Alia
est cognitio, que cadit super intentiones individuales; hec inest brutis et multis, et
hec est sensibilis virtutis, ut ipse dicit.

Deinde, utrum insit brutis habentibus animam sensibilem intentio rerum universalis et per modum universalis; id est, utrum universalia comprehendantur ab illis
prout accipiunt res individuales. Videtur sic.

[1] Omnis acceptio speciei rei non apropriate individue substantie rei est acceptio universalis. Sed acceptio intentionis speciei sic est in animabus brutorum.
Probatio: Omnis acceptio intentionis speciei rei nate applicari ad singulare, sub qua
accipiuntur multa singularia et nulli apropriatur, est acceptio universalis. Sed hec est
acceptio lupi ab agna, quia lupus, non quia iste lupus. Sed talis comprehensio est
universalis. Ergo et cetera.

[2] Preterea omnis apprehensio intentionis, que una existens ad multa nata est
applicari, est intentio universalis vel per modum universalis. Hoc patet, ut species
hominis, que in anima, nata est multis applicari; unde secundum substantiam cog-
noscitur quilibet homo. Sed intentiones, per quas bruta cognoscunt animalia, sunt
huiusmodi, ut agna per unam similitudinem lupi cognoscit omnes lupos. Similitudo
unius in multis faciebat universale. Ergo et cetera.

[3] Preterea omnis cognitio, que est circa intentiones solas individuales, habet
ortum ab individuo signato vel terminato. Cognitio intellectiva e contra, quia habet

ortum ab intentione communis rei absque intentionibus individualibus. Sed cognitio brutorum est que incipit ab ipsa specie et tendit ad individua. Agna enim cognoscit lupum, quem numquam vidit; similiter de aliis. Sed si sic cognoscit, necessarium est, quod prius cognoscat individuum. Quod non est verum. Unde cognoscit, licet numquam vidisset neque hanc neque aliam; cognoscit utrumque cognitione naturali. Ergo cognoscit ipsam per unem. Talis incipit ab universali et tendit ad particulare. Ergo et cetera.

[4] Preterea universale tripliciter consideratur. Uno modo secundum quod est exemplar efficientis. Secundo modo prout est perfectio rei, que fit. Alio modo secundum quod est exemplar operationis in rebus, ex quibus simile a simili. Quarto modo prout est exemplar cognoscendi postremum, sicut exemplar primi fuit primum et alia habent ab illo exemplar cognitionis. Unde quartus modus est exemplar cognitionis, per quod venimus ad exemplar primum. Universale non recipit multiplicationem nisi prout perficit rem, prout exemplar est et prout principium effectus cognitionis. Unde est unum in anima, multa in rebus. Sed omnis existentia universalis et in quantum exemplar efficientis vel cognoscentis est unum multa sub se comprehendens ut unum. Sed universale prout perficit est multa respectu multorum, quibus applicatur. Unde dico, quod artifex domus per unum exemplar facit multas domus. Acceptio universalis in particulari est acceptio eius non prout universale. Sed omne universale in bruto prout perficit est universalis acceptio ut est h <oc>; talis est acceptio particularis, ut Adam et Martinum. Sed per exemplar fuit cognitio universalis prout universale. Sed cognitio talis in aranea est huiusmodi. Ergo et cetera.

[5] Preterea quinta ratio: Dicunt doctores, quod universale dicitur tripliciter. Uno modo singul<ar>i applicatum, et videtur cum particularibus accidentibus prout hic et nunc. Secundo modo prout est quidditas pura; sic naturam universalis habet. Tertio modo prout est in anima; sic habet naturam spiritualem universalem denudatam accidentibus, et universale fit prout in anima est universalius; et secundum quod ordinantur res et intentiones rerum prout sub accidentibus individualibus, ut dicit Porphirius, accipietur ut individuum, et prout immune ab accidentibus accipietur universale ut universale. Sed bruta discernunt rem a re sine accidentibus, ut hominem ab asino, et discernunt hunc hominem ab illo sub accidentibus. Ergo sic discernunt bruta. Et h <oc> dicit Averroes, quod accipit ut sine accidentibus.

Sed contra. Averroes dicit: Virtus cognitiva duplex. Una distinguit intentiones universales; hec intellectus. Alia est, que distinguit intentiones individuales; hec sensitiva. Hec competit bruto. Sed nulla virtus, que non habet acceptionem universalis, discernit ea. Sensitiva huiusmodi, ut dicit Averroes. Hoc di<ci>t Avicenna et Algazel in multis locis.

Preterea sicut est ordo in virtutibus et rebus, similiter in receptione virtutum et rerum ipsarum. Sed acceptio intentionis individuorum est acceptio materialis prout res in materia corporali. Acceptio universalis in sua puritate est acceptio preter materiam. Hec fuit virtutis materialis, illa intellectus. Sed materialis est materialis acceptio. Talis est virtutis sensibilis. Ergo et cetera.

Dicendum, quod virtus sensitiva non accipit solum intentiones individuales, sed intentiones individuales elevatas. Iste tamen intentiones, quas accipit, non attingunt elevationem, que apud intellectum, sed distant per gradus.

Ad rationem dico sic: Acceptio intentionis universalis duplex. Una, que abstrahit a materia et a principiis materialibus; hec debetur anime intellective, ut dicit Aristotiles, quod est ponere hominem sine carnibus, ossibus et nervis. Ideo cognoscit deum, angelum et huiusmodi. Alia est, que non erigitur ultra principia materialia. Unde si offeratur ei sub principiis spiritualibus res, non cognoscet. Et ista coniungit duo individualiter accipiendo, ut animam bovis cum corpore bovis. Alia est prout comparat formam communem ad particulare, ut agnam ad hanc agnam; hoc non fit sine materia, et hec est anime sensitive. Primo modo de corporali fit spirituale in accipiendo. Secundo modo extra cursum materie, sed tamen plus potest accedere ad unum quam ad aliud; h<ec> ratione individui. Alia ratione forme communis et materie; h<e>c communis huic agne et illi.

Ad aliud patet solutio.


## Translation


First, it is asked whether animals discern and cognise individual intentions of things and forms, because this is that in which their behaviours are grounded. When a dog obeys a human being, [the question is] whether it cognises that this is a human being, or whether it cognises this only accidentally. An example [is this]: a wolf attacks a dog and dismisses a wolf. It is asked whether it cognises its species. This seems to be the case.

[1] The first reason [is this]: as said before, in brute animals, there is a mutual glance[6] at other things such that they receive from others those [features] that are beneficial and harmful. These [features] do not come only from the [bodily] mixture but also concern the substance and the species. Therefore, a sheep discerns a wolf as well as other things, with respect to their species. Hence, etc. This is the same in the medical disciplines because they start from the species.[7]

[2] The second reason is the following: some things are perfected by the soul, others by nature. But in those that are perfected by the soul the control [of behaviour] is more discrete than in those [perfected] by nature. Those which discern by nature, discern the species by natural discrimination as, for instance, the magnet[8] [distinguishes] iron from gold. So, a brute discerns by natural discrimination and in addition it has something that goes beyond this, and this is cognition. Thus, it is necessary that it apprehends and cognises a thing, not only [its] accidents.

[3] The third reason [is]: every cognitive substance which – with respect to the species that is enclosed by the accidents – follows the apprehended thing, flees it,

---

[6] On this 'aspectus mutuus,' see Köhler (2014), 306.

[7] E.g. the 'species' of patients with particular symptoms such as fever.

[8] Literally, 'adamans' means 'diamond' or 'steel'. However, it was commonly applied to the magnetic material that separates, for instance, iron from gold; see Sander (2020), 26–28.

obeys or disobeys it, apprehends the concrete[9] substance of the thing, not only [its] accidents. The soul of a brute is of this kind. Hence, etc. This is clear because the soul of a lamb flees from a wolf with respect to [this being a] wolf; and it does not flee from a dog but rather follows it with respect to [this being] friendly. By all means, a sheep obeys a human being because it is a human being, and a lion obeys the tamer with respect to [this being] an individual person. Thus, the discrimination happens according to the species and with regard to the species. This goes beyond the accidents.

But against this [is the following argument]: Avicenna[10] and Al-Ghazali[11] say that there are two kinds of cognition. One is of a thing based on its true principles. But it exists only in the intellective soul. This proves that the intellect belongs to human beings. Therefore, it cognises the species not insofar as it is staying or anything like that. Another kind of cognition is based on accidents. This is sensory, as they say, because it cognises something insofar as it sits or anything like that. But the cognition of a brute is sensory. Hence, it cognises only accidents, not the substance.

One must say that brutes cognise the species of things and substances. Consequently, a donkey cognises a human being and its species by natural cognition. I claim the same regarding other things.

To the [counter-]argument [I reply as follows]: Averroes[12] provides a solution by distinguishing between two kinds of cognition of substance. One is that which covers the universal quiddities of things, that is, the universal intentions that are separated from all individual things and from all things depending on accidents. This is intellective. The other kind of cognition [of substance] covers individual intentions. This, he says, is found in many brutes as well, and it is brought about by a sensory power.

Furthermore, [it is asked] whether brutes with a sensory soul have a universal apprehension of things and in a universal mode. That is, whether universals are grasped by them just like they grasp individual things. This seems to be the case.

[1] Every grasp of the species of a thing, not specifically applying to the individual substance of the thing, is a universal grasp. Yet, this kind of grasp of the intention of the species can be found in the souls of brutes. The proof [is this]: every grasp of the intention of the species of a thing that can be applied to a singular thing, under which many singulars are grasped although it does not specifically apply to any of them, is a universal grasp. This is the grasp of a wolf by a lamb as [it grasps] wolf, not this wolf. But such a grasp is universal. Hence, etc.

[2] Moreover, every apprehension of an intention that exists as one, but can be applied to many, is a universal intention or [an apprehension] in a universal mode. This is evident with regard to the species 'human being' that exists in the soul, but

---

[9] I.e. the individual substance or simply the individual.

[10] Avicenna Latinus, *Liber de anima* I.5, ed. Van Riet (1972), 94 f.

[11] This might refer to Algazel, *Metaphysica* IV.5, ed. Muckle (1933), 173–175.

[12] Averroes, *Commentarium magnum in Aristotelis De anima* II.65, ed. Crawford (1953), 227–229.

can be applied to many individuals. Hence, any human being is cognised in virtue of its substance. The intentions by virtue of which brute animals cognise are of this kind. For instance, through a likeness of wolf, a lamb cognises all wolves. A likeness of one thing in many is what establishes a universal. Hence, etc.

[3] Moreover, every cognition that solely concerns individual intentions has its origin in a concrete and determinate individual. Intellective cognition is different because it originates from the intention of a common thing without individual intentions. But the cognition of brutes is such that it starts from such a species and extends to the individual. A lamb even cognises a wolf it has never seen before, and the same goes for other cases. But if that is how it cognises, it is necessary that it first cognises the individual. And this is not true. Hence, it cognises even what it has never seen before, neither this nor another thing, and it cognises each of them by natural cognition. So, it cognises such a thing through one [form]. Such [cognition] starts from the universal and extends to the particular. Hence, etc.

[4] Furthermore, 'universal' can be considered in [at least] three different ways. First, as an exemplar of an efficient [cause]. Second, as the perfection of the thing that is produced. Third, as an exemplar of the act of producing things; by this a similar thing is made from a similar thing. Fourth, as the last exemplar of what is cognised just like the exemplar of the first [thing cognised] came first; this is the one from which the others got their exemplar of cognition. Thus, the fourth way is the exemplar of cognition by which we arrive at the first model. A universal is not multiplied unless it perfects a thing, insofar as it is an exemplar, or insofar as it is the origin of the effect of cognition. Hence, it is one in the soul, but many in the things. Yet, every universal existence is one that comprises many things as one, in particular as it is an exemplar for someone who produces or cognises something. Yet, a universal insofar as it perfects something is many with regard to the many things to which it is applied. Therefore, I say that a house builder builds many houses from one model. The universal grasp of a particular thing is a grasp of this thing, [but] not insofar as it is a universal. Still, every universal in a brute is such a universal grasp insofar as it perfects. Such is a particular grasp like [when we grasp] Adam and Martin. But through the exemplar a universal cognition as universal is brought about. The cognition of a spider is of this kind.[13] Hence, etc.

[5] In addition, there is a fifth argument: the doctors say that 'universal' is employed in three ways. First, as applied to a singular thing and, as it seems, with particular accidents as [being] here and now. Second, as pure quiddity such that it has a universal nature. Third, as [being] in the soul such that it has a spiritual universal nature stripped of any accidents; the universal that is brought about in the soul is more universal. Now, according to Porphyry,[14] an individual is grasped insofar as things and intentions of things are arranged with regard to individual accidents; and

---

[13] The basic idea here is that, from one model of a net, a spider builds many particular nets.

[14] What Ps.-Peter possibly has in mind here is Porphyry's definition of an individual as unique collection of properties; see Porphyry, *Isagoge* 7.22–24, ed. Minio-Paluello (1966), 13f.

a universal [is grasped] as universal when accidents are not involved. Brutes, however, discern one thing from another, such as 'human being' from 'donkey', regardless of any accidents. And they discern this human being from that [human being] with regard to accidents. Hence, this is how brutes discern. And this is what Averroes means when he says that something is grasped without accidents.

But against this [there are the following arguments]: Averroes[15] says that there are two kinds of cognitive powers. One distinguishes universal intentions; this is the intellect. The other one is what distinguishes individual intentions; this is sensory and granted to brutes. Yet, no power that does not have a universal grasp discerns those [universal intentions]. The sensory [power] is of this kind, Averroes says, as do Avicenna[16] and Al-Ghazali[17] in many places.

Moreover, just as there is an order of powers and things, there is also [an order] of the reception of powers and such things. But the grasp of an intention of individual things is a material grasp because the thing exists in corporeal matter. The universal grasp in its purity is a grasp that goes beyond matter. The former is done by a material power, the latter by the intellect. A material grasp belongs to a material power, and the sensory power is such [a power]. Hence, etc.

One must say that a sensory power does not only grasp individual intentions but elevated individual intentions. However, those intentions which it grasps do not attain the same level of elevation as those in the intellect, from which they differ in degree.

Regarding the [counter-]argument, I say the following: there are two kinds of universal grasp of an intention. One abstracts from matter and material principles. This belongs to the intellective soul, as Aristotle[18] says, and he means to establish the human being without muscles, bones, and nerves. This is the way in which it cognises God, angels, and the like. The other kind is one that does not go beyond material principles. So, when it is confronted with a thing under spiritual conditions it does not cognise. The former joins two things together that have been grasped individually, such as the soul of an oxen and the body of an oxen. The latter compares a common form to a particular, such as [the common form of] lamb to this lamb. This is not done without matter and belongs to the sensory soul. In the first mode, something corporeal is turned into something spiritual when being grasped. The second mode goes beyond the sphere of matter. Nevertheless, it can be applied to one thing rather than to another, that is, to individuals. Moreover, [it can be applied] in terms of the common form and matter, such as what is common to this and that lamb. With regard to the latter, the solution is evident.

---

[15] See note 12.

[16] See note 10.

[17] See note 11.

[18] It was common to interpret Aristotle's theory of the intellect in this way, but there is no passage in his writings in which he clearly makes such a claim.

# Bibliography

## *Primary Sources*

Algazel. (1933). *Metaphysics: A medieval translation* (J. T. Muckle, Ed.). Toronto: St. Michael's College.

Averroes. (1953*). Commentarium magnum in Aristotelis De anima libros* (F. S. Crawford, Ed.). Cambridge, MA: The Mediaeval Academy of America.

Avicenna Latinus. (1972). *Liber de anima seu sextus de naturalibus I-II-III* (S. van Riet, Ed.). Louvain: Peeters/Leiden: Brill.

Peter of Spain. (2015). *Questiones super libro 'De Animalibus' Aristotelis: Critical edition with introduction* (F. Navarro Sánchez, Ed.). London/New York: Routledge.

Porphyry. (1966). *Isagoge translatio Boethii (Aristoteles Latinus I.6-7)* (L. Minio-Paluello, Ed.). Bruges/Paris: Desclée de Brouwer.

Pseudo-Peter of Spain. *Commentum super libros de animalibus* (Venetian redaction). Venice, Biblioteca Nazionale Marciana, Lat. VI, 234, fol. 1ra–303vb.

## *Secondary Sources*

Asúa, M. de. (1991). *The organization of discourse on animals in the thirteenth century: Peter of Spain, Albert the Great, and the commentaries on* 'De animalibus'. PhD Diss. Notre Dame, Ann Arbor.

Asúa, M. de. (1997). Peter of Spain, Albert the Great, and the *Quaestiones de animalibus. Physis, 34*, 1–30.

Asúa, M. de. (1999). Medicine and philosophy in Peter of Spain's commentary on De animalibus. In C. G. Steel, G. Guldentops, & P. Beullens (Eds.), *Aristotle's animals in the middle ages and renaissance* (pp. 189–211). Leuven: Leuven University Press.

De Leemans, P., & Klemm, M. (2007). Animals and anthropology in medieval philosophy. In B. Resl (Ed.), *A cultural history of animals in the medieval age* (pp. 153–177). Oxford/New York: Berg.

Köhler, T. W. (2000). *Grundlagen des philosophisch-anthropologischen Diskurses im dreizehnten Jahrhundert: Die Erkenntnisbemühung um den Menschen im zeitgenössischen Verständnis.* Leiden/Köln: Brill.

Köhler, T. W. (2008). *Homo animal nobilissimum: Konturen des spezifisch Menschlichen in der naturphilosophischen Aristoteleskommentierung des dreizehnten Jahrhunderts, Teilband 1.* Leiden/Boston: Brill.

Köhler, T. W. (2014). *Homo animal nobilissimum: Konturen des spezifisch Menschlichen in der naturphilosophischen Aristoteleskommentierung des dreizehnten Jahrhunderts, Teilband 2.1 und 2.2* (2 vols). Leiden/Boston: Brill.

Oelze, A. (2018). *Animal rationality: Later medieval theories 1250-1350.* Leiden/Boston: Brill.

Sander, C. (2020). *Magnes: Der Magnetstein und der Magnetismus in den Wissenschaften der Frühen Neuzeit.* Leiden/Boston: Brill.

# Chapter 10
# Reasoning and Thinking (Roger Bacon, *Perspectiva*, Part II, Distinction 3, Chapter 9)

**Abstract** In a passage of his treatise on optics, Roger Bacon discusses the so-called power of cogitation (*virtus cogitativa*). Contrary to other medieval thinkers, he ascribes this faculty to both humans and nonhuman animals. This is noteworthy insofar as it was usually taken to be a rational faculty. Bacon, however, claims that dogs, bees, monkeys, and many other animals are endowed with it. Still, he makes clear that this does not mean that they are capable of reasoning in the same way in which humans are. What they can do by virtue of this power is to perform basic inferences in order to structure and plan certain activities. Given Bacon's own examples and descriptions one could say that he presents a medieval version of modern accounts of nonlinguistic thinking.

## Introduction

Even though Roger Bacon might not be as famous as Thomas Aquinas or Albert the Great, he is undoubtedly one of the most important scholars of the thirteenth century. Like his contemporaries, he wrote texts on various themes and made substantial contributions regarding the reception of Islamic philosophy in the Latin West. As far as his biography and academic life are concerned, most information is based on estimates and conjectures.[1] Born in the village of Ilchester in Southwest England at some point between 1214 and 1220, he went to Oxford to study arts during his youth and became a lecturer on Aristotle. The writings of Aristotle were also central to his teaching activities in Paris, which he took up around the end of the 1230s. Presumably, it was during this time that he wrote texts on logic as well as his commentaries on Aristotle's *Physics* (see Chap. 11) and *Metaphysics*. Around the middle of the 1240s, Bacon returned to Oxford and began to focus on the so-called *quadrivium* (i.e. four of the seven liberal arts, namely, arithmetic, geometry, astronomy, and music) but also on alchemy and optics. However, another twenty years

---

[1] On his biography, his works, and his academic life, see Hackett (1997); Clegg (2003); Raizman-Kedar (2011).

© The Author(s), under exclusive license to Springer Nature
Switzerland AG 2021
A. Oelze, *Animal Minds in Medieval Latin Philosophy*, Studies in the History of Philosophy of Mind 27, https://doi.org/10.1007/978-3-030-67012-2_10

passed by until he wrote his major works: the *Opus maius*, the *Opus minus*, and the *Opus tertius*. One of the main reasons for the relatively late production of these works is that Bacon had become a member of the Franciscan order in Paris in 1255/57. The order was rather sceptical of his scientific activities and tried to suppress his publications. This conflict reached its climax in 1278 when the order forbade the publication all of his writings and placed him under arrest. Bacon finally returned to Oxford and died there in 1292.

The quarrel with the Franciscan authorities and Bacon's relatively harsh criticism of contemporaries led to a comparatively poor reception of his works. It was only in the nineteenth century that scholars began to appreciate his achievements and celebrated him as the first scientist in the Western world. Regardless of whether or not this appraisal was disproportionate, Bacon's works contain various interesting and original views, particularly in the field of natural philosophy. Although his commentary on the *De animalibus* has been lost, there are several texts in which he discusses the cognitive capacities of nonhuman animals. One is a chapter of his treatise on optics (which was originally contained in his *Opus maius*), called *Perspectiva* in Latin.[2] In this work, Bacon adopts several ideas of the Arab mathematician, physicist, and astronomer Alhacen, who wrote one of the most influential texts on optics (known as *De aspectibus* to Latin thinkers). One of Alhacen's ideas is that there are various modes of seeing which differ in complexity. Although Bacon agrees with this view, he wonders which power of the soul is responsible for the more complex modes of seeing. It is in this context that he discusses the so-called power of cogitation (*virtus cogitativa*). Contrary to other medieval thinkers, he ascribes this faculty to both humans and nonhuman animals. This is noteworthy insofar as it was usually taken to be a rational faculty. Bacon, however, claims that dogs, bees, monkeys, and many other animals are endowed with it. Still, he makes clear that this does not mean that they are capable of reasoning in the same way in which humans are.[3] What they can do by virtue of this power is to perform basic inferences in order to structure and plan certain activities. This is nicely illustrated by the passage translated in the following. Given Bacon's own examples and descriptions one could say that he presents a medieval version of modern accounts of nonlinguistic thinking. These accounts claim that nonhuman animals can also engage in some sort of thought process.[4]

---

[2] For a closer analysis and discussion, see Sobol (1993), 114–117; Wood (2007), 39–45; Roling (2011), 244–246; Hackett (2013), 234–237; Köhler (2014), 371–373; Oelze (2018), 142–149; Toivanen (2018), 140f.

[3] Surprisingly or not, a more elaborate version of the distinction Bacon draws between full-fledged human reasoning and nonhuman animals' quasi-reasoning, has made it into the contemporary study of reasoning as 'dual process theory'; see Mercier & Sperber (2018), 44–46.

[4] For modern accounts of nonlinguistic thinking, see Bermúdez (2003) and Tomasello (2014).

## Bibliographical Note

The English translation is based on the following critical edition (also containing an alternative English translation) of the Latin text: Roger Bacon. (1996). *Roger Bacon and the origins of* Perspectiva *in the middle ages: A critical edition and English translation of Bacon's* Perspectiva *with introduction and notes* (D. C. Lindberg, Ed. and Trans.) (pp. 246–250). Oxford: Clarendon Press.


## Translation

Now, at the end of this talk about the mode of seeing by means of straight lines according to the three modes of sight (by sense alone, by knowledge, and by syllogism)[5] it can rightly be held to be a matter of doubt which power of the soul it is that, in the case of knowledge and syllogism, deals with the visible things mediated by the sense of sight. If we employ 'knowledge' and 'syllogism' as in logic, natural philosophy, and metaphysics, as it is the custom of the mass of ordinary people doing philosophy, it is necessary that it is the rational soul, because syllogism and knowledge, as they are employed in the aforementioned disciplines, pertain to it alone. And Alhacen calls this part of the soul the 'discerning power'[6] which, according to him, reasons and understands. Indeed, sometimes these words and similar expressions are found [to be employed in such a way] that it literally seems to be the intellective and rational soul [which operates in this case].

But it is certain that a dog recognises a human being it has seen before when it sees it again, and monkeys and many beasts do this. And they distinguish between things they have seen, of which they have memory, and they cognise one universal[7] from another, such as human from dog or from wood; and they distinguish individuals of the same species. And, therefore, the [kind of] cognition which the perspectivists[8] call '[cognition] by knowledge' belongs to brutes and humans. Hence, it is brought about by a power of the sensory soul.

Similarly, this is obvious for the cognition which is called '[cognition] by syllogism,' because motion is cognised by it. A dog runs away when somebody raises a stick to beat it.[9] And it would not do this unless it perceived the stick to change its position and to come closer to it. Similarly, when a brute, such as a dog or a cat or a wolf or anything else, holds an animal upon which it feeds, the predator remains

---

[5] Bacon explains these modes in *Perspectiva* I.10.3, but scrutinises them in this chapter.

[6] Alhacen, *De aspectibus*, b. II, ch. 3, ed. Smith (2001), 100.

[7] What Bacon has in mind here is a so-called 'vague particular' rather than a universal concept. That is, animals are capable of distinguishing, for instance, *this particular* human being they have seen before from *some* human being they see for the very first time; see Oelze (2018), 82–87.

[8] I.e. scientists working on optics.

[9] This example is found in Avicenna, *Liber de anima* IV.3, ed. van Riet (1968), 39; see Chap. 5.

motionless, as long as the prey is calm. But when the animal that has been caught flees, then the one hunting follows [it] until it catches it, if it can. And it would not do this unless it perceived that the position of the prey has changed with respect to itself. And so, it perceives motion, rest, and distance.

And it must be admitted that brutes have some of these kinds of cognition by a certain natural industry and by an instinct of nature without deliberation. And the power by which this works is the cogitative [power] which is the ruler of the powers and uses the other powers of the soul. For here a recollection of such things seen is required because of the distinction between universals and particulars. And as said before,[10] this recollection belongs to the imagination itself if it concerns light and colour and the twenty common sensibles,[11] because imagination is the repository of the [sensory] species[12] coming from these. But if it is [a recollection] of things which belong to estimation or memory, then that [power of] memory is used here for recollecting. For although a lamb flees a wolf which it has not seen before, it still flees much faster and more carefully when it has seen it before and sees it again. And so, there happens to be a distinction by the cogitative [power] mediated by memory which is the repository of the insensible intentions concerning sensory matter, as explained before.[13] And, therefore, the [kind of] cognition, by virtue of which things seen before are distinguished from other things, is found in brutes. But since there is no proper term for this mode of cognising, an equivocation,[14] which rather is a mistranslation, is used here. Similarly, it is necessary to narrow [the term] 'syllogism' for the present purpose. Yet, without doubt there is no reason by which it can be neglected that brutes perceive the distances of things and motion and rest, even though this is not the case regarding other common sensibles.

However, for the sake of the argument[15] it must be noted that the arrangement of an argument into a [syllogistic] figure[16] and the distinction of the conclusion from the premises pertains to nothing but the rational soul. But a certain gathering of many things into one by natural industry and by instinct of nature (in which the many things resemble premises and the one is similar to a conclusion, because it is gathered from those [many things]) can well be found in brutes.[17] For we see that monkeys which have been offended ambush humans. And for this they arrange many things in order to get revenge. Therefore, they gather the one thing they intend from many things. We also see spiders arrange a web, and not only in one way but in various geometrical forms, so that flies get caught quite easily. And a wolf devours earth in order to be more weighty when it catches a horse, a bull, or a deer by the

---

[10] *Perspectiva* I.1.2, 6–9.

[11] E.g. number, motion, rest, position, and size; see *Perspectiva* I.1.3, 8–11.

[12] The form of an object that is abstracted from matter in the process of perception.

[13] *Perspectiva* I.1.4, 14f.

[14] This means that the term 'syllogism' is (misleadingly) applied in a different sense.

[15] I.e. the claim that nonhuman animals have a cogitative power capable of reasoning; see note 6.

[16] A certain arrangement of a logical argument.

[17] Bacon adopts the idea of inference in perception from Alhacen; see Sabra (1978).

nostrils, because by the power of the weight of the earth it can press down and hold on the animal more easily. Moreover, I have seen a cat that longed for some fish which swam in a large, stony tank. And since it could not get hold of them because of the water, it pulled the stopper out and let the water out until the tank was drained, so that it found the fish on the dry ground. Thus, for this it conceived of several steps to reach the desired goal. And the bee builds all combs hexagonal, that is, it selects one of the forms which most fills out the space, so that no empty space remains between the combs. And it does not want this [empty] space because otherwise honey or young bees fall out of the hive and perish. Thus, for [achieving] this aim, which resembles a conclusion, it gathers many things in its cogitation that resemble premises. And this occurs in infinitely many cases in which brute animals cogitate about many things in a certain order with respect to the one thing they intend as if they inferred by themselves a conclusion from premises. Yet, neither do they arrange the discourse of their cogitation in mode and figure[18] nor do they distinguish the latter from the former by deliberation. Just as little do they perceive themselves to bring about this kind of discourse, because their cogitation proceeds by natural instinct alone. And this discourse is similar to an argument and a syllogism, which is why the authors of *perspectiva*[19] call them 'argument' and 'syllogism'. And they certainly call this cogitation more properly 'syllogistic' than they call the distinction between universals and particulars seen before 'cognition by knowledge'.

# Bibliography

## *Primary Sources*

Alhacen. (2001). *Alhacen's theory of visual perception* (A. M. Smith, Ed.). 2 vols. Philadelphia: American Philosophical Society.

Avicenna Latinus. (1968). *Liber de anima seu sextus de naturalibus IV-V* (S. van Riet, Ed.). Louvain/Leiden: Peeters/Brill.

Bacon, R. (1996). *Roger Bacon and the origins of* Perspectiva *in the middle ages: A critical edition and English translation of Bacon's* Perspectiva *with introduction and notes* (D. C. Lindberg, Ed. and Trans.). Oxford: Clarendon Press.

## *Secondary Sources*

Bermúdez, J. L. (2003). *Thinking without words*. Oxford/New York: Oxford University Press.

Clegg, B. (2003). *The first scientist: A life of Roger Bacon*. London: Constable.

Hackett, J. (Ed.). (1997). *Roger Bacon and the sciences: Commemorative essays*. Leiden/New York/Köln: Brill.

---

[18] See note 16.

[19] I.e. (treatises on) the science of optics.

Hackett, J. (2013). Animal and human knowledge in the *Perspectiva* (*Opus maius*, part five) of Roger Bacon. In L. X. López-Farjeat & J. A. Tellkamp (Eds.), *Philosophical psychology in Arabic thought and the Latin Aristotelianism of the 13th century* (pp. 222–241). Paris: Vrin.

Köhler, T. W. (2014). *Homo animal nobilissimum: Konturen des spezifisch Menschlichen in der naturphilosophischen Aristoteleskommentierung des dreizehnten Jahrhunderts. Teilband 2.1.* Leiden/Boston: Brill.

Mercier, H., & Sperber, D. (2018). *The enigma of reason*. London: Penguin.

Oelze, A. (2018). *Animal rationality: Later medieval theories 1250–1350*. Leiden/Boston: Brill.

Raizman-Kedar, Y. (2011). Roger Bacon. In H. Lagerlund (Ed.), *Encyclopedia of medieval philosophy: Philosophy between 500 and 1500* (Vol. 2, pp. 1155–1160). Dordrecht: Springer.

Roling, B. (2011). Syllogismus brutorum: Die Diskussion der animalischen Rationalität bei Albertus Magnus und ihre Rezeption im Mittelalter und in der Frühen Neuzeit. *Recherches de théologie et philosophie médiévales, 78*(1), 221–275.

Sabra, A. I. (1978). Sensation and inference in Alhazen's theory of visual perception. In P. K. Machamer & R. G. Turnbull (Eds.), *Studies in perception: Interrelations in the history of philosophy and science* (pp. 160–185). Columbus: Ohio State University Press.

Sobol, P. G. (1993). The shadow of reason: Explanations of intelligent animal behaviour in the thirteenth century. In J. E. Salisbury (Ed.), *The medieval world of nature: A book of essays* (pp. 109–128). New York/London: Garland.

Toivanen, J. (2018). Marking the boundaries: Animals in medieval Latin philosophy. In G. F. Edwards & P. Adamson (Eds.), *Animals: A history* (pp. 121–150). Oxford: Oxford University Press.

Tomasello, M. (2014). *A natural history of human thinking*. Cambridge, MA/London: Harvard University Press.

Wood, R. (2007). Imagination and experience in the sensory soul and beyond: Richard Rufus, Roger Bacon and their contemporaries. In H. Lagerlund (Ed.), *Forming the mind: Essays on the internal senses and the mind/body problem from Avicenna to the medical enlightenment* (pp. 27–57). Dordrecht: Springer.

# Chapter 11
# Foresight and Deliberation (Roger Bacon, *Questiones super libros quatuor Physicorum*, Book II)

**Abstract** According to Aristotle, nonhuman animals lack the faculties of intellect and reason. Therefore, it seems that one cannot account for their behaviour by rational causes. However, in his commentary on Aristotle's *Physics*, Bacon spends several pages discussing the question of why nonhuman animal behaviour that looks rational to us is not actually brought about by reason and deliberation rather than by natural instinct. In particular, he examines cases of prudential or foresightful behaviour, such as the ants' collecting of grain for the winter during the summer. By and large, he does not deviate from Aristotle's denial of reason and deliberation to nonhuman animals. Nevertheless, he introduces some subtle and interesting terminological distinctions in order to capture the cognitive capacities of ants, spiders, and other animals.

## Introduction

Besides his comprehensive treatise on optics (see Chap. 10), Roger Bacon wrote several commentaries on influential texts of Aristotle. One of these texts is Aristotle's treatise on natural philosophy, the *Physics*. In the second book, Aristotle makes a distinction between different kinds of causes: *natural* and *rational*. For example, when snow has fallen during the night but is gone the next day, this might have a natural cause, namely, that the sun made it melt away. However, it could also have a rational cause, for example, a human being who rationally and deliberately decided to shovel the snow. The question now is whether this distinction of different causes can also be employed for explaining nonhuman animal behaviour.

According to Aristotle, nonhuman animals lack the faculties of intellect and reason. Therefore, it seems that one cannot account for their behaviour by rational causes. However, in his commentary on Aristotle's *Physics*, Bacon spends several pages discussing the question of why nonhuman animal behaviour that looks rational to us is not actually brought about by reason and deliberation rather than by natural instinct. In particular, he examines cases of prudential or foresightful behaviour, such as the ants' collecting of grain for the winter during the summer. By and

A. Oelze, *Animal Minds in Medieval Latin Philosophy*, Studies in the History of Philosophy of Mind 27, https://doi.org/10.1007/978-3-030-67012-2_11

large, he does not deviate from Aristotle's denial of reason and deliberation to non-human animals. Nevertheless, he introduces some subtle and interesting terminological distinctions in order to capture the cognitive capacities of ants, spiders, and other animals.[1]

## Bibliographical Note

The English translation is based on the following critical edition of the Latin text: Roger Bacon. (1928). *Questiones super libros quatuor Physicorum* (*Opera hactenus inedita* 8) (R. Steele, Ed.) (pp. 120–125). Oxford: Clarendon Press.

## Translation

The tenth question is about the activities of non-rational animals which, even if they do something with regard to some goal, do not do it by art or deliberation, as mentioned in the text.[2] Therefore, some wonder whether they do such things by virtue of the intellect. And so, the question is whether the spider produces webs, ants collect grain, and birds build nests by nature or intellect, and by art or reason and deliberation. And what will be said about one of these kinds of animals applies to all.

It seems that such animals do not do things by nature: those things which are always done are [done] by nature. But these kinds of animals do not always engage in such activities. For birds do not always build nests, therefore etc. The major premise appears in this second[3] [book of Aristotle's *Physics*].

To the same point: Nature does nothing in vain, as has often been written by Aristotle in this book[4] and in *On the Soul*.[5] But whenever birds build nests in vain – because they do not always lay [eggs] – they fail. Therefore, etc.

Against [this argument]: Each operation of a sensory power happens with regard to some proper natural object, not with regard to something artificial or something that has been placed by the intellect. This is self-evident. But the activities of such animals originate from a sensory power, because in them sense is the ultimate perfection. Hence, such activities are natural ones and [brought about] by nature.

It seems that such activities are brought about by intellect or reason and art: there are three kinds of cognition corresponding to three kinds of cognisable things. For some cognisable things are present, and these are cognised by sense; some lie in the

---

[1] For a closer analysis of this text, see Oelze (2018), 189–191.

[2] Aristotle, *Physica* II.8, 199a20–23.

[3] Ibid., 199b25f.

[4] This principle is found in *De caelo* I.4, 271a33, but not literally in the *Physics*.

[5] Aristotle, *De anima* III.9, 432b21–23.

past, and these are grasped by cognition through memory; others lie in the future, hence they are apprehended by some other power because they are different from the other things. But this [power] is no other power than the intellect, hence future things are cognised by the intellect. But these kinds of animals engage in such activities by virtue of cognition of a future [point of] time, hence such animals engage in their activities by intellect or reason. The minor premise is clear: What would birds build nests for if they did not preconceive the future summer? For in the winter their young cannot survive. Similarly, during the summer the ant collects grain on which it feeds in the winter, which it has preconceived as something future. Thus, the major premise can be confirmed as follows: The most excellent cognition originates from the most excellent power. But the most excellent cognition is of future things because it is more difficult, more subtle, and much harder to cognise future things than other things. Hence, the cognition of future things is done by the intellect.

To the same point: deliberating belongs to the intellect alone. But these kinds of animals deliberate, and hence possess an intellect. Therefore, etc. The major premise is evident since choosing, distinguishing, and discriminating the suitable and good from the unsuitable and bad and, similarly, foreseeing and deliberating are acts of reason and intellect. The minor premise is clear because ants collect grain, and with great deliberation they put it in places where it can be easily protected.

To the same point: It is written in the first [book] of the *Metaphysics*[6] that all animals which, besides hearing, have memory are capable of learning. But such animals are animals of this kind. Therefore, etc. The minor premise is clear because such animals remember the food that they have stored in holes in the ground and in knotholes; and to this [food] they return when winter comes. Thus, they provide for future situations and conceive past things. And in accordance with the fact that the cold is much stronger and longer-lasting in the winter, they collect more food for future times. Thus, such animals are capable of learning. But no animals are capable of learning except those which have an intellect. Hence, such animals have an intellect. And so, their activities are brought about by intellect or reason.

The opposite can be proven by several arguments and authorities. For it is this by which non-rational animals differ from humans, [namely], that humans possess an intellect whereas these do not. Hence, sense is the ultimate perfection of animals.

The solution: To this [argument] it must be said that such animals engage in their activities by nature since they [engage in them] by the intellect of nature, by nature, or by a diligence upon which they have been bestowed by nature. The reason for this is that the latter is the perfection in them. But the sensory operation is a natural operation. And since such animals lack reason and intellect, nature, which has been very concerned with caring for their preservation, has given them natural diligence for the guidance of their life and the production of offspring. Therefore, nature itself, which has been very concerned with the continuation and preservation of all [animals], has given diligence in care to the weaker and less perfect animals rather

---

[6] Aristotle, *Metaphysica* I.1, 980a27–b25. On the connection between hearing, memory, and learning, see Chaps. 7 and 8 in this volume.

than to the more excellent and perfect [animals] to balance their deficits. That is, it has bestowed more natural diligence to spiders, ants, and these kinds [of animals] than to horses, cattle, or sheep. For if such animals, which rank quite lowly [on the ladder of nature] and are of little use, would not have greater diligence than the others, they would soon perish from a lack of food because the genus of humans does not care for these kinds [of animals]. And so, the power of created nature[7] would not only be manifest in itself, but also by what it has not done.

To the first argument against this [argument] it must be said that those things which are done by nature are always done with relation to a cause, although they are sometimes rarely done because of the rarity[8] of time. Therefore, ants always collect grain, and birds build nests because they are subject to the [natural] disposition existing in them. Thus, it is something natural that a woman is pregnant; but still she does not always bear children, but only at a certain point of time, and being subject to the natural disposition existing in her.

To the second [argument] it must be said that nature does nothing in vain insofar as it is a cause by itself. Nevertheless, it can do something in vain because of some corruption existing in the principle or in the seed or in something impeding [the natural process] from the outside. In this sense, I say that by natural appetite and by their proper nature birds do not build nests in vain. But if they do not always lay [eggs] or if they do not always have young, this is because of some impediment from outside or inside. Therefore, this defect must not be attributed to nature but rather to a corruption of the principle out of which nature works.

To the second part of the question, that is, [the question of] whether animals engage in such activities by intellect or reason, it must be said that, as has been seen, they do not [engage in such activities by intellect and reason] but by the natural diligence which has been given to them. Therefore, it must be admitted that such activities are brought about by art.

Yet, it must be noted that there are two kinds of art. One is that which is the principle of an operation by which a model is produced through the application of the features of sensible things, such as the art of carpentry. And in such an art the one who is acting acts with deliberation, purpose, and the use of reason. The other thing called 'art' is some instinct of nature or some capacity given by nature or an innate diligence. And by this kind of art such animals do things, as has been said. And the more this [kind of art] is in them, the more they are removed from the perfection of humans, which is why the spider builds itself a web by a strong imagination, as long as nothing extrinsic hinders it.

To the first argument it has to be said that there are three kinds of cognition of future things. The first of them is the one which is found in the substance of the

---

[7] I.e. the creatures. The creator, by contrast, is the '*natura naturans*'. On this terminology and its history, see Weijers (1978).

[8] Bacon distinguishes two kinds of rarity: causal and temporal. The latter refers to events which rarely occur from a temporal point of view; see *Questiones supra libros quatuor Physicorum Aristotelis*, ed. Steele (1928), 97.

[divine] cogniser; all future things are in his power.[9] And in this way, the first cause cognises everything by looking into itself, which is the mirror of eternity. And another [substance], that is, an intelligence which itself has been created, also cognises future things by looking into the divine model. However, [it does not cognise] all future things, because certain future things are accessible only to divine providence. And this [divine providence] does not want to reveal them to any creature, but not because it is bearing ill will or because it is greedy, but because the creature is incapable of such apprehension, as there is in itself a deficit and inborn defect. The second mode is the cognition of future things which lies in the substance of the one who cognises; by his diligence, deliberation, and perspicacity future things come about, but not all of them. And in this way, humans, by using reason and intellect, and by looking at the causes and signs of future things, have foreknowledge of many future things just like astronomers, by looking at the stars which regulate the world (and to the lower of which they ascribe life and preservation), preconceive their circular motions and many other things. And together with the preceding [kind of cognition] this cognition derives from intellect and reason. Nevertheless, they are different, as has been seen. The third mode of cognition of future things derives from an instinct of nature alone or from diligence. And this cognition is found in brute animals, about which we talk in this context, for the guidance of their life and preservation and for the continuation of their own species. And this kind of cognition of future things does not derive from intellect and reason, as has been seen.

To the second [argument] it must be said that such animals do not deliberate because for deliberating two things are needed, namely, foreseeing future and perceiving past things. But such animals do not foresee. In order to understand this, it must be noted that certain animals act towards and for the future as, for instance, humans. And such animals foresee [the future]. The others are those which operate only towards the future but not for the future, like the brute animals about which we talk. And to these [animals] foresight is not ascribed. Note also that acting[10] towards, but not for, the future means to act or to produce something in the present which the one who acts might need or will need in the future, even though she neither preconceives the future nor discriminates different points of time. And brute animals act in this way. From this it is also clear what it means to act towards the future and for the future.

But against this it can be argued as follows: brute animals such as ants perceive what is present and future either as one thing or as different things. But [they do not perceive them] as one thing, because they would not collect grain in the summer nor put them in a place for the sake of preservation so that they do not lack [grain in the winter], if they would take the present summer and the future winter to be one and the same thing. And so, it is clear that they perceive what is present and what is

---

[9] I.e. God.

[10] Note that Bacon himself employs the term 'acting' (*agere*) instead of 'operating' (*operari*) in this passage although this term was usually applied to rational beings alone.

future as different things. But they cannot perceive in this way unless by distinguishing and discerning one thing from another; and if they do this they can foresee and deliberate. To this it must be said that such brute animals perceive what is present and future as different things; but [they do so only] in an accidental mode or accidentally and not in an essential mode or essentially. Yet, to perceive [the future] in this way does not suffice for foresight and deliberation. This can be demonstrated by the following example: the vegetative soul has two tasks, namely, nourishing and propagating. For the semen comes from the vegetative soul; but by the separation [of the semen] it happens that the continuity is universal. Yet, the vegetative soul did not essentially aim at this [universal continuity] but at propagation alone. But the aim that such continuance is established by propagation happens to be in the vegetative soul. Similarly, ants collect grain in the present summer essentially aiming at their preservation. Still, they do not cognise that the winter is [something] future. Hence, just as they use food and eat grain in the summer for the present preservation, they do in a similar way engage in that collecting of grain for the sake of the present preservation. For if they would not do this, they would expect[11] to perish soon. And so, if from such collecting of grain a preservation and guidance of their life in the future occur, this cognition and intention of theirs is accidental, and so they essentially perceive what is present and what is future as one thing, still [they perceive them] accidentally as two things.

To the third argument it must be said that such animals do not have complete memory which works by deliberation and by the discrimination of [different] parts of time. Therefore, they do not relate what is present to what is past, as humans [do], but they have only incomplete memory which is based on the presence of the sensible thing. This, however, does not suffice for receiving instruction. All activities of such animals have to be understood in this way.

# Bibliography

## *Primary Sources*

Aristotle. (1936). *De caelo* (D. J. Allan, Ed.). Oxford: Clarendon Press.
Aristotle. (1950). *Physica* (W. D. Ross, Ed.). Oxford: Clarendon Press.
Aristotle. (1957). *Metaphysica* (W. Jaeger, Ed.). Oxford: Clarendon Press.
Aristotle. (1961). *De anima* (W. D. Ross, Ed.). Oxford: Clarendon Press.
Bacon, R. (1928). *Questiones super libros quatuor Physicorum* (*Opera hactenus inedita* 8) (R. Steele, Ed.). Oxford: Clarendon Press.

---

[11] Since the Latin term is '*estimare*,' this expectation is presumably formed by the faculty of estimation.

## *Secondary Sources*

Oelze, A. (2018). *Animal rationality: Later medieval theories 1250–1350*. Leiden/ Boston: Brill.

Weijers, O. (1978). Contribution à l'histoire des termes 'natura naturans' et 'natura naturata' jusqu'à Spinoza. *Vivarium, 16*(1), 70–80.

# Chapter 12
# Inner Senses (Thomas Aquinas, *Summa theologiae*, Part I, Question 78, Article 4)

**Abstract**  Question 78 of the first part of Aquinas' famous *Summa theologiae* concerns human psychology, in particular the 'powers' (*potentiae*) or faculties of the human soul. In article 4, Aquinas wonders whether the sensory part of the human soul has been properly divided into a certain number of external senses, such as sight or hearing, and a certain number of so-called internal or inner senses, such as imagination, memory, and estimation. Generally speaking, the inner senses process the information received by the external senses. Since humans share many, if not all, sensory powers with nonhuman animals, Aquinas tries to determine the commonalities and differences between human and nonhuman animal cognition. His article is not the only late-medieval text on this subject, but its great popularity makes it a cornerstone of medieval philosophy of animal minds.

## Introduction

Thomas Aquinas is certainly one of, if not *the*, most famous medieval philosopher. Although he was born as the youngest son of rather poor parents near Aquino in central Italy in 1225, he created one of the richest and most influential oeuvres in medieval theology and philosophy.[1] His education started at the age of five in the convent school of the famous monastery of Monte Cassino, and continued at the University of Naples at the age of fourteen. At the arts faculty, Aquinas came into contact with Aristotle's works on natural philosophy which had just been (and in some cases were still being) translated from Greek and Arabic into Latin. It was this rediscovery and reception of Aristotle that shaped Aquinas' works and academic career. He found a spiritual home in the newly founded order of the Dominicans, which he joined in 1244. What followed was a life filled with productivity and travels: First, Aquinas went to Paris (for his novitiate), then to Cologne (to study with Albert the Great from 1248–52). Back in Paris, he began teaching as a bachelor

---

[1] On his life and works, see, for instance, Weisheipl (1974) and Porro (2016).

(mainly in theology), before he became a master in theology and got his own chair at the university. After that he spent several years at the papal courts at Orvieto and Rome, but then returned to Paris, and finally to Naples, where he died in 1274 at the age of forty-nine.

Despite his comparatively early death, Aquinas produced a huge number of texts (roughly one hundred have been identified as authentic works). They include commentaries on Peter Lombard's *Sentences* (one of the most important textbooks in the Middle Ages) as well as commentaries on various Aristotelian works and extensive theological *summae*. The text translated in the following is taken from one of these *summae*, the famous *Summa theologiae*. It comprises several volumes and covers almost every theological topic, from discussions on the trinity and Christology, to anthropology and angelology. The text is divided into various parts. Each of them contains an entire body of questions on a certain subject. Each question is further divided into articles, and so each article addresses a particular detail in the context of a specific question.

The selected passage is taken from a part that focuses on human nature. Question 78 concerns human psychology, in particular the 'powers' (*potentiae*) or faculties of the human soul. In this context, Aquinas wonders whether the sensory part of the human soul has been properly divided into a certain number of external senses, such as sight or hearing, and a certain number of so-called internal or inner senses, such as imagination, memory, and estimation. Generally speaking, the inner senses process the information received by the external senses (see Chaps. 4 and 5).[2] Since humans share many, if not all, sensory powers with nonhuman animals, Aquinas tries to determine the commonalities and differences between human and nonhuman animal cognition. His article is not the only late-medieval text on this subject, but its great popularity makes it a cornerstone of medieval philosophy of animal minds.

## Bibliographical Note

The English translation is based on the following edition of the Latin text: Thomas Aquinas. (1889). *Pars prima Summae theologiae, qq. 50–119 (Opera omnia 5)* (pp. 255–257). Rome. There are numerous English translations of this text, for instance, Thomas Aquinas. (2002). *The treatise on human nature.* Summa theologiae *1a75-89* (R. Pasnau, Trans.) (pp.73– 77). Indianapolis/Cambridge: Hackett Publishing.

---

[2] On the history of the theory (or theories) of inner senses, see Wolfson (1935). For an analysis of Aquinas' theory in particular, see, for instance, Klubertanz (1952); Tellkamp (1999); Lisska (2016).

# Translation

Fourth article: Whether the inner senses have been properly distinguished.

Regarding the fourth article, we proceed as follows: It seems that the inner senses are not properly distinguished.

1. For what is common is not distinguished from what is proper. Therefore, the common sense must not be classified amongst the internal sensory powers, apart from the proper external senses.

2. Furthermore, it is not necessary to posit any kind of inner apprehensive power for that for which the proper and external sense suffice. Yet, the proper and external senses suffice for judging about sensible things, because each single sense[3] judges about a proper object.[4] Similarly, they also seem to suffice for perceiving their own acts.[5] For since the action of a sense is somehow in between the [sense] power and the object, it seems that sight can perceive its [act of] seeing much more than a colour, because [this act is] something closer to itself. And this applies to others as well. So, it was unnecessary to posit an inner power for this purpose which is called 'common sense'.

3. Moreover, according to the Philosopher,[6] phantasy and memory are acts of the first sensory power.[7] Yet, an act is not distinguished from a subject. Hence, memory and phantasy must not be posited as separate powers, apart from sense.

4. Furthermore, the intellect depends on sense less than any other power of the sensory part [of the soul]. Yet, the intellect cognises nothing unless by acquiring [it] from the sense. This is why it is said in the first book of the *Posterior [Analytics]*[8] that those who miss one sense miss one particular kind of knowledge. Therefore, even less must a power of the sensory part, which they call 'estimative [power],' be posited for perceiving intentions, which sense does not perceive.

5. Moreover, the act of the cogitative [power] consists in gathering, combining, and dividing, and the act of the recollective [power] consists in employing some sort of syllogism for searching [for past impressions]. These [acts] differ more from the act of the estimative [power] and memory than the act of the estimative [power differs] from the act of phantasy. Thus, either the cogitative and the recollective must be posited as separate powers, apart from the estimative and memory, or the estimative and memory must not be posited as separate powers, apart from phantasy.

---

[3] E.g. sight.

[4] E.g. colour.

[5] E.g. the act of seeing.

[6] I.e. Aristotle.

[7] I.e. the common sense which bundles the information received through the proper senses.

[8] Aristotle, *Analytica posteriora* I.18, 81a38.

6.  In addition, in the twelfth book of *On the Literal Meaning of Genesis,*[9] Augustine
    posits three kinds of seeing, namely, corporeal, which is brought about by sense;
    spiritual, which is brought about by imagination or phantasy; and intellectual,
    which is brought about by the intellect. So, there is no inner power which is in
    between sense and intellect, except for the imaginative.

But [what can be said] against this is that Avicenna, in his *Book on the Soul,*[10]
posits five internal sensory powers, namely, *common sense, phantasy, imaginative
[power], estimative [power]*, and *memory*.

I reply by saying that since nature does not fail in necessary things, there must
necessarily be as many actions of the sensory soul as suffice for the life of a perfect[11]
animal. And any of these actions that cannot be reduced to one cause require distinct
powers, because a power of the soul is nothing else but the nearest origin of the
operation of the soul.

However, it must be taken into account that what is required for the life of a perfect animal is that it apprehends a thing not only when it is sensorily present but also
when it is absent. Otherwise, an animal would not be moved toward searching for
something absent, because the movement and the activity of an animal follow an
apprehension. The opposite of this is most clearly found in perfect animals which
move by progressive motion.[12] For they are moved toward something absent that has
been apprehended. Thus, it is necessary that by the sensory soul an animal not only
receives the species[13] of sensible things, when it is presently affected by them, but
also retains and preserves them. Yet, in the realm of corporeal things reception and
retention are reduced to different causes: humid matters receive well and retain
badly; the contrary is the case for dry things. Therefore – since a sensory power is
the act of a corporeal organ – it is necessary that the power which receives a species
is distinct from the one which stores it. In addition, it must be taken into account that
if an animal would be moved only by something that is delightful or distressful for
sense, it would not be necessary to posit anything else in an animal but the apprehension of forms which sense perceives, and in which it takes delight or by which it
is terrified. However, it is necessary for an animal that it searches for things or flees
from things not only because they are pleasing or unpleasing when sensed, but also
because of some other advantages and benefits or harms. For instance, a sheep
which sees that a wolf is coming flees not because of the ugliness of its colour or
shape, but as if it were an enemy by nature. Similarly, a bird collects a straw not
because it pleases the sense but because it is useful for building a nest. Thus, it is

---

[9] Augustine, *De Genesi ad litteram* XII.6 f., ed. Migne (1887) (= PL 34), 458–460.

[10] Avicenna, *Liber de anima* I.5, ed. Van Riet (1972), 85–90 (see Chap. 4); *Liber de anima* IV.1, ed.
Van Riet (1968), 1–11.

[11] I.e. an animal which has all external and internal sense powers.

[12] I.e. by locomotion.

[13] I.e. the sensory forms.

necessary for an animal that it perceives such intentions[14] which an external sense does not perceive. And this kind of perception must necessarily have some other cause. So, if the perception of the forms of sensible things happens by a sensory alteration,[15] the perception of the aforementioned intentions does not.

So, the proper senses and the common sense, the distinction of which will be discussed later, are arranged for the reception of forms of sensible things. – Phantasy or imagination, which are the same [faculty], have been arranged for the retention and preservation of these forms.[16] For phantasy or imagination are like some sort of treasury of forms which have been grasped by sense. – Yet, for apprehending the intentions which are not grasped by sense the estimative power has been arranged. – The power of memory, which is some sort of treasury of such intentions, [has been arranged] for preserving these [intentions]. A sign for this is that, in animals, remembering originates from any intention of this kind as, for instance, [the intention] that something is harmful or suitable. And even the notion of the past, to which memory pays attention, is counted among this kind of intention.

However, it must be taken into account that, with regard to [the perception of] sensible forms, there is no difference between a human being and other animals since they are affected by external sensible things in a similar manner. But there is a difference with regard to the aforementioned intentions because other animals perceive such intentions only by a certain natural instinct. A human being, by contrast, [perceives them] also by a certain comparison. Hence, what is called 'natural estimative [power]' in other animals is called 'cogitative [power]' in humans; it finds such intentions by a certain comparison.[17] Therefore, it is also called 'particular reason'.[18] Physicians assign a specific organ to it, namely, the middle part of the head. For it compares individual intentions as reason comprehends universal intentions. – Yet, from the faculty of memory [a human being] has not only memory, which other animals have, [which consists] in an immediate recalling of past things, but also recollection, that is, memory of past things by a quasi-syllogistic enquiry concerning individual intentions.

Avicenna, however, posits a fifth power in between the estimative and the imaginative [power] which combines and separates imaginary forms. This is evident when we create one form of a golden mountain from the imagined form of gold and the imagined form of a mountain.[19] But this operation does not appear in other ani-

---

[14] Aquinas adopts this concept from (the Latin translation of) Avicenna's *Liber de anima* (see Chaps. 4 and 5). It refers to a cognitive vehicle, so to speak, and so its meaning is not to be confused with the modern meaning of the term. On intentions see also Chaps. 6 and 9.

[15] The idea here is that by the reception of a sensory form a sensory organ is altered to some extent.

[16] Aquinas rejects Avicenna's distinction between phantasy and imagination. On his concept of imagination, see Brennan (1941); Stump (1999); Black (2000); Frede (2001).

[17] On the role of estimation in animal cognition according to Aquinas, see Manzanedo (1990); De Haan (2014); Juanola (2015).

[18] Aquinas adopts this terminology from Averroes; see Di Martino (2008).

[19] See Avicenna Latinus, *Liber de anima* I.5, ed. Van Riet 1972), 89 (see Chap. 4); IV.1, ed. Van Riet (1968), 6. However, Avicenna does not mention the example of the golden mountain in these passages. For a closer analysis, see Black (2013).

mals, apart from humans, in whom the imaginative power suffices for this [kind of operation]. Averroes also ascribes this operation to imagination in a certain book he wrote *On Sense and What Is Sensed.*[20]

And so, it is unnecessary to posit more than four inner powers of the sensory part, namely, common sense and imagination, estimative [power] and memory.

So, to the first argument it must be said that the inner sense is not called 'common' by predication as a genus,[21] but rather as the common root and origin of the external senses.

To the second argument it must be said that a proper sense judges about a proper sensible by discriminating this [proper] sensible from others which fall within the scope of the same sense, for instance, by discriminating white from black or green. However, discerning white from sweet can be done neither by sight nor by taste, because it is necessary that the one which discriminates them cognises each of them. Therefore, it is necessary that a judgment of discrimination pertains to the common sense, to which all apprehensions of the senses are led to as to a common terminus. And by this [common sense] the intentions of the senses are also perceived, as when somebody sees himself seeing. For this [meta-cognition] cannot be brought about by a proper sense that cognises nothing but the form of a sensible thing by which it is affected. In this alteration sight is completed, and from this alteration follows another alteration of the common sense which perceives [the act of] seeing [itself].

To the third argument it must be said that one power originates from the soul, mediated by another [power], as said before.[22] Likewise, the soul [itself] is also subject to another power, mediated by another [power]. And in this way, phantasy and memory are called 'acts of the first sensory [power]'.

To the fourth argument it must be said that even though the operation of the intellect originates from sense, nevertheless, in a thing that has been apprehended by sense the intellect cognises much that sense itself cannot perceive. And similarly, [so does] the estimative [power], but in a lesser way.

To the fifth argument it must be said that the cogitative [power] and memory excel in a human being not because of what is a particular feature of the sensory part, but by some affinity and proximity to universal reason in respect of a certain flowing back.[23] Therefore, they are not different, but the same powers [as in other animals]. However, they are more perfect than in other animals.

---

[20] See Averroes, *Compendium libri Aristotelis De sensu et sensato*, ed. Shields (1949), 38–40.

[21] A genus (e.g. 'animal') is common by predication insofar as it can be predicated of different animals.

[22] *Summa theologiae* I.77.7.

[23] It is controversial what '*refluentia*' means in this context. However, it seems that what Aquinas has in mind here is some sort of flow of cognitive information from a higher cognitive power, such as the intellect, back to a lower power, such as cogitation; see Rubini (2020), 283–286. Aquinas likely received this concept from Albert the Great who apparently adopted it from Moses Maimonides; see Schwartz (2011), 283f.

To the sixth argument it must be said that Augustine says that spiritual vision is what is brought about by the likenesses of bodies in the absence of [these] bodies. Therefore, it is clear that it is common to all inner apprehensions.

# Bibliography

## *Primary Sources*

Aristotle. (1964). *Analytica priora et posteriora* (W. D. Ross, Ed.). Oxford: Clarendon Press.
Augustine. (1887). *De Genesi ad litteram libri XII* (J.-P. Migne, Ed.) ( = PL 34). Paris.
Avicenna Latinus. (1968–1972). *Liber de anima seu sextus de naturalibus.* 2 vols. (S. van Riet, Ed.). Louvain: Peeters/Leiden: Brill.
Averroes. (1949). Compendium libri Aristotelis De sensu et sensato. In A. L. Shields (Ed.), *Averroes Cordubensis, Compendia librorum Aristotelis qui Parva naturalia vocantur* (pp. 3–44). Cambridge, MA: The Mediaeval Academy of America.
Thomas Aquinas. (1889). *Pars prima Summae theologiae, qq. 50-119 (Opera omnia 5).* Rome.
Thomas Aquinas. (2002). *The treatise on human nature.* Summa theologiae *1a75-89* (R. Pasnau, Trans.) (pp. 73–77). Indianapolis/Cambridge: Hackett Publishing.

## *Secondary Sources*

Black, D. L. (2000). Imagination and estimation: Arabic paradigms and Western transformations. *Topoi, 19*(1), 59–75.
Black, D. L. (2013). Rational imagination: Avicenna on the cogitative power. In L. X. López-Farjeat & J. A. Tellkamp (Eds.), *Philosophical psychology in Arabic thought and the Latin aristotelianism of the 13th century* (pp. 59–81). Paris: Vrin.
Brennan, R. E. (1941). The Thomistic concept of imagination. *The New Scholasticism, 15*(2), 149–161.
De Haan, D. D. (2014). Perception and the *vis vogitativa*: A Thomistic analysis of aspectual, actional, and affectional percepts. *American Catholic Philosophical Quarterly, 88*(3), 397–437.
Di Martino, C. (2008). *Ratio particularis: La doctrine des sens internes d'Avicenne à Thomas d'Aquin: Contribution à l'étude de la tradition arabo-latine de la psychologie d'Aristote.* Paris: Vrin.
Frede, D. (2001). Aquinas on phantasia. In D. Perler (Ed.), *Ancient and medieval theories of intentionality* (pp. 155–183). Leiden/Boston/Köln: Brill.
Juanola, J. D. A. (2015). Inteligencia animal y *vis aestimativa* en Avicena y Tomás de Aquino. *Espíritu. Cuadernos del instituto filosófico de Balmesiana, 64*(150), 341–362.
Klubertanz, G. P. (1952). *The discursive power: Sources and doctrine of the vis cogitativa according to St. Thomas Aquinas.* St. Louis: The Modern Schoolman.
Lisska, A. J. (2016). *Aquinas's theory of perception: An analytic reconstruction.* Oxford: Oxford University Press.
Manzanedo, M. F. (1990). La cogitativa del hombre y la inteligencia de los animales. *Angelicum, 67*(3), 329–363.
Porro, P. (2016). *Thomas Aquinas: A historical and philosophical profile* (J. G. Trabbic & R. W. Nutt, Trans.). Washington, DC: The Catholic University of America Press.

Rubini, P. (2020). 'Accidental perception' and 'cogitative power' in Thomas Aquinas and John of Jandun. In E. Băltuţă (Ed.), *Medieval perceptual puzzles: Theories of sense perception in the 13th and 14th centuries* (pp. 269–303). Leiden/Boston: Brill.

Schwartz, Y. (2011). The Latin encounter with Arabic Aristotelian cosmology. In L. Honnefelder (Ed.), *Albertus Magnus und der Ursprung der Universitätsidee: Die Begegnung der Wissenschaftskulturen im 13. Jahrhundert und die Entdeckung des Konzepts der Bildung durch Wissenschaft* (pp. 277–298). Berlin: Berlin University Press.

Stump, E. (1999). Aquinas on the mechanisms of cognition: Sense and phantasia. In S. Ebbesen & R. L. Friedman (Eds.), *Medieval analyses of language and cognition* (pp. 377–395). Copenhagen: C.A. Reitzels.

Tellkamp, J. A. (1999). *Sinne, Gegenstände und Sensibilia: Zur Wahrnehmungslehre des Thomas von Aquin.* Leiden/Boston/Köln: Brill.

Weisheipl, J. A. (1974). *Friar Thomas d'Aquino: His life, thought, and work.* Garden City: Doubleday.

Wolfson, H. A. (1935). The internal senses in Latin, Arabic, and Hebrew philosophic texts. *The Harvard Theological Review, 28*(2), 69–133.

# Chapter 13
# Prudence (John Duns Scotus, *Quaestiones super libros Metaphysicorum Aristotelis*, Book I, Question 3)

**Abstract** Like Albert the Great and Thomas Aquinas, John Duns Scotus was a highly important and influential thinker in the later Middle Ages. Yet, unlike Albert and Aquinas, he was a Franciscan friar. Unfortunately, we are in the dark regarding most details of his biography. Although the last part of his name identifies him as a Scot, the precise place and date of his birth are unknown. Since he was ordained as priest on March 17, 1291 in Northampton, England, and since ordination usually did not take place before the age of twenty-five, it is likely that Scotus was born at some point before March 1266. Furthermore, it is known that he studied philosophy and theology at Oxford, before he left for Paris in 1302. There he lectured on Peter Lombard's *Sentences*, one of the most important texts of the Middle Ages. In 1305, Scotus became a doctor of philosophy. In 1307, he moved to the *studium generale* at Cologne, founded more than fifty years earlier by Albert the Great. However, his teaching activities at Cologne did not last for long, since he suddenly died in 1308. In his commentary on Aristotle's *Metaphysics*, John Duns Scotus addresses the question of whether nonhuman animals are capable of employing prudence (prudentia). In his reply, he devotes much space to explaining why such animals are prudent only in a metaphorical way of speaking. Therefore, his text is an important medieval contribution to the discussion of anthropomorphic language. This debate still prevails in the contemporary debate over animal minds.

## Introduction

Like Albert the Great and Thomas Aquinas, John Duns Scotus was a highly important and influential thinker in the later Middle Ages. Yet, unlike Albert and Aquinas, he was a Franciscan friar. Unfortunately, we are in the dark regarding most details of his biography.[1] Although the last part of his name identifies him as a Scot, the precise place and date of his birth are unknown. Since he was ordained as priest on

---

[1] On his life and his works, see Cross (1999).

A. Oelze, *Animal Minds in Medieval Latin Philosophy*, Studies in the History of Philosophy of Mind 27, https://doi.org/10.1007/978-3-030-67012-2_13

March 17, 1291 in Northampton, England, and since ordination usually did not take place before the age of twenty-five, it is likely that Scotus was born at some point before March 1266. Furthermore, it is known that he studied philosophy and theology at Oxford, before he left for Paris in 1302. There he lectured on Peter Lombard's *Sentences*, one of the most important texts of the Middle Ages. In 1305, Scotus became a doctor of philosophy. In 1307, he moved to the *studium generale* at Cologne, founded more than fifty years earlier by Albert the Great.[2] However, his teaching activities at Cologne did not last for long, since he suddenly died in 1308.

As regards Scotus' position within later medieval thought, he is often considered to be a counterpart to the Dominican Aquinas, on the one hand (especially in the field of theology), and to the Franciscan William of Ockham, on the other (in particular with respect to the field of philosophy and the debate over the ontological status of universals). In general, his extensive commentary on the *Sentences* is what gained him his fame, although he also produced several question commentaries on different texts by Aristotle. Some of these are particularly interesting with regard to the philosophy of animal minds. Like Albert the Great (see Chap. 7), Scotus commented on Aristotle's *Metaphysics* and, also like Albert, he addressed the question of whether nonhuman animals are capable of employing prudence (*prudentia*).[3] However, his commentary differs from Albert's in at least two regards. First, he does not comment on Aristotle word by word but discusses various questions arising from the original text. Second, in his reply to the question of whether nonhuman animals can be called prudent, he devotes much space to explaining why they are prudent only in a metaphorical way of speaking. Therefore, his text is an important medieval contribution to the discussion of anthropomorphic language. This debate still prevails in the contemporary debate over animal minds.

## Bibliographical Note

The English translation is based on the following critical edition of the Latin text: John Duns Scotus. (1997). *Quaestiones super libros Metaphysicorum Aristotelis, Libri I-V* (R. Andrews et al., Eds.) (pp. 87–94). St. Bonaventure, N.Y.: The Franciscan Institute, St. Bonaventure University. An alternative English translation can be found in John Duns Scotus. (1997). *Questions on the Metaphysics of Aristotle, Volume I: Books 1–5* (G. J. Etzkorn & A. Wolter, Trans.) (pp. 75–81). St. Bonaventure, NY: The Franciscan Institute, St. Bonaventure University.

---

[2] See the introduction to Chap. 7.

[3] For an analysis of this passage, see Oelze (2018), 199–202.

# Translation

[Question 3: Whether prudence exists in brute animals]
[The question is] whether prudence exists in brute animals.

[It seems] that [it does] not [for the following reasons]:

First, because, [according to] book VI of the *Ethics,*[4] "prudence is the right reason about things to be done"; [but] brute animals do not possess reason.

Moreover, because prudence involves provision for the future from memory of the past. This cannot work without comparing the past to the future; comparing, however, belongs to reason itself.

In addition, because they do not cognise anything unless by sense. Sensation in itself concerns only proper and common sensibles.[5] The harmful and the useful, which is what prudence is about, are neither proper nor common sensibles, therefore, etc.

The Philosopher[6] literally claims the contrary.

[I. To the question]

I reply that prudence exists in brutes metaphorically, that is, not with regard to those things which they pursue or flee by natural instinct (like a lamb follows its mother and flees a wolf, or like a swallow builds a nest, or like an ant collects grain for the winter), because these things are not done by memory (for an ant born in the summer never recalls the winter, and [nevertheless] it collects grain). Memory, however, is a [cognitive] component of the prudence of brute animals (this is literally [Aristotle[7]]). Moreover, such things which arise from natural instinct are necessarily adopted by the entire species. And so, with regard to them, it does not happen that they are done in one way or another.

However, prudence – as it is found in us – is a deliberative habit.[8] It does not regard an end, but regards the means arranged for [achieving an] end; and it does not concern necessary but contingent matters. And so, in these cases [prudence] is about those things that can be done in one way or another: for instance, that it[9] collects or stores [grain] in this or that place, and [takes] from this or that heap – by memory of the place in which it stored the first piece of grain and [by memory] of the heap from which it took the first –, and that a spider rather builds a web in a place where there is a larger amount of flies, or a swallow [builds] a nest [in a place] to which the access is more difficult.

---

[4] Aristotle, *Nicomachean Ethics* VI.5, 1140b3–4; VI.13, 1144a28–44b1.

[5] A proper sensible is the sensible thing (or quality) proper to each sense, e.g. colour for sight. Common sensibles such as size or shape can be perceived by more than one sense.

[6] Aristotle, *Metaphysica* I.1, 980b22–24.

[7] See note 6.

[8] I.e. a cognitive capacity that is acquired by habituation.

[9] I.e. the ant.

[II. To the initial arguments]

To the arguments.

To the first [argument]: That this [definition of prudence as "the right reason about things to be done"] is the definition of prudence properly speaking.

To the other [argument]: [In *Metaphysics* I.1, Aristotle] literally [says that] "they participate in experience to a minor degree". And so, just like they have experience in one way, [they have the capacity of] comparing in another way, that is, not that [kind of comparing] which is applied by reason and which works by [rational] discourse from the known to the unknown.

To the third [argument]: By internal sensory cognition something can be cognised that cannot be cognised by an external sense, although the species[10] of that [thing cognised] clearly is in the external sense, as it is claimed about the cognition of substance which happens by virtue of the intellect, not by sense. According to some people,[11] however, substance multiplies its species, together with the species of an accident. Yet, sense does not cognise [substance] by means of such a species, even though it is in that [species]. And this is because of a deficiency of the cognitive power, not because of the species of what is represented. For instance, the medium[12] does not see colour although the species of colour is there.

[III. Objection regarding the comparison of the past and the future in brutes]

Against the reply to the second argument [the following objection might be raised]: brutes do many things by cognition in the same way in which they are done by a human being who cognises by a discourse of reason. Thus, they seem to have similar cognition. The premise is evident: A human being reasons by way of syllogising that 'by [taking] the shorter way one reaches the goal; this is shorter, therefore, etc.'; and based on such a discourse one chooses the shorter [way] to obtain something. Now, a dog seems to choose in a similar way when chasing a hare. And the same [happens] in other cases.

To this [objection] it is said that they do something in a way similar to what a human being does by deliberation. However, it is not necessarily the case that they have similar cognition. For that which is chosen by deliberation can also be chosen not by deliberation but by a sensory appetite alone. And so, each of them produces a visible action in a similar way, but they are not similarly masters of their actions.

Against this: Thus, in the same way brutes can act as if they possessed prudence or the [capacity of] of comparing the past to the future although they possess none [of these capacities]. For an ant makes provisions for the winter as if it cognised the future winter. Yet, since this does not seem to be cognising – because it[13] does not have a being in itself but only in its cause (or in a necessity if it is necessary, or in a contingency if it is contingent) –, it does not seem that a future thing can be cog-

---

[10] I.e., broadly speaking, the form of a thing cognised.

[11] E.g. Roger Bacon, *De multiplicatione specierum* I.2, ed. Lindberg (1983), 24.

[12] I.e. the air.

[13] I.e. what is cognised.

nised (necessarily or by way of guessing with a degree of probability) by someone to whom it is a future thing, unless from the cause. However, cognition of the effect from the cause is based on comparison properly speaking. This is denied to brutes. Thus, prudence in the way in which it exists in them does not seem to be provision for the future by memory of the past.

[IV. Additional reply]

I reply that it can be admitted that since animals are acted upon in every action and do not act,[14] and, therefore, are not the proper masters of any action, they do not act with provision for the future by memory of the past. Still, they seem to [act with provision] because they act in a similar way by nature as they would if they acted self-determinedly.

Against [this reply the following objection can be raised]: In what way does Aristotle posit [different] grades of cognition in brutes? – The reply [is]: that, according to the truth, all brutes lack provision for the future by cognition. However, some cognise only things present and do not have any instinct for doing things which are useful in the future. Others have an instinct for operating as if they provided for the future, together with the cognition of things present. Still, they act by necessity, not by foreknowledge or freely. Therefore, they are prudent only by analogy.

But you resolutely ask why such [behaviours] are not adopted by the entire species. – The reply [is]: what is diverse pertains to sense as, for instance, to collect grain from this heap and to store them here. Yet, what is uniform is brought about by an instinct of nature as, for instance, to collect straightforwardly as if providing [for the future]. Therefore, sense regulates natural instinct.

But from this it seems to follow that those that [act] diversely are less prudent than those that [act] uniformly, because nobody situates prudence in sensory apprehension. But what is diverse there precisely pertains to sense.

However, there is another way in which Aristotle's opinion can be saved, because he himself never speaks of provision for the future but only of memory. And from this he infers: "And for this reason others [that have memory] are prudent," as if that [grade of cognition] would not be another grade beyond memory.

Thus, it must be noted that he does not make a distinction: neither between phantasy and memory nor between sense and estimative [power]. And each apprehensive power has a correspondent appetitive power. So, each animal has two kinds of appetite: one [is] sensory, the other estimative. And so, each animal has sense just like it also has some sort of estimative [capacity].

But where these powers exist without other retentive [powers] there is neither apprehension of nor striving for a suitable sensible thing or for something that is pleasurable by nature. Instead, [there is] only [apprehension of or striving for] a sensible thing that pertains to the estimative [power], and only if this sensible thing

---

[14] This is based on John of Damascus, *De fide orthodoxa*, c. 41 (= II.27), ed. Buytaert (1955), 153.

is present. Yet, nobody grants prudence proper or by analogy to someone who seeks only what is present.

In those, however, which possess phantasy, retaining the species of a sensible thing, and [which possess] memory, retaining the species of what has been judged to be suitable, it will, by virtue of a [cognitive] act, also be judged what is suitable if, by virtue of an act, a sensible thing is imagined in the absence [of that thing]. And even though the appetite of phantasy is not stimulated – because what is strongly imagined is not pleasurable for the sense – the appetite of the estimative [power] is nevertheless stimulated if it is suitable by nature. And so, by this kind of memory and estimation and appetite the act of a brute seeking something absent (not pleasurable for the sense, but suitable by nature) is similar to the act of prudence in us, because it is similar with respect to the execution.

If we would seek something, not out of prudence but after the apprehension of something suitable (and that it is suitable we would have determined by extensive deliberation), we would seek such a thing not because it is pleasurable. Hence, it does not seem that they lack anything except that [capacity of] deliberation. But because of this [lack] there is no dissimilarity in seeking something. As said before, we do many things without deliberating, but in a similar way, as if we had deliberated. The highest [degree of] similarity is [reached] if this suitable thing is suitable to be used by them, not in the very moment when they search it, but in the future. For then they seem to provide [for the future]. But they never do this based on cognition of the future, but based on a current cognition of something present or past in the estimative [power].

But to this one can object as follows: Why is one phantasm more stimulating for them than another? – Reply: After the motions of external sensible things have stopped, that [object] occurs first which has been impressed more strongly [in the senses].

Furthermore, it is argued: Why are phantasy and estimative [power] not moved now as at other times? For in the winter an ant does not collect grain. – Moreover, why does a dolphin flee storms given that it has not sensed them before? – Furthermore, whenever the stronger sensible things cease outside, phantasy and estimative [power] impel [one to do something]; and any animal would always do the same. – Moreover, it never cognises something past with a concept of the past or at least as present, like it belongs to phantasy to cognise. Search for answers.

# Bibliography

## *Primary Sources*

Aristotle. (1894). *Ethica Nicomachea* (I. Bywater, Ed.). Oxford: Clarendon Press.
Aristotle. (1957). *Metaphysica* (W. Jaeger, Ed.). Oxford: Clarendon Press.
John Duns Scotus. (1997a). *Quaestiones super libros Metaphysicorum Aristotelis, Libri I-V* (R. Andrews et al., Eds.). St. Bonaventure: The Franciscan Institute, St. Bonaventure University.

John Duns Scotus. (1997b). *Questions on the Metaphysics of Aristotle, Volume I: Books 1–5* (G. J. Etzkorn & A. Wolter, Trans.). St. Bonaventure: The Franciscan Institute, St. Bonaventure University.

John of Damascus. (1955). *De fide orthodoxa: Versions of Burgundius and Cerbanus* (E. M. Buytaert, Ed.). St. Bonaventure: The Franciscan Institute.

Bacon, R. (1983). *Roger Bacon's philosophy of nature: A critical edition, with English translation, introduction, and notes, of* De multiplicatione specierum *and* De speculis comburentibus (D. C. Lindberg, Ed. and Trans.). Oxford: Clarendon Press.

## *Secondary Sources*

Cross, R. (1999). *Duns Scotus*. New York/Oxford: Oxford University Press.

Oelze, A. (2018). *Animal rationality: Later medieval theories 1250–1350*. Boston/Leiden: Brill.

# Chapter 14
# Erring (Adam Wodeham, *Lectura secunda in librum primum Sententiarum*, Prologue, Question 4, §8)

**Abstract** In his commentary on the *Sentences*, Adam Wodeham tries to account for sensory illusions. In his view, they result from erroneous judgments. However, he has to address the question of how nonhuman animals can also fall prey to such an illusion. Because if illusions are erroneous judgments and if animals fall prey to illusions, it follows that they are capable of judging. This means that they can affirm or negate that something is the case by 'complex propositions' (as judgments were defined by William Ockham). This view leads to various consequences which Wodeham is not ready to accept. Instead, he develops an interesting and intricate argument for a more parsimonious and less anthropomorphic explanation of animal behaviour.

## Introduction

Adam Wodeham is quite often primarily referred to as student and secretary of the famous William of Ockham. However, he was an important fourteenth-century philosopher and theologian in his own right.[1] Born near Southampton, England, around 1295 he entered the Franciscan order at a relatively young age and first studied philosophy at their *studium* (some sort of small university of the order) in London. It was during this time that he met Ockham, under whom he studied, before working as an assistant in preparing Ockham's comprehensive *Sum of Logic*. When Ockham moved to Avignon in 1324, Wodeham went to Oxford to study theology. One of the duties of academic theologians during that time was to lecture on the so-called *Sentences*, the most important medieval textbook on theology, written by Peter Lombard in the middle of the twelfth century. Already in the thirteenth century, Albert the Great, Thomas Aquinas, and John Duns Scotus had produced commentaries on the *Sentences*. Wodeham did the same by giving lectures on the *Sentences* in London, Norwich, and Oxford. His commentaries, in particular the so-called

---

[1] On his life and works, see Courtenay (1978); Wood (2003); Lahey (2011).

A. Oelze, *Animal Minds in Medieval Latin Philosophy*, Studies in the History of Philosophy of Mind 27, https://doi.org/10.1007/978-3-030-67012-2_14

*Lectura secunda*, produced at Norwich, and the *Ordinatio Oxoniensis*, a revised version of his Oxford lecture, remained influential after his death in 1358.

When Adam Wodeham commented on the *Sentences*, *Sentences* commentaries had already developed into an independent and original genre of texts. Around 1240, commenting on the *Sentences* had become a requirement for all candidates in theology. The commentary tradition reached its peak around the middle of the fourteenth century. One of the most obvious differences between earlier and later commentaries is that later authors used the commentaries as a vehicle to discuss and communicate subjects that went well beyond Peter Lombard's original text. A good example of this kind of digression is the debate between Adam Wodeham and Gregory of Rimini (see Chap. 15) over animals' capacity of judging.[2] The general context of this debate has actually nothing (or not much) to do with animal cognition. Rather, the starting point is Peter Auriol's theory of 'apparent being' (*esse apparens*). According to Auriol, cognitive powers such as the sense organs or the intellect transform the object of cognition in such a way that it takes on a special form of existence. This form is different from the form of existence of the object in the extra-mental (or 'extra-cognitive') world. One of the examples by which Auriol claims to prove his theory is the illusion of moving trees at the shore, when seen from a ship that is moving.[3] Since the motion of the trees is neither in the act of seeing nor in the trees nor in the air, Auriol argues that it can only be explained by an apparent being into which the powers of cognition have put the trees.[4] Adam Wodeham, however, disagrees with Auriol.[5] In his view, the explanation of illusions does not require a theory of apparent existence. Instead, he thinks that an illusion such as the motion of trees is the result of an erroneous judgment. This is where animals come into play. For Wodeham has to address the question of how to explain that nonhuman animals can also fall prey to such an illusion: if illusions are erroneous judgments and if animals fall prey to illusions, it follows that they are capable of judging. This means that they can affirm or negate that something is the case by 'complex propositions' (as judgments were defined by Ockham). This view leads to various consequences which Wodeham is not ready to accept. Instead, he develops an interesting and intricate argument for a more parsimonious and less anthropomorphic explanation of animal behaviour. It becomes even more interesting when

---

[2] For a reconstruction, analysis, and evaluation, see Reina (1986); Tachau (1993), 665; Michon (2001), 326f.; Perler (2006), 89–94; Oelze (2018a), 121–129; Oelze (2018b), 189–194.

[3] This example was quite popular even in antiquity. Auriol presumably took it from Aristotle, *De insomniis* 2, 460b26f., a short treatise transmitted as part of the so-called '*Parva naturalia*'. The example can also be found in Ptolemy's *Optics*; see Smith (1996), 124. This text was translated into Latin in the twelfth century, see ibid., 7f.

[4] See Peter Auriol, *Scriptum super primum Sententiarum*, d. 3, s. 14, a. 1, n. 31, ed. Buytaert (1956), 696. Wodeham reproduces this explanation in *Lectura secunda in librum primum Sententiarum*, prol., q. 4, §7, ed. Wood (1990), 97.

[5] On this debate in particular, see Adriaenssen (2019). On Wodeham's concept of judging, see also Perler (2008) and Pickavé (2012).

read through the eyes of Gregory of Rimini who openly attacked Wodeham's position (see Chap. 15).

## Bibliographical Note

The English translation is based on the following critical edition of the Latin text: Adam Wodeham. (1990). *Lectura secunda in librum primum Sententiarum* (R. Wood, Ed.) (pp. 98–100). St. Bonaventure, NY: St. Bonaventure University. To date, the Latin has not been translated into English.

## Translation

[Three objections against the explanation of the first experience[6]]

Against [this explanation I argue as follows]: The impression because of which it appears to a human being that the trees move is a sensory act. However, for you[7] no judgment by which it is accepted that something is somehow or behaves in a certain way is a sensory act. Therefore [that impression cannot be a judgment]. The first premise is proven because, also to brutes, the trees appear to move. For when the ship moves towards the trees, they run away [as] if these [trees] are something frightening to them. […]

[Reply to the first objection: Whether brutes can form a judgment]

To the first [objection I reply as follows]: The assumption [that the impression that the trees move is a sensory act] must be denied. However, to a certain degree, it can well be the case that by visual perceptions, which are sensory acts, the trees appear to move to a human being. For the proof [of this] I admit that brutes have simple visual perceptions. Naturally, these [perceptions] would be followed by a judgment; by this [judgment] it has been established in a complex and objective way that the trees appear to move, supposing that this kind of gathered or objectively formed perception is available to them. But we cannot know whether they have it unless by making guesses based on the effects and movements following such simple visual perceptions. However, taking such visual perceptions for granted, it is certain that they sometimes flee certain things seen and at other times pursue them. From this it seems to follow with a certain degree of probability that these things would not appear to them only in this way, but that they would rather appear to them

---

[6]This refers to Peter Auriol, *Scriptum super primum Sententiarum*, d. 3, s. 14, a. 1, n. 31, ed. Buytaert (1956), 696, and his theory of apparent being; see the introduction above.

[7]I.e. William Ockham.

to be harmful or useful. And so, they would have a complex, objective perception or, formally, [the capacity of] composition and division. For, as it seems, we do not pursue or flee anything except those things which we judge [to be] good or bad. And in their case it seems to work in the same way.

But if they would have been moved by this it would consequently be necessary to ascribe practical reason to them, that is, a practical order concerning choosing and reacting, pursuing and fleeing. For they behave as if they had [the capacity of coming up with an] order [concerning how to behave]. And then I do not see why they should not be called 'rational animals'. Thus, I say instead that brutes "are acted upon rather than acting"[8] because this seems more plausible to me. That is, they do not only not freely pursue or flee useful and harmful things, but also neither deliberate nor judge by a complex objective judgment that something agreeable exists, that something is harmful and must be fled, or [is useful and] must be pursued. Rather, they immediately flee at the simple apprehension of this thing that is harmful; or they pursue [at the simple apprehension of] that thing that is agreeable.

And if this kind of pursuit naturally exists in all individuals of some species, then the first simple apprehension that is caused by the thing present suffices for [triggering] such a pursuit or flight. However, if they seem to provide for the future, as it is the case with the ant that collects grain for the winter, or [with] the spider that builds a web in which flies are caught, this is not brought about by some cognition or memory which the ant has of the winter, or by the experience that it would otherwise lack food, because an ant that has been born in the summer shows the same kind of gathering behaviour; instead, this is brought about by an instinct of nature.

However, where one individual of a species flees or pursues something present or absent that another individual [of the same species neither] pursues [nor flees], this comes from the memory and imagination of punishment or pleasure that arises by contact with a similar object. So, even there is no such objective composition. Instead, it pursues or flees immediately at the act of apprehension of a present thing in combination with the imagination or memory of simple punishment or previously experienced pleasure. This is not unfavourable for a brute, as we experience even in our own case, because we frequently do many things at a single act of simple apprehension without any other deliberation or complex apprehension. For instance, we scratch our head or rub our beard when we feel an itch. And we make many other gestures and movements without any deliberation or previous judgment.

Also, it is very clear that a judgment or deliberation is required for strongly desiring something, whereas for desiring something unconditionally a simple apprehension usually suffices. So, why should it not [suffice] in the same way for what a brute desires or demands? It pursues [something] whenever nothing is in the way,

---

[8] John of Damascus, *De fide orthodoxa* II (27), c. 41, n. 1, transl. Burgundii, ed. Buytaert (1955), 153.

such as simply an obstacle or the memory of a punishment resulting from [the contact with] another [similar object]. Thus, it must be said that brutes possess no [capacity of forming a] composite, objective judgment. But, as suggested, by virtue of one or several visual perceptions they well apprehend the trees and the distance as such and such and as suddenly smaller or greater. And at such [cognitive] acts flight or pursuit naturally follow in a brute without any composite judgment that something is agreeable or disagreeable, so long as it apprehends what is truly agreeable or disagreeable in a thing.

# Bibliography

## *Primary Sources*

Adam Wodeham. (1990). *Lectura secunda in librum primum Sententiarum* (R. Wood, Ed.). St. Bonaventure, NY: St. Bonaventure University.
Aristotle. (1955). *Parva naturalia* (W. D. Ross, Ed.). Oxford: Clarendon Press.
John of Damascus. (1955). *De fide orthodoxa* (E. M. Buytaert, Ed.). St. Bonaventure: The Franciscan Institute.
Peter Auriol. (1952–1956). *Scriptum super primum Sententiarum* (E. M. Buytaert, Ed.). 2 vols. St. Bonaventure: The Franciscan Institute.

## *Secondary Sources*

Adriaenssen, H. T. (2019). Peter Auriol and Adam Wodeham on perception and judgment. In B. Glenney & J. F. Silva (Eds.), *The senses and the history of philosophy* (pp. 149–162). Abingdon/New York: Routledge.
Courtenay, W. J. (1978). *Adam Wodeham: An introduction to his life and writings.* Leiden: Brill.
Lahey, S. E. (2011). Adam Wodeham. In H. Lagerlund (Ed.), *Encyclopedia of medieval philosophy: Philosophy between 500 and 1500* (Vol. 1, pp. 20–24). Dordrecht: Springer.
Michon, C. (2001). Intentionality and proto-thoughts. In D. Perler (Ed.), *Ancient and medieval theories of intentionality* (pp. 325–341). Leiden/Boston/Köln: Brill.
Oelze, A. (2018a). *Animal rationality: Later medieval theories 1250–1350.* Leiden/Boston: Brill.
Oelze, A. (2018b). Können Tiere irren? Philosophische Antworten aus dem 13. und 14. Jahrhundert. In A. Speer & M. Mauriège (Eds.), *Irrtum – Error – Erreur* (pp. 179–194). Berlin/Boston: De Gruyter.
Perler, D. (2006). Intentionality and action: Medieval discussions on the cognitive capacities of animals. In M. C. Pacheco & J. F. Meirinhos (Eds.), *Intellect et imagination dans la philosophie médiévale* (Vol. 1, pp. 72–98). Turnhout: Brepols.
Perler, D. (2008). Seeing and judging: Ockham and Wodeham on sensory cognition. In S. Knuuttila & P. Kärkkäinen (Eds.), *Theories of perception in medieval and early modern philosophy* (pp. 151–169). Dordrecht: Springer.
Pickavé, M. (2012). Emotion and cognition in later medieval philosophy: The case of Adam Wodeham. In M. Pickavé & L. Shapiro (Eds.), *Emotion and cognitive life in medieval and early modern philosophy* (pp. 94–115). Oxford: Oxford University Press.

Reina, M. E. (1986). Un abozzo di polemica sulla psicologia animale: Gregorio da Rimini contro Adamo Wodeham. In C. Wenin (Ed.), *L'homme et son univers au Moyen Âge* (pp. 598–609). Louvain: Publications de l'Institut Supérieur de Philosophie.

Smith, A. M. (1996). *Ptolemy's theory of visual perception: An English translation of the optics.* Philadelphia: American Philosophical Society.

Tachau, K. H. (1993). What senses and intellect do: Argument and judgment in late medieval theories of knowledge. In K. Jacobi (Ed.), *Argumentationstheorie: Scholastische Forschungen zu den logischen und semantischen Regeln korrekten Folgerns* (pp. 653–668). Leiden: Brill.

Wood, R. (2003). Adam of Wodeham. In J. J. E. Gracia & T. B. Noone (Eds.), *A companion to philosophy in the middle ages* (pp. 77–85). Malden: Blackwell.

# Chapter 15
# Judging (Gregory of Rimini, *Lectura super primum Sententiarum*, Distinction 3, Question 1, Article 1)

**Abstract** In a passage of his commentary on the *Sentences*, Gregory of Rimini tries to define different forms of knowledge (*notitia*) and discusses the differences between human and nonhuman knowledge. Most of his answer to the question of whether nonhuman animals have what he calls 'complex knowledge' (*notitia complexa*) is a critique of Wodeham's argument against the ascription of the capacity of judging to nonhuman animals. Contrary to Wodeham, Gregory sees no problem in ascribing this capacity to other animals, as long as one makes certain distinctions between the judgments of humans and nonhuman animals. His debate with Wodeham is one of the few, if not the only, late-medieval example of a direct exchange of arguments regarding a specific cognitive capacity of animals. For this reason, his text is particularly interesting to read.

## Introduction

Gregory of Rimini was a contemporary of Adam Wodeham (see Chap. 14). His influence on later medieval philosophy also stems mainly from his commentary on the *Sentences*. Yet, unlike Wodeham, he was not a Franciscan, but a member of the order of the Hermits of Saint Augustine. Nevertheless, he played an important role in the reception and discussion of Franciscans such as William of Ockham, Adam Wodeham, and Peter Auriol. Born in Rimini, Italy, around 1300, Gregory came in touch with the thought of Peter Auriol, in particular during his studies at the university of Paris.[1] He then taught theology at various places in Italy, where he seems to have become familiar with the ideas of Ockham and Wodeham. Around the beginning of the 1340s, he returned to Paris and lectured on Peter Lombard's *Sentences*. In 1345, he became Master of Theology and moved back to Italy in order to teach at Padua, for example. He died in Vienna in 1358, that is, roughly one year after he had been elected prior general of the Augustinians.

---

[1] On his life and works, see Zupko (2002) and Friedman and Schabel (2011).

A. Oelze, *Animal Minds in Medieval Latin Philosophy*, Studies in the History of
Philosophy of Mind 27, https://doi.org/10.1007/978-3-030-67012-2_15

From Gregory's commentary on the *Sentences* only the parts on the first two books have survived (it is not even clear whether he also wrote commentaries on books 3 and 4). Nevertheless, this provides enough material for awarding him an important place in later medieval thought, especially because he reunited the different strands of tradition from Oxford and Paris. His debate with Adam Wodeham (see Chap. 14) over animals' capacity of judging arises in the larger context of epistemology. One of the main questions Gregory aims to answer is what kind of knowledge of God humans can have. In this context, he tries to define different forms of knowledge (*notitia*) and discusses the differences between human and nonhuman knowledge. Most of his answer to the question of whether nonhuman animals have what he calls 'complex knowledge' (*notitia complexa*) is a critique of Wodeham's argument against the ascription of the capacity of judging to nonhuman animals. Contrary to Wodeham, Gregory sees no problem in ascribing this capacity to other animals, as long as one makes certain distinctions between the judgments of humans and nonhuman animals. His debate with Wodeham is one of the few, if not the only, late-medieval example of a direct exchange of arguments regarding a specific cognitive capacity of animals. For this reason, his text is particularly interesting to read.[2]

## Bibliographical Note

The English translation is based on the following critical edition of the Latin text: Gregory of Rimini. (1981). *Lectura super primum et secundum Sententiarum* (A. D. Trapp and V. Marcolino, Eds.) (vol. 1, pp. 304–306). Berlin/New York: Walter de Gruyter. The Latin text has not yet been translated into English.

## Translation

[Whether animals have complex knowledge[3]]
Yet, here it is very suitably asked whether non-rational animals, too, have some sort of complex knowledge of sensible things; because there is no doubt that they have simple [knowledge of sensible things].
And here I say that even though this cannot be fully known to us naturally, we can nevertheless infer with a certain degree of probability that they have such knowledge from the things we perceive. This can be proven, first, because, as we see, a brute at some time apprehends some sensible thing, such as a bread, and

---

[2] For secondary literature on this debate, see the references in the introduction to Chap. 14.

[3] Knowledge in terms of '*notitia*' is different from knowledge in terms of '*scientia*'. While '*scientia*' refers to knowledge of the causes of something, '*notitia*' can also include some sort of familiarity, for instance, when one knows something because one has seen it before.

moves towards it. At some other time, however, it apprehends the same [kind of] thing and does not move towards it. Thus, since this movement is caused by an animal appetite, and since such an appetite follows an apprehension, it requires a sensory judgment, apart from the simple apprehension. By this [sensory judgment] it is judged that this thing is useful or necessary or such and such.

Second, [it is proven] because sometimes an animal that desires something sweet or something else with regard to taste moves towards a particular thing, the colour of which it has apprehended. This, however, would not happen, as it seems, if it would not judge that this thing is sweet. And this is confirmed by the fact that if it later tastes and does not find that this is what it has been looking for, it walks away from that thing. This argument is put forward by Avicenna[4] in [book] 6 of his *Natural Philosophy*, part 4, chapter 1, in which he demonstrates that animals possess a common sense. Therefore, he says that "if they[5] would not be joined in the [faculty of] imagination of animals that lack intellect, they[6] would not desire to eat when they see it, that is, that this thing which has such a shape is sweet, when they have an inclination towards sweetness by a proper desire". And later on[7] he concludes that if such a faculty would not exist in animals "life would be difficult for them if smell would not reveal something about flavour and if sound would not reveal something about flavour etc".

Third, the same thing is proven by experience [some have] had of hounds.[8] When they come to a fork [in the path] while they are chasing wild game that flees, they sniff at one way. And if they do not perceive on it the smell of the one fleeing, they immediately proceed by the other [way], without sniffing at it. It seems that this cannot come from another source than [from the fact] that they judge that the game did not cross over [onto] this [path], at which they have sniffed. And from this they judge – as if they would reason – that it crossed over [onto] another [path].

Fourth, [the argument is proven] because learning cannot occur without complex knowledge. Certain animals, however, are capable of learning, as experience shows; therefore, etc.

In this regard, the authority is also Avicenna's [book] 6 on *Natural Philosophy*, part 1, chapter 5. There he talks about the estimative [power] and gives an example, saying that this is "the power which exists in the sheep, and which judges that this wolf must be fled or that this lamb must be cared for."[9] However, it is clear, that all these kinds of knowledge are complex.

---

[4] Avicenna Latinus, *Liber de anima* IV.1, ed. van Riet (1968), 2.

[5] I.e. the different sensibles such as taste and colour.

[6] I.e. the animals.

[7] See note 4.

[8] This famous example is known as 'Chrysippus' dog' (named after the Stoic logician Chrysippus). On its history, see Floridi (1997). For a contemporary analysis, see Rescorla (2009). See also text 23.

[9] Avicenna Latinus, *Liber de anima* I.5, ed. Van Riet (1972), 89; see Chap. 4.

The argument of a certain doctor[10] who says that, according to this [argument], such animals would possess practical intellect, and that such animals would need to be called 'rational beings,' does not hold. For these things do not follow when talking about such things in the sense in which we say that a human being is rational or possesses practical intellect. For human beings do not only have particular but also universal judgments, and not only judgments about sensible things but also about non-sensible things. And based on such [judgments] they reason and are called 'rational' in the proper sense of the term. Similarly, whenever the practical intellect deliberates, it draws not only on particulars but also on other universals. Also, it compares past to present and future things. And one could refer to various other differences because of which that conclusion does not hold. This is also confirmed because, according to the Commentator,[11] [book] 3 of *On the Soul*, commentary number 6, the cogitative power possesses such particular judgments. Still, for the same reason he says that from this it does not follow that it is a rational power. This will become clear in the demonstration of the third conclusion.[12] But if you still want to call these [animals] 'rational,' too, you can; because words are arbitrary. And so, one could also deny any simple knowledge to them and conclude that others are rational, if one wants to call all beings that have cognition 'rational'.

# Bibliography

## *Primary Sources*

Adam Wodeham. (1990). *Lectura secunda in librum primum Sententiarum* (R. Wood, Ed.). St. Bonaventure, NY: St. Bonaventure University.
Gregory of Rimini. (1981). *Lectura super primum et secundum Sententiarum* (A. D. Trapp and V. Marcolino, Eds.). 2 vols. Berlin/New York: Walter de Gruyter.

## *Secondary Sources*

Floridi, L. (1997). Scepticism and animal rationality: The fortune of Chrysippus' dog in the history of western thought. *Archiv für Geschichte der Philosophie, 79*(1), 27–57.
Friedman, R. L., & Schabel, C. (2011). Gregory of Rimini. In H. Lagerlund (Ed.), *Encyclopedia of medieval philosophy: Philosophy between 500 and 1500* (Vol. 1, pp. 439–444). Dordrecht: Springer.
Rescorla, M. (2009). Chrysippus' dog as a case study in non-linguistic cognition. In R. W. Lurz (Ed.), *The philosophy of animal minds* (pp. 52–71). Cambridge: Cambridge University Press.
Zupko, J. (2002). Gregory of Rimini. In J. J. E. Gracia & T. B. Noone (Eds.), *A companion to philosophy in the middle ages* (pp. 283–290). Malden: Blackwell.

---

[10] I.e. Adam Wodeham, *Lectura secunda in librum primum Sententiarum*, prol., q. 4, §8, ed. Wood (1990), 99; see Chap. 14.

[11] Averroes, *Commentarium magnum in Aristotelis De anima libros* III.6, ed. Crawford (1953), 415 f.

[12] See Gregory of Rimini, *Lectura super primum Sententiarum*, d. 3, q. 1, a. 1, eds. Trapp & Marcolino (1981), 309.

# Part II
# Emotion

# Chapter 16
# Friendship, Enmity, and Fear (Albert the Great, *Quaestiones super De animalibus*, Book 8, Questions 1–3)

**Abstract** In his question commentary on Aristotle's writings on animals, Albert the Great also raises some questions regarding the emotional life of animals. Although friendship and enmity, which are the topics of questions 1 and 2 of book 8, do not strictly speaking qualify as emotions, it is clear that they are based on certain feelings such as pleasure or fear. As Albert also emphasises, questions of the emotions are deeply intertwined with issues of cognition, insofar as an emotion such as pleasure usually seems to require a preceding cognitive operation, for instance, the perception of something pleasurable. However, the question is whether an emotional reaction to or qualification of an object (e.g. as pleasurable) surpasses the level of the sensory soul and thus goes beyond the mental abilities of nonhuman animals. This is one of the fundamental questions Albert tries to answer.

## Introduction

Albert the Great's '*De animalibus*' (see Chap. 8), is largely a literal commentary of Aristotle's most important writings on animals. However, he has also written a so-called 'question commentary'. In this commentary, he goes through the Aristotelian text by discussing various questions concerning the physiology and psychology of animals. In this context, he also raises some questions regarding the emotional life of animals or their 'passions' (*passiones*), as medieval philosophers called them. Although friendship and enmity, which are the topics of questions 1 and 2 of book 8, do not strictly speaking qualify as emotions, it is clear that they are based on certain feelings such as pleasure or fear. As Albert also emphasises, questions of the emotions are deeply intertwined with issues of cognition, insofar as an emotion such as pleasure usually seems to require a preceding cognitive operation, for instance, the perception of something pleasurable. However, the question is whether an emotional reaction to or qualification of an object (e.g. *as* pleasurable) surpasses the level of the sensory soul and thus goes beyond the mental abilities of nonhuman animals. This is one of the fundamental questions Albert tries to answer in the questions translated in the following.

A. Oelze, *Animal Minds in Medieval Latin Philosophy*, Studies in the History of Philosophy of Mind 27, https://doi.org/10.1007/978-3-030-67012-2_16

## Bibliographical Note

The English translation is based on the following critical edition of the Latin text: Albert the Great. (1955). *Quaestiones super De animalibus* (F. Filthaut, Ed.) (*Opera omnia* 12) (pp. 188–189). Münster: Aschendorff. For an alternative English translation see: Albert the Great. (2008). *Questions concerning Aristotle's On animals* (I. M. Resnick & K. F. Kitchell, Jr., Trans.) (pp. 268–271). Washington, D.C.: The Catholic University of America Press.


## Translation

Question 1: Whether friendship and enmity exist in brutes.

*However, the characters of animals differ*[1] etc. In this eighth book [of the *History of Animals*] the Philosopher[2] determines the question of friendship and enmity in animals. Hence, it is asked whether friendship and enmity exist in brutes.

(1) And it seems that [they do] not [exist among them]. Those passions that go beyond the sensory faculties and operations do not exist in animals unless they possess a faculty that is raised above sense. However, friendship and enmity go beyond the sensory operations. Therefore, they do not exist in brutes.

(2) Furthermore, in those [animals] whose operations are directed toward one thing, friendship and enmity do not exist because they occur with respect to many things. However, the operations of brutes are directed towards one thing because they are not endowed with reason which has the ability [of being directed] towards opposites. Therefore, etc.

The Philosopher claims the contrary.

It must be said that friendship and enmity are found in brutes. And the reason for this is that friendship consists in the perception of what is pleasant, and enmity in the perception of what is harmful. Yet, these [kinds of perception] are found in brutes. Therefore, etc. For birds perceive a grain as something pleasant to them, and a sheep or lamb perceives a wolf as something that is harmful to it and a human being or the shepherd as friendly.

(1) [Reply] to the arguments: To the first [argument] it must be said that there are two types of sensory faculty: internal and external; external such as sight, hearing, and the like; internal such as common sense, imaginative power, estimative power, and memory. Hence, it is possible that friendship and enmity are not

---

[1] Aristotle, *Historia animalium* IX.1, 608a11. This refers to the Greek text since the volume of the Latin translation (in the *Aristoteles Latinus*) has not yet been published.

[2] I.e. Aristotle.

perceived by the external senses but are still perceived by the estimative power, because the estimative power is properly perceptive of invisible[3] intentions that do not fall within the scope of sense or that do not move sense per se.[4]

(2) To the second argument it must be said that it is possible that the faculty of brutes does not relate to contraries, insofar as they are contraries, as [do] reason and will. Still, the faculty of brutes relates to different things: to one by choice, to another by flight.

Question 2: Whether friendship and enmity exist in all brutes.

Furthermore, it is asked whether they exist in all brutes.

(1) And it seems that [they do] not. Friendship and enmity do not exist in those [animals] in which there is no estimative power. Yet, many brutes lack an estimative power. For it is said in the first book of the *Metaphysics*[5] that the life of animals is guided by sense alone, and the life of humans by art and reason. Therefore, etc.

(2) Moreover, those [animals] in which friendship and enmity exist perceive objects from a distance. But there are many animals, such as immobile ones,[6] that lack sight, hearing, and smell. Therefore, etc.

On the contrary: Every animal is pleased by what is pleasant and saddened by what is harmful. But where there are pain, pleasure, and sadness, there are friendship and enmity. Therefore, etc.

It must be said that there is some sort of natural harmony; and this is found between non-living things, for instance, between fire and fire or a stone and a stone. The other [kind of] harmony is the one that is based on sense, or is perceived by sense, and friendship consists in this kind of harmony. Thus, even though a stone harmonises with a stone, the stone, however, does not perceive that harmony. But there is no animal that does not perceive what is pleasant to it and equally what is harmful, because immobile animals spread and spill over towards pleasant things. And if they are touched by unpleasant things they withdraw from them. And, therefore, by natural instinct they regard the former as friendly and the latter as hostile, etc.

Question 3: Whether a lamb would flee a wolf without perception of what is harmful in it.

Furthermore, it is asked whether a lamb would flee a wolf without perception of what is harmful in it.

---

[3] Contrary to the critical Latin edition, I read '*invisibilis*' instead of '*indivisibilis*' here, because to speak of intentions as 'invisible' is more common and makes more sense than calling them 'indivisible'.

[4] Proper sensibles (e.g. colours) move a sense (e.g. sight) *per se*; intentions move sense *per accidens*.

[5] Aristotle, *Metaphysica* I.1, 980b25–28.

[6] E.g. molluscs and sponges (in Aristotle's taxonomy).

And it seems that [the lamb would] not [do this], because as there is an intellective faculty in a human being there is a sensory faculty in a brute. Yet, nothing is grasped by the intellect of a human being that has not been in the sense before.[7] And so does a brute even much less grasp what has not been in the sense before, and consequently something harmful. That is why a lamb flees a wolf, because it has been in the sense before.

On the contrary: A lamb does not perceive anything in the wolf but the colour and common sensibles.[8] But many times it perceives something more frighteningly coloured and shaped, which it, nevertheless, does not flee. Thus, it perceives nothing harmful before it flees.

It must be said that the estimative power of a brute works in three different ways, namely, by way of apprehension, by way of experience, and by way of [comparing] likenesses[9]: By way of apprehension as an infant seeks and sucks a teat which it has not seen before. Similarly, a lamb flees a wolf which it has never seen before. For while the colour and the shape of the wolf move the external sense, and then the internal sense, the internal sense naturally grasps the intention of enmity. Therefore, the grasp of being harmful or harm precedes its flight. Sometimes it works by way of experience as a bird flies away when someone threatens to throw a stone or when someone pulls out or moves a stick, because it often happened that it has been caught or that troubles resulted from this kind of motion. A sign for this is that a young bird does not fear this [kind of motion] until it has experienced for itself something bad from this, or until it has been taught by its father or mother to fly away, etc. [And it works] by way of [comparing] likenesses as a bird flees masks or the image of a human being or a figure designed in the likeness of someone holding a bow.

Given these [examples], the replies to the arguments are clear.

# Bibliography

## *Primary Sources*

Albert the Great. (1955). *Quaestiones super De animalibus* (F. Filthaut, Ed.) (*Opera omnia* 12). Münster: Aschendorff.
Albert the Great. (2008). *Questions concerning Aristotle's On animals* (I. M. Resnick & K. F. Kitchell, Jr., Trans.). Washington, DC: The Catholic University of America Press.
Aristotle. (1957). *Metaphysica* (W. Jaeger, Ed.). Oxford: Clarendon Press.

---

[7] This statement was common among medieval philosophers. It is often attributed to Aristotle in some of whose writings the notion (but not the phrasing) is present indeed; see Cranefield (1970), 79n16.

[8] E.g. shape, size, and number.

[9] Albert certainly adopts this classification from Avicenna, *Liber de anima* IV.3, ed. Van Riet (1968), 37–40; see Chap. 5 in this volume.

Aristotle. (2002). *Historia animalium, Vol. 1, Books I-X: Text* (D. M. Balme & A. Gotthelf, Eds.). Cambridge: Cambridge University Press.

Avicenna Latinus. (1968). *Liber de anima seu sextus de naturalibus IV-V* (S. van Riet, Ed.). Louvain: Peeters/Leiden: Brill.

## *Secondary Sources*

Cranefield, P. F. (1970). On the origin of the phrase 'Nihil est in intellectu quod non prius fuerit in sensu'. *Journal of the History of Medicine and Allied Sciences, XXV*(1), 77–80.

# Chapter 17
# Appetites and Emotions (Thomas Aquinas, *Summa theologiae*, Part I, Question 81, Articles 2-3)

**Abstract** In Thomas Aquinas' theory of emotions, emotions (or *'passiones,'* as they are called in Latin) are embedded in a larger psychological framework. They are features (or acts) of so-called *appetitive* powers. Contrary to *apprehensive* powers, which make a being cognitively apprehend something, appetitive powers make a being strive for something. They are further divided into *sensory* and *intellective*. Sensory appetite, in turn, is divided into *concupiscible* and *irascible*. As Aquinas makes clear in the passage of the *Summa theologiae* translated in the following, an appetite is concupiscible if the object is simply good or bad or, differently speaking, if it is easily attained or rejected. An appetite is irascible if the object is *arduous*, that is, if it is not so easily attained or rejected. Consequently, Aquinas classifies emotions depending on the appetite to which they belong. Enjoyment, for instance, is brought about by the concupiscible appetite. Hope and despair are irascible emotions. Thus, the answers he gives to the question of whether nonhuman animals have emotions are based on this fundamental psychological distinction.

## Introduction

In Thomas Aquinas' theory of emotions, emotions (or *'passiones,'* as they are called in Latin) are embedded in a larger psychological framework.[1] They are features (or acts) of so-called *appetitive* powers. Contrary to *apprehensive* powers, which make a being cognitively apprehend something, appetitive powers make a being strive for something. They are further divided into *sensory* and *intellective*. Sensory appetite, in turn, is divided into *concupiscible* and *irascible*. As Aquinas makes clear in the passage of the *Summa theologiae* translated in the following, an appetite is concupiscible if the object is simply good or bad or, differently speaking, if it is easily attained or rejected. An appetite is irascible if the object is *arduous*, that is, if it is not so easily attained or rejected. Consequently, Aquinas classifies emotions depending

---

[1] See Knuuttila (2004), 239–255; King (2012); Perler (2018), 37–53.

© The Author(s), under exclusive license to Springer Nature
Switzerland AG 2021
A. Oelze, *Animal Minds in Medieval Latin Philosophy*, Studies in the History of
Philosophy of Mind 27, https://doi.org/10.1007/978-3-030-67012-2_17

on the appetite to which they belong. Enjoyment, for instance (see text 17), is brought about by the concupiscible appetite. Hope and despair (see text 18) are irascible emotions. Thus, the answers he gives to the question of whether nonhuman animals have emotions are based on this fundamental psychological distinction.

## Bibliographical Note

The English translation is based on the following edition of the Latin text: Thomas Aquinas. (1889). *Pars prima Summae theologiae, qq. 50–119 (Opera omnia 5)* (pp. 289–291). Rome. For an alternative English translation see, for instance, Thomas Aquinas. (1970). *Summa theologiae. Vol. 11: Man (1a. 75–83)* (T. Suttor, Trans.) (pp. 207–215). London: Blackfriars.

## Translation

Article 2: Whether the sensory appetite should be divided into irascible and concupiscible as separate powers

Regarding the second [article], we proceed as follows.

1. It seems that the sensory appetite should not be divided into irascible and concupiscible as separate powers. For a power of the soul is one and the same regarding contrariety, such as sight with regard to black and white, as is said in the second [book] of *On the Soul*.[2] Yet, pleasant and harmful are contraries. And so, since the concupiscible concerns what is pleasant, the irascible, however, what is harmful, it seems that the same power of the soul is irascible and concupiscible.
2. Moreover, sensory appetite is not concerned with things unless they are pleasant to sense. But what is pleasant to sense is the object of the concupiscible. Hence, the sensory appetite is in no way different from the concupiscible.
3. Moreover, hatred is in the irascible. For, in *On Matthew*, Hieronymus says that "in the irascible we hold the vice of hatred".[3] But hatred is [also] in the concupiscible because it is opposed to love. Thus, concupiscible and irascible are the same power.

Yet, contrary to this is that Gregory of Nyssa[4] and the Damascene[5] posit different powers – irascible and concupiscible – as parts of sensory appetite.

---

[2] Aristotle, *De anima* II.11, 422b23f.

[3] Hieronymus, *Commentariorum in Matheum libri IV*, II.13,33, eds. Hurst & Adriaen (1969), 109.

[4] This is a common misattribution; see Dobler (2000), 101. The correct reference is Nemesius of Emesa, *De natura hominis* 15, eds. Verbeke & Moncho (1975), 92.

[5] John of Damascus, *De fide orthodoxa*, c. 26 (= II.12), ed. Buytaert (1955), 119.

I reply that – generically – sensory appetite is one power which is called 'sensibility'. But it is divided into two powers which are kinds of sensory appetite, namely, irascible and concupiscible. In order to show this, it is necessary to consider that in natural, corruptible things there has to be not only an inclination to seek pleasant and flee harmful things, but also to resist harms and obstacles that produce impediments for pleasant things and cause harms. Fire, for instance, has a natural inclination not only to move away from a lower place that is not pleasant for it to a higher place that is pleasant, but also to resist harms and obstacles. And so, since sensory appetite is an inclination following a sensory apprehension as natural appetite is an inclination following a natural form,[6] it is necessary that there are two appetitive powers in the sensory part: one by which the soul is inclined to seek things pleasant to sense and to flee harmful things, and this [power] is called 'concupiscible'; and another by which an animal resists attacks that destroy pleasant things and cause harms, and this [power] is called 'irascible'. For this reason it is said that their object is something *arduous* because it is directed at what overcomes obstacles and stands out above them.

However, these two inclinations cannot be reduced to one origin because sometimes the soul brings about sad feelings against the inclination of the concupiscible so that it can fight against obstacles according to the inclination of the irascible. Therefore, the passions of the irascible also seem to be in opposition to the passions of the concupiscible because a rising desire diminishes anger and rising anger diminishes desire, as [can be seen] in many cases. From this it also becomes clear that the irascible is something like the protectress and defender of the concupiscible, as long as it rises up against those things that impede pleasant things, which the concupiscible desires, and [against those] that produce harmful things, which the concupiscible flees. And for this reason all passions of the irascible begin with passions of the concupiscible and terminate in them, as, for instance, anger arises from sadness and, if overcome, ends with pleasure. For the same reason the fights of animals are about concupiscible things, namely, feeding and mating, as is said in [book] VIII of *On Animals*.[7]

To the first argument it must be said that the concupiscible power concerns both pleasant and unpleasant things. But the irascible exists for resisting something unpleasant that is in opposition.

To the second argument it must be said that just as there is a certain estimative power among the apprehensive powers in the sensory part [of the soul], that is, a power which is capable of perceiving what does not alter the [external] senses, as said above,[8] there is also in the sensory appetite a certain power of striving for something that is not pleasant in terms of pleasure for the senses, but insofar as it is useful for the animal's defence. And this is the irascible power.

---

[6] This means that, for instance, a stone cannot *not* fall down to earth when thrown.

[7] Aristotle, *Historia animalium* VIII.1, 589a2–5.

[8] Thomas Aquinas, *Summa theologiae* I.78.4, Editio Leonina (1889), 256; see Chap. 12 in this volume.

To the third argument it must be said that hatred as such pertains to the concupiscible but it can pertain to the irascible in terms of an attack that is caused by hatred.

Article 3: Whether irascible and concupiscible obey reason

The third question proceeds as follows.

1. It seems that the irascible and concupiscible do not obey reason. For the irascible and concupiscible are parts of sensibility. But sensibility does not obey reason, hence it is symbolised by the snake, as Augustine says in [book] XII of *On the Trinity*.[9] Thus, the irascible and concupiscible do not obey reason.
2. Furthermore, what obeys something does not act against it. Yet, irascible and concupiscible act against reason, according to the apostle [Paul] in *Romans* 7[10]: *I see another law in my limbs acting against the law of my mind*. Thus, the irascible and concupiscible do not obey reason.
3. Furthermore, as the appetitive power is inferior to the rational part of the soul, so is the sensory power, too. But the sensory part of the soul does not obey reason, for we do not hear nor see whenever we want. And so, similarly, the powers of sensory appetite, that is, irascible and concupiscible, do not obey reason either.

But contrary to this is what the Damascene[11] says, [namely], that what obeys and what can be persuaded by reason is divided into desire and hatred.

I reply that the irascible and concupiscible obey the superior part [of the soul], in which there is intellect or reason and will, in two ways: in one way with respect to reason; but in another way with regard to will. Reason they somehow obey with regard to their own acts. This belongs to reason because in some other animals, sensory appetite is naturally moved by the estimative power. For instance, when the sheep, evaluating the wolf as hostile, fears it.[12] However, as said above,[13] in place of the estimative power there is the cogitative power in humans which is called 'particular reason' by some, insofar as it is capable of comparing individual intentions. Therefore, in humans the sensory appetite is naturally moved by it. However, particular reason itself is naturally moved and guided by universal reason. Therefore, in syllogisms singular conclusions are drawn from universal premises. And, therefore, it is clear that universal reason commands the sensory appetite, which is distinguished into concupiscible and irascible, and this appetite obeys it. And since inferring singular conclusions from universal principles is not the work of the simple intellect but of reason, the irascible and concupiscible are said to obey reason rather than the intellect. This can also be experienced by anybody in herself or himself. For by applying some universal considerations hatred or fear or anything else like this are mitigated or roused.

---

[9] Augustine, *De trinitate* XII.12, ed. Mountain (1968), 371.

[10] *Romans* 7:23.

[11] John of Damascus, *De fide orthodoxa*, c. 26 (= II.12), ed. Buytaert (1955), 119.

[12] For a discussion of this example see King (2012), 213–215, and Perler (2012).

[13] See note 8.

The sensory appetite is also subject to the will, [namely], with regard to the execution which is done by the moving power. For in other animals, movement immediately follows a concupiscible or irascible appetite. For instance, the sheep that fears the wolf immediately flees because there is in them no superior appetite that is in opposition [to these emotions].[14] A human being, however, is not immediately moved by an irascible or concupiscible appetite but waits for the command of the will which is the superior appetite. For in all cases in which something depends on the moving powers, whatever moves does not move unless by the power of the first mover. Therefore, the inferior appetite does not suffice for moving unless the superior appetite consents. And this is what the Philosopher[15] says in [book] III of *On the Soul*, that *the superior appetite moves the inferior appetite as a superior sphere [moves] an inferior [sphere].*[16] Thus, in this way the irascible and concupiscible are put under reason.

To the first argument it must be said that sensibility is symbolised by the *snake* with respect to what is its proper feature on the part of the sensitive part [of the soul]. Sensory appetite, however, is called 'irascible' and 'concupiscible' rather on the part of the act to which they are brought by reason, as has been said.

To the second argument it must be said that, as the Philosopher says in the first [book] of the *Politics,*[17] *despotic and politic*[18] *rule can be observed in animals: for the soul somehow rules the body by despotic rule; the intellect, however, [rules] the appetite politically and monarchically.* For the rule called 'despotic' is that by which somebody rules slaves who do not have the power to resist the command of the commander because they do not own anything. However, the rule called 'politic' and 'monarchic' is that by which somebody rules free people who, even though they are subdued to the command of the ruler, still possess some sort of proper [power] by which they can resist the command of the ruler. Thus, in this way the soul is said to rule the body by despotic rule, because the limbs of the body can in no way resist the commands of the soul but hands and feet immediately move upon the appetite of the soul, and any kind of limb that naturally moves is moved willingly. Intellect or reason, however, are said to rule the irascible and concupiscible by politic rule because the sensory appetite has something on its own, hence it can resist the command of reason. For sensory appetite is naturally moved not only by the estimative power in other animals, and by the cogitative [power] in a human being, which is guided by universal reason, but also by the imaginative [power] and sense. Therefore, we experience the irascible and concupiscible to be in opposition to reason when we perceive or imagine something pleasurable which is prohibited by reason or

---

[14] I.e. the sheep cannot *not* be afraid of the wolf.

[15] Aristotle, *De anima* III.11, 434a12–15.

[16] This analogy is based on Aristotle's cosmological theory, according to which the universe consists of a hierarchy of spheres; see, for instance, Pellegrin (2009). The movement of lower (or interior) spheres results from the movement of higher (or exterior) spheres.

[17] Aristotle, *Politica* I.5, 1254b2–6.

[18] I.e. the kind of rule by which equal people rule over equal people.

something sad which reason commands. And so, by the fact that the irascible and concupiscible are somehow in opposition to reason it is not excluded that they obey it.

To the third argument it must be said that for their acts the external senses require external sensibles by which they are altered, whose presence is not in the power of reason. But the internal powers – appetitive as well as apprehensive ones – do not require external things and, therefore, they are subject to the command of reason, which can not only rouse or mitigate the affections of the appetitive power, but also form the phantasms of the imaginative power.

# Bibliography

## *Primary Sources*

Aristotle. (1957). *Politica* (W. D. Ross, Ed.). Oxford: Clarendon Press.
Aristotle. (1961). *De anima* (W. D. Ross, Ed.). Oxford: Clarendon Press.
Aristotle. (2002). *Historia animalium, Vol. 1, Books I-X: Text* (D. M. Balme & A. Gotthelf, Eds.). Cambridge: Cambridge University Press.
Augustine. (1968). *De trinitate libri XV (libri I–XII)* (W. J. Mountain, Ed.) (*Opera* 16/1) (Corpus Christianorum Series Latina 50). Turnhout: Brepols.
Hieronymus. (1969). *Commentariorum in Matheum libri IV* (D. Hurst and M. Adriaen, Eds.) (*Opera* 1/7) (Corpus Christianorum Series Latina 77). Turnhout: Brepols.
John of Damascus. (1955). *De fide orthodoxa: Versions of Burgundius and Cerbanus* (E. M. Buytaert, Ed.). St. Bonaventure, NY: The Franciscan Institute.
Nemesius of Emesa. (1975). *De natura hominis: Traduction de Burgundio de Pise* (G. Verbeke and J. R. Moncho, Eds.). Leiden: Brill.
Thomas Aquinas. (1889). *Pars prima Summae theologiae, qq. 50–119* (*Opera omnia* 5). Rome.
Thomas Aquinas. (2002). *The treatise on human nature:* Summa theologiae *1a 75–89* (R. Pasnau, Trans.). Indianapolis/Cambridge: Hackett Publishing.

## *Secondary Sources*

Dobler, E. (2000). *Indirekte Nemesiuszitate bei Thomas von Aquin: Johannes von Damaskus als Vermittler von Nemesiustexten.* Freiburg: Universitätsverlag.
King, P. (2012). Emotions. In B. Davies & E. Stump (Eds.), *The Oxford handbook to Aquinas* (pp. 209–226). Oxford: Oxford University Press.
Knuuttila, S. (2004). *Emotions in ancient and medieval philosophy.* Oxford: Clarendon Press.
Pellegrin, P. (2009). The argument for the sphericity of the universe in Aristotle's *De caelo*: Astronomy and physics. In A. C. Bowen & C. Wildberg (Eds.), *New Perspectives on Aristotle's De caelo* (pp. 163–185). Brill: Leiden/Boston.
Perler, D. (2012). Why is the sheep afraid of the wolf? Medieval debates on animal passions. In M. Pickavé & L. Shapiro (Eds.), *Emotion and cognitive life in medieval and early modern philosophy* (pp. 32–52). Oxford: Oxford University Press.
Perler, D. (2018). Feelings transformed: Philosophical theories of the emotions, 1270–1670 (T. Crawford, Trans.). Oxford/New York: Oxford University Press.

# Chapter 18
# Enjoyment (Thomas Aquinas, *Summa theologiae*, Part I-II, Question 11, Article 2)

**Abstract** In his *Summa theologiae*, Thomas Aquinas also raises fundamental psychological questions that go beyond the field of theology. One of these questions concerns the character of enjoyment (*fruitio*) and its possible existence in nonhuman animals. From a folk psychological point of view, it seems obvious that not only humans but also other animals are capable of enjoying things such as food. Yet, Aquinas wonders whether nonhuman animals are endowed with the kind of cognitive prerequisites that are necessary for enjoying something. This question becomes more plausible with regard to his distinction of three kinds of pleasure: *delectatio* and *gaudium* are emotions that arise when the concupiscible appetite rests in a good apprehended by the external senses, and respectively by the internal senses. *Fruitio* is the kind of pleasure that is produced when the will rests in a good apprehended by the intellect. Since nonhuman animals lack the intellect, the question is whether they can enjoy something in the full sense of the term. The distinction between perfect and imperfect enjoyment which Aquinas introduces in this context might seem typically scholastic but provides an interesting alternative to a plain denial of an emotion such as enjoyment to other animals.

## Introduction

In his *Summa theologiae*, Thomas Aquinas discusses a wide range of topics, including the nature of emotions (see also Chaps. 17 and 19 in this volume). His main motivation for doing this is theological. However, he proceeds with philosophical diligence and raises fundamental psychological questions that go beyond the field of theology. One of these questions concerns the character of enjoyment (*fruitio*) and its possible existence in nonhuman animals. From a folk psychological point of view, it seems obvious that not only humans but also other animals are capable of enjoying things such as food.[1] Yet, Aquinas wonders whether nonhuman animals

---

[1] This question has also been addressed in recent biology; see North (2015).

© The Author(s), under exclusive license to Springer Nature
Switzerland AG 2021
A. Oelze, *Animal Minds in Medieval Latin Philosophy*, Studies in the History of
Philosophy of Mind 27, https://doi.org/10.1007/978-3-030-67012-2_18

are endowed with the kind of cognitive prerequisites that are necessary for enjoying something. This question becomes more plausible with regard to his distinction of three kinds of pleasure[2]: *delectatio* and *gaudium* are emotions that arise when the concupiscible appetite[3] rests in a good apprehended by the external senses, and respectively by the internal senses. *Fruitio* is the kind of pleasure that is produced when the will rests in a good apprehended by the intellect. Since nonhuman animals lack the intellect, the question is whether they can enjoy something in the full sense of the term. The distinction between perfect and imperfect enjoyment which Aquinas introduces in this context might seem typically scholastic but provides an interesting alternative to a plain denial of an emotion such as enjoyment to other animals.

## Bibliographical Note

The English translation is based on the following edition of the Latin text: Thomas Aquinas. (1891). *Prima secundae Summae theologiae, qq. 1–70 (Opera omnia* 6) (p. 91). Rome. For an alternative English translation, see, for instance, Thomas Aquinas. (1970). *Summa theologiae, Vol. 17: Psychology of human acts (1a2ae. 6–17)* (T. Gilby, Trans.) (pp. 101–103). London: Blackfriars.

## Translation

Article 2: Whether enjoying something can be found only in rational creatures or also in brute animals.

Concerning the second [article], we proceed as follows.

1. It seems that enjoying something belongs exclusively to humans. For, in book I of *On Christian Doctrine*,[4] Augustine says that *we are humans who enjoy and take advantage of something.* Thus, other animals cannot enjoy something.
2. Furthermore, enjoying is about an ultimate goal.[5] Yet, brute animals cannot attain an ultimate goal. Therefore, enjoying does not belong to them.
3. Furthermore, as the sensory ranks below the intellective appetite, the natural[6] appetite ranks below the sensory. So, if enjoying pertains to the sensory appe-

---

[2] On this distinction, see De Haan (2015).

[3] On the concupiscible appetite, see Chap. 17.

[4] Augustine, *De doctrina christiana* I.22.20, ed. Martin (1962), 16.

[5] For Aristotelians an ultimate goal is something like happiness.

[6] I.e. the power of striving for something possessed by beings lacking cognition.

tite it seems that it could pertain to the natural appetite for the same reason. This is clearly false because being pleased does not belong to it. Hence, enjoying does not belong to the sensory appetite. And so, it cannot be found in brute animals.

However, the refutation is what Augustine says in the book *Eighty-three Questions*[7]: *It is not absurd to think that beasts, too, enjoy some food or some bodily pleasure.*

I reply by saying that, as it follows from what has been said before,[8] enjoying is not an act of a power that arrives at a goal like an executing power, but [an act] of a power which commands the execution; for it has been said that this is the appetitive power. However, in things lacking cognition one finds a certain power attaining a goal by way of execution as, for instance, what is heavy tends downwards and what is light upwards. Yet, the power to which the goal pertains by way of commanding cannot be found in them. However, [it can be found] in some superior nature which moves the whole nature by [its] command as the appetite moves the other powers for its acts in those beings having cognition. Therefore, it is obvious that in those lacking cognition the enjoyment of a goal cannot be found, even though they arrive at a goal; but [it can be found] only in those that have cognition.

However, the cognition of a goal is of two kinds: perfect and imperfect. Perfect [cognition] is the one by which not only the goal and the good, but also the universal sense of the goal and the good, are cognised; and such cognition belongs to a rational nature alone. Imperfect cognition, however, is the one by which the goal and the good is partially cognised, and such cognition is present in brute animals. Moreover, their appetitive powers are not free in giving commands, but they move towards the things that have been apprehended according to natural instinct. Therefore, enjoyment in the perfect sense is found in a rational creature; in an imperfect sense, however, [it is] in brute animals; but [it is] in other creatures in no sense at all.

Thus, to the first argument it must be said that Augustine speaks of perfect enjoyment.

To the second argument it must be said that enjoyment is not necessarily about an ultimate goal per se but about what is had by anyone when [achieving] an ultimate goal.

To the third argument it must be said that sensory appetite follows some cognition, yet not the natural appetite, particularly insofar as it is in those which lack cognition.

To the fourth argument it must be said that there Augustine speaks of imperfect enjoyment. This is clear from the way of speaking, because he says that it is much less absurd to think that beasts enjoy, too, than it would be to say that they take advantage of something.

---

[7] Augustine, *De diversis quaestionibus octoginta tribus*, q. 30, ed. Mutzenbecher (1975), 39.

[8] In article 1 of the same question.

# Bibliography

## *Primary Sources*

Augustine. (1962). *De doctrina christiana* (J. Martin, Ed.) (*Opera* 4/1) (= CCSL 32). Turnhout: Brepols.

Augustine. (1975). *De diversis quaestionibus octoginta tribus* (A. Mutzenbecher, Ed.) (*Opera* 13/2) (= CCSL 44A). Turnhout: Brepols.

Thomas Aquinas. (1891). *Prima secundae Summae theologiae, qq. 1–70* (*Opera omnia* 6). Rome.

Thomas Aquinas. (1970). *Summa theologiae, Vol. 17: Psychology of human acts (1a2ae. 6–17)* (T. Gilby, Trans.). London: Blackfriars.

## *Secondary Sources*

De Haan, D. (2015). Delectatio, gaudium, fruitio: Three kinds of pleasure for three kinds of knowledge in Thomas Aquinas. *Quaestio, 15*, 543–552.

North, G. (Ed.) (2015). *The biology of fun and the fun of biology. Current biology: 25th anniversary special issue, 25*(1).

# Chapter 19
# Hope and Despair (Thomas Aquinas, *Summa theologiae*, Part I-II, Question 40, Article 3)

**Abstract** In *Summa theologiae* I-II.40.3, Thomas Aquinas discusses whether non-human animals possess the emotion of hope (*spes*) and despair (*desperatio*). According to his division of emotions, humans have hope when they try to attain a good that is absent but attainable. Despair, by contrast, is felt when one longs for something that is absent and unattainable. The question now is whether nonhuman animals also have such feelings. Aquinas introduces ordinary observations of animal behaviour that support the ascription of an emotion such as hope to nonhuman animals. A dog, for instance, seems to hope that it can catch a hare. Otherwise, it would not even try to catch it. Still, the question is whether hoping for something requires a notion of future states or events (namely, those states and events we hope for), and if so, whether animals are endowed with this kind of cognitive prerequisite. Contrary to his answer to the question of enjoyment in nonhuman animals, Aquinas does not introduce a terminological distinction between perfect and imperfect types of such emotions. Rather, he distinguishes between the ways in which they are sensed by humans and nonhuman animals. This finally allows him to justify the ascription of hope and despair to nonhuman animals without neglecting the fact that they have a different nature in such animals than they have in rational beings.

## Introduction

In *Summa theologiae* I-II.11.2, Thomas Aquinas discusses whether nonhuman animals possess the emotion of enjoyment (see Chap. 18). In another question, he directs his attention to hope (*spes*) and despair (*desperatio*).[1] According to Aquinas' division of emotions, humans have hope when they try to attain a good that is absent but attainable. Despair, by contrast, is felt when one longs for something that is absent and unattainable. The question now is whether nonhuman animals also have such feelings. Aquinas introduces ordinary observations of animal behaviour that

---

[1] For Aquinas' division of emotions, see King (1998) and (2012).

A. Oelze, *Animal Minds in Medieval Latin Philosophy*, Studies in the History of Philosophy of Mind 27, https://doi.org/10.1007/978-3-030-67012-2_19

support the ascription of an emotion such as hope to nonhuman animals. A dog, for instance, seems to hope that it can catch a hare. Otherwise, it would not even try to catch it. Still, the question is whether hoping for something requires a notion of future states or events (namely, those states and events we hope for), and if so, whether animals are endowed with this kind of cognitive prerequisite. Contrary to his answer to the question of enjoyment in nonhuman animals, Aquinas does not introduce a terminological distinction between perfect and imperfect types of such emotions. Rather, he distinguishes between the ways in which they are sensed by humans and nonhuman animals. This finally allows him to justify the ascription of hope and despair to nonhuman animals without neglecting the fact that they have a different nature in such animals than they have in rational beings.[2]

## Bibliographical Note

The English translation is based on the following edition of the Latin text: Thomas Aquinas. (1891). *Prima secundae Summae theologiae, qq. 1–70* (*Opera omnia* 6) (p. 267). Rome. For an alternative English translation see, for example, Thomas Aquinas. (1965). *Summa theologiae, Vol. 21: Fear and anger (1a2ae. 40–48)* (J. P. Reid, Trans.) (pp. 9–11). London: Blackfriars.

## Translation

Article 3: Whether hope exists in brute animals

Regarding the third [article], we proceed as follows

1. It seems that hope does not exist in brute animals. For hope is about a future good, as the Damascene[3] says. Yet, to cognise something lying in the future does not pertain to brute animals. They only possess sensory cognition that does not concern future things. So, hope does not exist in brute animals.
2. Furthermore, the object of hope is a good that can possibly be attained. Yet, possible and impossible is some sort of distinction between true and false that exists only in the mind, as the Philosopher says in book VI of the *Metaphysics*.[4] So, hope does not exist in brute animals in which there is no mind.

---

[2] For an analysis of this passage, see Hünemörder (1988), 203f.; Roberts (1992), 294; Loughlin (2001), 52–54; Miner (2009), 218f.; Perler (2012), 81, and (2018), 41; Köhler (2014), 214; Davids (2017), 210f.; Oelze (2018), 183–188.

[3] John of Damascus, *De fide orthodoxa*, c. 43, ed. Buytaert (1955), 158.

[4] This distinction is not found in book VI but V; see Aristotle, *Metaphysica* V.12, 1019b22–34.

3. Moreover, in *On the Literal Meaning of Genesis*, Augustine says that *animals are moved by things seen*.[5] But hope is not about what is seen. *For why does someone hope for what he sees?*, as it is asked in *Romans*, chap. 8.[6] So hope does not exist in brute animals.

Yet, on the other hand, hope is a passion of the irascible[7] [appetite]. But the irascible [appetite] exists in brute animals, hence hope does, as well.

I reply by saying that the internal passions of animals can be inferred from the external movements. From these it is clear that hope exists in brute animals. For when a dog sees a hare, or a hawk a bird, that is too far away, it does not move towards it as if did not hope that it could catch it. Yet, if it is nearby it moves [towards it] as if [it were] in the hope of catching it. For, as has been said above,[8] the sensory appetite of brute animals, and also the natural appetite of things lacking sensory perception, follows the grasp of some intellect as [does] the appetite of an intellective nature which is called 'will'. Yet, the difference here is that the will is moved by a grasp of the intellect that is conjoined [to it]. But the movement of the natural appetite follows a grasp of the separated intellect[9] that has created nature, and similarly, the sensory appetite of brute animals that also act by a certain natural instinct. Therefore, a similar process occurs in the works of brute animals and of other natural things as in the works of art. And in this sense, hope and despair exist in brute animals.

To the first [argument] it must be said that even though brute animals do not cognise future things, an animal is nevertheless moved by natural instinct towards something lying in the future as if it would foresee the future. For this kind of instinct has been given to them by the divine intellect which foresees future things.

To the second [argument] it must be said that the object of hope is not something possible insofar as it is some sort of distinction of what is true. For this is based on the application of a predicate to a subject. Yet, the object of hope is something possible that is called 'possible' with regard to some potency. For this is how the possible is distinguished in book V of the *Metaphysics*,[10] namely, in the two kinds of possible things mentioned before.

To the third [argument] it must be said that even though what lies in the future does not fall within the scope of sight, the appetite is still moved towards something futural or something that must be pursued, or is [moved] away from something that must be avoided by what an animal sees in the present.

---

[5] Augustine, *De Genesi ad litteram* IX.14.25, ed. Migne (1887), 402.

[6] *Romans* 8:24.

[7] On this appetite see Chap. 17.

[8] E.g. *ST* I-II.1.2.

[9] I.e. God.

[10] See, for instance, Aristotle, *Metaphysica* V.12, 1019a15–33.

# Bibliography

## Primary Sources

Aristotle. (1957). *Metaphysica* (W. Jaeger, Ed.). Oxford: Clarendon Press.

Augustine. (1887). *De Genesi ad litteram libri XII* (J.-P. Migne, Ed.) (Patrologia Latina 34, 245–486). Paris.

John of Damascus. (1955). *De fide orthodoxa: Versions of Burgundius and Cerbanus* (E. M. Buytaert, Ed.). St. Bonaventure: The Franciscan Institute.

Thomas Aquinas. (1891). *Prima secundae Summae theologiae, qq. 1–70* (*Opera omnia* 6). Rome.

Thomas Aquinas. (1965). *Summa theologiae, Vol. 21: Fear and anger (1a2ae. 40–48)* (J. P. Reid, Trans.). London: Blackfriars.

## Secondary Sources

Davids, T. (2017). *Anthropologische Differenz und animalische Konvenienz: Tierphilosophie bei Thomas von Aquin.* Leiden/Boston: Brill.

Hünemörder, C. (1988). Thomas von Aquin und die Tiere. In A. Zimmermann & C. Kopp (Eds.), *Thomas von Aquin: Werk und Wirkung im Licht neuerer Forschungen* (pp. 379–392). Berlin/New York: Walter de Gruyter.

King, P. (1998). Aquinas on the passions. In S. MacDonald & E. Stump (Eds.), *Aquinas's moral theory: Essays in Honor of Norman Kretzmann* (pp. 101–132). Ithaca/London: Cornell University Press.

King, P. (2012). Emotions. In B. Davies & E. Stump (Eds.), *The Oxford handbook to Aquinas* (pp. 209–226). Oxford: Oxford University Press.

Köhler, T. W. (2014). *Homo animal nobilissimum: Konturen des spezifisch Menschlichen in der naturphilosophischen Aristoteleskommentierung des dreizehnten Jahrhunderts, Teilband 2.1 und 2.2.* 2 vols. Leiden/Boston: Brill.

Loughlin, S. (2001). Similarities and differences between human and animal emotion in Aquinas's thought. *The Thomist, 65,* 45–65.

Miner, R. (2009). *Thomas Aquinas on the passions: A study of Summa theologiae 1a2ae 22–48.* Cambridge: Cambridge University Press.

Oelze, A. (2018). *Animal rationality: Later medieval theories 1250–1350.* Leiden/Boston: Brill.

Perler, D. (2012). Die kognitive Struktur von Hoffnung: Zwei mittelalterliche Erklärungsmodelle. *Deutsche Zeitschrift für Philosophie, 60*(1), 73–89.

Perler, D. (2018). *Feelings transformed: Philosophical theories of the emotions, 1270–1670* (T. Crawford, Trans.). Oxford/New York: Oxford University Press.

Roberts, R. C. (1992). Thomas Aquinas on the morality of emotions. *History of Philosophy Quarterly, 9*(3), 287–305.

# Chapter 20
# Pleasure (Peter of Abano, *Expositio problematum Aristotelis*, Chapter 38, Problem 7)

**Abstract** In his commentary on the *Problemata* (which were usually misattributed to Aristotle), Peter of Abano addresses the question of why the term 'incontinence' (*incontinentia*) is employed for pleasures (*delectationes*) deriving from touch and taste, but not from smelling, sight, and hearing. One suggestion is that, since touch and taste are shared by humans and almost all nonhuman animals, they are inferior to other senses. Hence, the pleasures connected to them are more blameworthy. Although this argument seems to throw a typically Christian light on certain emotions, Peter's text nicely shows that most ideas regarding the blameworthiness and moral inferiority of certain feelings are already found in Aristotle. Furthermore, Peter elucidates the somatic character of emotions that is also emphasised in modern theories, and he sets out to scrutinise the connection between lower- and higher-level cognition and emotion in humans and nonhuman animals.

## Introduction

The thirteenth-century philosopher and physician Peter of Abano (also called Pietro d'Abano or Petrus de Abano) has received increasing scholarly attention in recent years. Still, not much is known about his life.[1] The main reason for the lack of biographical information is that, unlike most of his contemporaries, he does not seem to have produced the usual scholarly texts (e.g. a *Sentences* commentary) that could help to shed light on certain stages of his career. All we know is that he was born in Abano (near Padua) around 1250, presumably taught at the University of Paris, and later returned to Padua where he taught philosophy and medicine until his death around 1315.

Although Peter is mainly known for his *Conciliator*, an encyclopaedic compilation of various authorities on medical topics, his influence on later thinkers also derives from a commentary on the so-called *Problemata*. This work was

---

[1] For a brief overview, see Klemm and Leemans (2005); Lagerlund (2011).

© The Author(s), under exclusive license to Springer Nature
Switzerland AG 2021
A. Oelze, *Animal Minds in Medieval Latin Philosophy*, Studies in the History of Philosophy of Mind 27, https://doi.org/10.1007/978-3-030-67012-2_20

misattributed to Aristotle for a very long time. Even though it was not amongst the Aristotelian writings that had a place in later medieval university curricula, Peter's commentary received a great deal of attention as it was the first comprehensive commentary in Latin (published in 1310).[2] The passage translated in the following is a literal commentary on chapter 7 of book 28 of the *Problemata*. This chapter resembles large portions of chapter 13 of book 3 of Aristotle's *Nicomachean Ethics*. In both texts, the question is why the term 'incontinence' (*incontinentia*) is employed for pleasures (*delectationes*) deriving from touch and taste, but not from smelling, sight, and hearing.[3] One suggestion is that, since touch and taste are shared by humans and almost all nonhuman animals, they are inferior to other senses. Hence, the pleasures connected to them are more blameworthy. Although this argument seems to throw a typically Christian light on certain emotions, Peter's text nicely shows that most ideas regarding the blameworthiness and moral inferiority of certain feelings are already found in Aristotle. Furthermore, Peter elucidates the somatic character of emotions that is also emphasised in modern theories.[4] This aspect is closely linked to their function: as fear makes an animal flee, and hence ensures its survival, the feeling of pleasure increases the interest in feeding and propagating. Since the latter are mainly connected with the sense of touch and taste, Peter claims that it is only through these senses that nonhuman animals can feel pleasure proper. However, he also presents some examples of animals which seem to be pleased by smelling, hearing, and seeing per se. And so, he sets out to scrutinise the connection between lower- and higher-level cognition and emotion in humans and nonhuman animals.

## Bibliographical Note

The Latin text is a transcription of the following edition: Peter of Abano. (1475). *Expositio problematum Aristotelis cum textu* (foll. 258ra-258va). Mantua. It has not yet been translated into English.

## Text

Septimum problema

   *Propter quid qui secundum delectationes tactus atque gustus quo itaque super-habundaverunt incontinentes dicuntur. Qui enim circa venerea luxuriosi, qui autem*

---

[2] For a short introduction, see Siraisi (1970). On the medieval reception of Aristotle's *Problemata*, see De Leemans and Goyens (2006). On Peter's role in particular, see De Leemans and Hoenen (2016).

[3] On the passage and its context, see Klemm (2006).

[4] An overview of such theories is provided by Barrett et al. (2016).

*circa delectationes cibi, eorum autem que sunt secundum cibum, a quibusdam qui-*
*dem in lingua est delectabile, a quibusdam vero in gutture, propter quid et*
*Phyloxenus gruis guttur orabat habere, alii autem secundum visum et auditum non*
*amplius. Aut quia delectationes que fiunt ab hiis communes sunt nobis et aliis ani-*
*malibus, ergo sicut existentibus communibus inhonorabilissimi sunt et maxime*
*atque sole obprobiosi quare eum qui ab hiis vincitur vituperamus et incontinentem*
*et vituperatum dicimus, propter id quod a pessimis delectationibus vincitur.*
*Existentibus autem sensibus quinque, alia autem animalia exuta predictis delectan-*
*tur, secundum alias autem aut omnino non delectantur, aut secundum accidens hec*
*patiuntur. Videmus enim videns aut odorans gaudet quia fruitur, et quando replebi-*
*tur, neque talia delectabilia ipsi, sic neque nobis cibi odor quando non habemus*
*appetitum commedendi, quando autem indigentes sumus dele<c>tabilis. Qui vero*
*est rosa semper delectabilis.*

Repetit secundum problema ut amplius declaretur d<icens> quare quando super-
habundaverint et excesserint in voluptate que est secundum tactum magis quantum
ad luxuriam que est in choytu et secundum gustum quo ad illam que gule. Triplicem
enim distinguit Boetius de scolastica disciplina. Hiis enim adiungit eam que in
ornatu vestium dicuntur incontinentes et intemperati.

Et exponit, nam qui sunt circa venerea dicuntur luxuriosi, qui vero circa voluptates ciborum et potuum gulosi seu lecatores. Et iterum eorum quibus est delectatio
circa cibum quidam habent eam in lingue superiori pellicula, propter eius multam
sensibilitatem alii vero solum in ea., sed amplius $2°$ totum guttur.

Et ideo lecator dictus Phylo<xe>nus Eri<x>ius. Pulti vorax existens deprecaba-
tur venerem, que est ciborum dea et potuum, ut guttur eius efficeretur longius quam
illud gruis. $3°$ etiam Ethi<corum>. Secundum quidem alios sensus, puta visum,
auditum et odoratum non contingit per amplius concupiscentiam fieri. Unde ibidem
qui gaudent colore et figuris non dicuntur temperati aut intemperati et similiter in
hiis que circa auditum nam superhabundanter gaudentes melodiis nullus intempera-
tus dicitur, neque similiter circa ea. que odoris nisi forte per accidens. Non enim
congaudentes odoribus rosam aut talium dicuntur intemperanti, sed magis illi qui
gaudent odoribus unguentorum et pulmentorum fit eis concupiscibilium memoria.
Unde exurientes gaudent ciborum odoribus non autem saturati, similiter etiam alia
animalium non delectantur circa hos tres sensus nisi per accidens. Non enim canes
gaudent odoribus leporum, sed cibatione, nam odor causat in eis sensum cibativum,
neque etiam leo voce bovis, sed commextione, sed neque videns cervum visione
gaudet, sed cibi fruitione futuri. Vidi tamen aviculas cantantes, maxime phylome-
nas, gaudere cantu humano et ad illum accedere ut principaliter ipso mote. Dicitur
et pavonem delectari in visione pulcritudinis pennarum suarum et tristari in ea. que
pedum. Fertur etiam quod unicornis odore virginis delectatur puelle. Unde sermo
Aristo<telis> verificabitur ut ad multum. Notandum quod per guttur non intelligitur
epiglotis que est organus proprius vocativa ut particula $xi^a$, sed magis cum os aperi-
tur et lingua deorsum plicatur quod apparet ante foramina epiglotis et isofagi cum
parte etiam ipsius aliquali ut indicat Phylosenus.

Deinde 'Aut quia' solvit et prius assignat magis causam quesiti d<icens> primo
causam esse quia voluptates que consistunt in hiis duobus sensibus, scilicet tactu et

gustu, communes sunt nobis et aliis animalibus etiam vilioribus. Propter quorum communitatem inhonorabilissimi sunt, ipsi et maxime vel soli obprobiosi. Et ideo qui detinetur et vincitur ab eis incontinentem et vituperatum nominamus eo quod a pessimis et brutalibus vincatur et subpedicetur voluptatibus que animam fedant et corpus coinquinant, ex quibus contingit ipsus omnia exercere prava. Nosce quod licet in gustu sit voluptas immensa abhominabilis amplius tamen in tactu. Unde Ethi<corum> tertio communissimus autem tactus sensivum secundum quem intemperantia quod merito videbitur ex probabilis quia non secundum quod homines existunt ver<o> secundum quod animalia talibus utique hominibus est gaudere et maxime diligere bestiale. Notandum quod tactum contingit potissime delectari consequenter circa gustum deinde odoratum, postea auditum, et tandem circa visum minime, quia tactus ceteris materialior hic atque spiritualior. Medii autem mediocriter se habent 4° de accedenti.

Deinde – 'Existentibus' – comparat 2° delectationes sensuum ad invicem d<icens> primo, quod cum sensus sint 5, puta tactus, gustus, odoratus, auditus et visus, alia quidem animalia exuta et remota a delectationibus visus et auditus vel separata a nobis. Carent enim ratione quam habemus soli. Et ideo ipsa delectantur solum secundum predictos sensus, tactum, scilicet et gustum, secundum vero aliquos tres aut totaliter non delectantur vel si delectantur per accidens evenit id pati sive delectari. Quod ostenditur, nam conspicimus quod illud quod videt: atque odorat congaudet eo quod fruitur in cibo postea sed cum fretum fuerit et repletum visus et odor predictorum non sunt ei delectabilia ut antea, priusquam esset repletum, quod etiam nos patimur. Non enim cibus nobis delectabilis est odore cum fuerimus saciati taliter, ut cesset appetitus commedendi, cum tamen esset antea odor delectabilis cum indigebamus ipso.

Deinde 'Qui vero' prevenit 2° dubitationi quia crederet aliquis quod odor rose et talium aromatum non esset aliquando delectabilis cum quis multociens fuerit ipso post repletionem assuetus. Quare subdit quod odor rose ac his semper est delectabilis: nunquam enim replet eo quod ipse recipitur sub quadam effumatione spirituali non receptione subiecti ipsius interius sicut odor cibi et potus recipitur cum eius subiecto. Et hic quidem odor amplius respicit animam et spiritum. Omnis enim odor bonus cibus est illius. Aristo<teles>. Alexander. Cibus autem corpus. Unde de sensu et sensato quidam odores secundum seipsos sunt delectabiles quemadmodum illi qui florum quidam vero ratione nutrimenti sub eis occultati. Unde tertio Ethi<corum> secundum alios quidem sensus, puta visum, auditum et odoratum non contingit per amplius concupiscentiam fieri. Notandum etiam quod potest alia causa dari quare animalium alia sunt ceteris a tactu et gustu non gaudentia nisi per accidentia, quia cum homo sit sapientissimum animalium et prudentissimum: Polliti<corum> primo et secundo De anima indiguit instrumentis quibus posset sapientiam et prudentiam exercere. His autem sunt visus, auditus et odoratus, ut patet De sensu et sensato. Hii enim faciunt ad scientiam et ad bene esse, alii vero ad esse simpliciter. Quare homo in hiis delectatur, ut possit eorum delectatione sapientiam et prudentiam acquirere cum delectatio propria perficiat operationem, Ethi<corum> 4° et quia animalium alia non habent sapientiam et prudentiam hiis non nisi fortasse per accidens delectabuntur.

# Translation

Seventh question

*Concerning[5] the reason why those who enjoy a great excess of the pleasures con-nected with touch or taste are called 'incontinent'. For those who are excessive regarding sexual intercourse, but also those [who are excessive] regarding the plea-sures of food, [are called 'incontinent']; and of those [pleasures] which concern food, part of the pleasurable [feeling] is on the tongue, but part of it is in the throat. This is also why Philoxenus[6] wished to have the throat of a crane. However, it is not applied to other [pleasures] concerning sight and hearing. And since the pleasures which are produced by those [senses] are common to us and other animals, the commonly existing ones are utterly dishonourable and highly or solely disgraceful. This is why we criticise those who are overcome by them and call them 'incontinent' and 'sinful,' because they are overcome by the worst pleasures. However, there are five senses. Yet, other animals without [these senses] get pleasure from those men-tioned before. But with regard to other senses, they either find no pleasure at all or [only] insofar as they are affected by this accidentally.[7] For we see that somebody who sees or smells [something] rejoices because she enjoys [it]; and when one is saturated the same things are no longer pleasurable, just like the smell of food is not as pleasant for us when we do not have the desire to eat something as when we are hungry. Yet, a rose is always pleasant.*

In order to make this point fully clear he[8] returns to the problem by saying why people are more excessive and immoderate in the pleasure deriving from touch, particularly the excess that lies in sexual intercourse, and [in the pleasure deriving] from taste in somebody who swallows something. For in *On Scholastic Teaching*, Boethius[9] makes a threefold distinction, because to these [pleasures] he adds those who are called 'incontinent' and 'intemperate' in matters related to clothing.

And he[10] explains that those who are [excessive] regarding sexual intercourse are called 'immoderate'. But those [who are excessive] regarding the pleasures of foods and drinks [are called] 'gluttons' or 'lechers'. And of those in whom there is plea-sure regarding food, some feel this [pleasure] in the tip of the tongue because of its high degree of sensibility (and some even [feel it] only there), but more [people feel it] in the entire throat.

---

[5] The paragraph printed in italics is the original (Pseudo-)Aristotelian text.

[6] Famous glutton, mentioned in various ancient comedies as well as by Aristotle in *Ethica Eudemia* III.2, 1231a15-17 and *Ethica Nicomachea* III.13, 1118a32f.

[7] I.e. in combination with something else such as the taste of food or hunger.

[8] I.e. (Pseudo-)Aristotle.

[9] This actually refers to Pseudo-Boethius, *De disciplina scolarium* 2.7–14, ed. Weijers (1976), 101–104.

[10] I.e. (Pseudo-)Aristotle.

And, therefore, Philoxenus,[11] [the son of] Eryxis, has been called a 'glutton'. Being voracious as a foal he prayed to Venus, who is the goddess of foods and drinks, so that she would give him a throat that is longer than that of a crane, as [is] also [mentioned] in the third book of the *Ethics*.[12] Regarding certain other senses, such as sight, hearing, and smell, it does not happen that a stronger desire is caused. Hence, those who take much pleasure in colour and form are not called 'temperate' or 'intemperate'. Similarly, in those matters concerning hearing none of those who are greatly pleased by melodies is called 'intemperate,' nor similarly in those matters concerning smell, unless very much by accident. For those rejoicing in the odours of a rose or anything like this are not called 'intemperate,' but rather those who take pleasure in the odours of perfumes and condiments which make them remember the objects of their desires. Therefore, those who eat, but not the ones who are sated, are pleased by the odours of food.

Similarly, other animals, too, are not pleased with regard to these three senses, unless by accident. For dogs do not take pleasure in the odours of a hare but in the meal, as the odour stimulates the dietary sense in them; [and] neither is a lion pleased by the voice of an ox, but by the consumption, nor by the sight when seeing a deer, but by the enjoyment of the future meal. However, I[13] have seen that small songbirds, mainly nightingales, are pleased by the song of a human and approach it, principally moved by the very same. It is also said that the peacock is pleased by seeing the beauty of its feathers and saddened if it has lost one of these. Moreover, it has been passed on that the unicorn is pleased by the odour of virgins. Hence, Aristotle's talk will be established as true in many other cases.

It must be noted that 'throat' does not refer to the epiglottis, which is the organ required for speaking, as [has been said] in chapter 11[14]. Rather, [it refers] to what appears in front of the opening of the epiglottis and the oesophagus, together with some part of the same, when the mouth is opened and the tongue pressed down, as [the case of] Philoxenus shows.[15]

After that [comes the passage beginning with] 'And since' [in which] he provides a solution and first specifies the main argument of the question by saying that the first argument is that the pleasures which derive from these two senses, that is, touch and taste, are common to us and the other animals, including little ones. Because of their commonality they are dishonourable and highly or solely disgraceful. And, therefore, we call someone who is caught and overcome by them 'incontinent' and 'sinful,' because he is overcome and subdued by the worst and most brutish pleasures that damage and mutilate the body. And from this it follows that indulging in

---

[11] See note 6.

[12] See note 6.

[13] A similar observation is described by Albert the Great, *De animalibus* VIII.6.1, ed. Stadler (1916), 667. On ego-statements in Peter of Abano, see De Leemans and Coucke (2011).

[14] Chapter 11, Problem 1; see *Expositio problematum Aristotelis cum textu* (Mantua, 1475), fol. 139vb.

[15] Peter aims to make clear that the throat is more than the part that covers the larynx while swallowing.

all of them is bad. However, one needs to be aware of the fact that even though there is endless pleasure in taste, [the pleasure deriving from] touch is still more abominable. Hence, according to the third [book] of the *Ethics*,[16] the sense of touch is common [to humans and other animals] with regard to intemperance. This seems correct, based on the assumption that [it is common] not insofar as they are humans, but insofar as they are animals. And to enjoy or love any of these is highly beastly for humans. It must be noted that touch causes the greatest amount of pleasure, followed by taste and smell, then [comes] hearing; but the least [amount is caused] by sight because, in comparison to the others, touch is more material, while the latter is more spiritual. The middle [senses], however, are more moderate, as [is mentioned in] the fourth book of *On Accidents*.[17]

Then, [in the passage beginning with] 'There are,' he compares one sensory pleasure after another. First, he says that even though there are five senses, namely, touch, taste, smell, hearing, and sight, other animals lack some of them and are further away from the pleasures of sight and hearing, or they are different compared to us. For they lack [the faculty of] reason which only we possess. And so, they are pleased only by the senses mentioned before, that is, touch and taste. But by the other three [senses] they are not pleased at all; and if they are pleased it happens by accident that they are affected or pleased. This is shown when we observe that someone who, during a meal, seeing or smelling [what she eats] rejoices in it. But later, when she is stuffed and sated, the sight and smell of the things mentioned above are not as pleasurable for her as before, that is, before she was sated. This is something we experience, too. For the smell of food is not pleasant for us when we are sated since the desire to eat has ceased, even though the smell was pleasant before when we were hungry.

After that [comes the passage beginning with] 'Yet' [in which] he anticipates a doubt, because somebody could think that the odour of a rose and of things scented in this way is no longer pleasant when someone has smelled this many times and, filled [with the odours], has become accustomed [to them]. The reason why he insinuates that the odour of a rose is always pleasant for this [person] [is the following]: For what is received under [the circumstances of] a certain spiritual evaporation and not received together with the subject – as the odour of food and drink is perceived together with the subject – does not itself satiate. And in this case an odour is much more related to the soul and the spirit [than to the body]. For every odour of good food is of this kind, as Aristotle and Alexander [of Aphrodisias say], but food [relates] to the body. Therefore, [it is said] in *On Sense and Sensibilia*[18] that some odours are pleasant in themselves as, for instance, those of flowers; others, however, because of the food that is behind them. Hence, [it is said] in the third

---

[16] Aristotle, *Ethica Nicomachea* III.13, 1118b1-3.

[17] Galen, *De symptomatum causis* I.VI.5, trans. Johnston (2006), 223.

[18] Aristotle, *De sensu et sensato* 5, 443b26f.

book of the *Ethics*[19] that with regard to other senses such as sight, hearing, and smell, no further heavy desire is created.

It must be noted that one can also provide another reason for why other animals do not find pleasure in the rest [of the senses], apart from touch and taste, unless by accident: because if humans are the wisest and most prudent animals, [as mentioned in] the first [book] of the *Politics*[20] and in the second [book] of *On the Soul*,[21] they need [cognitive] tools by virtue of which they can employ wisdom and prudence. These [tools], however, are sight, hearing, and smell, as is clear from *On Sense and Sensibilia*.[22] For they contribute to knowledge and well-being, but the others only to being per se. This is why humans find pleasure in these [senses] so that they can acquire wisdom and prudence through this pleasure, because proper pleasure brings an operation to perfection, [as mentioned in the] fourth [book] of the *Ethics*.[23] And since other animals do not possess wisdom and prudence, they can find no pleasure in those [senses] unless, perhaps, by accident.

# Bibliography

## *Primary Sources*

Aristotle. (1894). Ethica Nicomachea (I. Bywater, Ed.). Oxford: Clarendon Press.

Aristotle. (1955). *Parva naturalia* (W. D. Ross, Ed.). Oxford: Clarendon Press.

Aristotle. (1956). *De anima* (W. D. Ross, Ed.). Oxford: Clarendon Press.

Aristotle. (1957). *Politica* (W. D. Ross, Ed.). Oxford: Clarendon Press.

Aristotle. (1991). *Ethica Eudemia* (R. R. Walzer and Jean Mingay, Eds.). Oxford: Clarendon Press.

Albert the Great. (1916–1920). *De animalibus libri XXVI*. 2 vols. (H. Stadler, Ed.). Münster: Aschendorff.

Galen. (2006). *On diseases and symptoms* (I. Johnston, Trans.). Cambridge: Cambridge University Press.

Peter of Abano. (1475). *Expositio problematum Aristotelis cum textu*. Mantua.

Pseudo-Boethius. (1976). *De disciplina scolarium* (O. Weijers, Ed.). Leiden: Brill.

## *Secondary Literature*

Barrett, L. F., Lewis, M., & Haviland-Jones, J. M. (Eds.). (2016). *Handbook of emotions* (4th ed.). New York/London: The Guilford Press.

De Leemans, P., & Goyens, M. (Eds.). (2006). *Aristotle's Problemata in different times and tongues*. Leuven: Leuven University Press.

---

[19] Aristotle, *Ethica Nicomachea* III.13, 1118a1-23.

[20] Aristotle, *Politica* I.2, 1253a31-35.

[21] Aristotle, *De anima* II.3, 414b16-19.

[22] Aristotle, *De sensu et sensato* 1, 436b18–437a3.

[23] Aristotle, *Ethica Nicomachea* X.4, 1174b23.

De Leemans, P., & Coucke, G. (2011). Sicut vidi et tetigi… Ego-statements and experience in Pietro d'Abano's *Expositio Problematum Aristotelis*. In T. Bénatouïl & I. Draelants (Eds.), *Expertus sum: L'expérience par les sens dans la philosophie naturelle médiévale* (pp. 405–426). Firenze: SISMEL – Edizioni del Galluzzo.

De Leemans, P., & Hoenen, M. J. F. M. (Eds.). (2016). *Between text and tradition: Pietro d'Abano and the reception of Pseudo-Aristotle's Problemata Physica in the middle ages*. Leuven: Leuven University Press.

Klemm, M. (2006). Medicine and moral virtue in the *Expositio Problematum Aristotelis* of Peter of Abano. *Early Science and Medicine, 11*(3), 302–335.

Klemm, M., & De Leemans, P. (2005). Pietro d'Abano. In T. F. Glick, S. J. Livesey, & F. Wallis (Eds.), *Medieval science, technology, and medicine: An encyclopedia* (pp. 404–405). New York/ Abingdon: Routledge.

Lagerlund, H. (2011). Peter of Abano. In id (Ed.), *Encyclopedia of medieval philosophy: Philosophy between 500 and 1500* (Vol. 2, pp. 952–953). Dordrecht: Springer.

Siraisi, N. G. (1970). The *Expositio Problematum Aristotelis* of Peter of Abano. *Isis, 61*(3), 321–339.

# Part III
# Volition

# Chapter 21
# Free Choice, Free Judgment, and Free Appetite (Albert the Great, *De homine* I)

**Abstract** In his comprehensive treatise *On Human Beings*, Albert the Great discusses a large number of questions centring on the nature of humans. A fundamental question in this context is in what sense humans are unique. Therefore, Albert also raises various questions concerning the features and capacities of nonhuman animals. One of the features that Albert examines is what is commonly called 'free choice' (*liberum arbitrium*). His answer to the question of whether only humans or also nonhuman animals possess free choice focuses on various components of volition, namely, free appetite, free judgment, and free choice. For in order to choose something one needs to desire or to have an appetite for it. This, in turn, requires a judgment about what is desirable or not. Moreover, this appetite and this judgment must not be determined, because otherwise it could not be said that one has freely or voluntarily chosen something. Although Albert's answer to the question of whether nonhuman animals possess free will is negative, it is illuminating insofar as it scrutinises the assumptions lying behind an ascription of free choice to an animal.

## Introduction

In his comprehensive treatise *On Human Beings*, Albert the Great discusses a large number of questions centring on the nature of humans. A fundamental question in this context is in what sense humans are unique. Therefore, Albert also raises various questions concerning the features and capacities of nonhuman animals. The basic assumption here is that if a feature or capacity can be found in other animals as well, it is nothing specifically human. One of the features that Albert examines is what is commonly called 'free choice' (*liberum arbitrium*). The Latin expression is not easily translated into English and other modern languages, because there is always a question of whether what is named '*arbitrium*' produces an act of *judging* about an object, or an act of *choosing* that object.[1] Albert quotes a classical

---

[1] On this problem, see, for instance, Korolec (1982), 630.

© The Author(s), under exclusive license to Springer Nature                    177
Switzerland AG 2021
A. Oelze, *Animal Minds in Medieval Latin Philosophy*, Studies in the History of
Philosophy of Mind 27, https://doi.org/10.1007/978-3-030-67012-2_21

definition, according to which *arbitrium* is both a faculty of reason and of will. So, for him it is clear that it somehow unites these two acts. Consequently, his answer to the question of whether only humans or also nonhuman animals possess free choice focuses on various components of volition, namely, free appetite, free judgment, and free choice. For in order to choose something one needs to desire or to have an appetite for it. This, in turn, requires a judgment about what is desirable or not. Moreover, this appetite and this judgment must not be determined, because otherwise it could not be said that one has freely or voluntarily chosen something. Although Albert's answer to the question of whether nonhuman animals possess free will is negative, it is illuminating insofar as it scrutinises the assumptions lying behind an ascription of free choice to an animal.

## Bibliographical Note

The English translation is based on the following critical edition of the Latin text: Albert the Great. (2008). *De homine* (H. Anzulewicz & J. Söder, Eds.) (*Opera omnia* 27/2) (pp. 507–508). Münster: Aschendorff. The Latin text has not yet been translated into English.

## Translation

Whether free choice exists only in rational beings or also in brutes.
     Regarding the first [question], we proceed as follows:

1. Everything which has the power to judge about opposites and to turn towards whatever it wants, has free choice. In many brutes the sensory soul is of this kind. Hence, it has free choice. The first [premise] is proven by the definition of Bernard[2] who, in *On Free Choice*, says that free choice is the power to do what one wants. The second [premise], however, is proven by what has been said above[3]. There it has been established that the judgment of phantasy and, similarly, of the appetite is about opposites and is not bound to any of these by necessity.

2. Moreover, in everything in which there is the power to strive for something good or bad by itself, without the coercion to [strive for] any of them, there is also freedom of appetite. This kind of appetite is in many brutes. Hence, there will be free appetite in many brutes. The first [premise] is proven in the first [book] of the *Metaphysics*[4]. There it is said that [what is] free is what has its own cause.

---

[2] Bernard of Clairvaux, *De gratia et libero arbitrio* VI.16, ed. Leclercq & Rochais (1963), 177f.

[3] Albert the Great, *De homine*, eds. Anzulewicz & Söder (2008), 487.

[4] Aristotle, *Metaphysica* I.1, 982b25f.

The second premise is proven by what has been said before[5]. Therefore, the following [is true]: In anything in which there is free appetite, there is the freedom of striving for what it wants. This is nothing else but free choice, according to the saints[6]. In brutes free appetite exists. Hence, there exists in them the freedom of striving for what they want. This is identical with free choice.

If, by chance, it would be said that they have a certain free appetite but do not have free choice (for the fact that they do not decide what is desirable), [there is] a counter-argument: There is no appetite without a judgment about what is desirable. Brutes have appetite. Hence, they have a judgment about what is desirable. But judging means deciding. Hence, they have [the capacity of making a] decision[7], and so they have the two things it takes to have free choice.

If it would be said that choice is similar to reason and will, in which free choice mainly consists, since Augustine says that "free choice is a faculty of reason and will"[8], [there is] a counter-argument. According to this [argument], there is no difference between humans and brutes in this regard, apart from the fact that in brutes the judgment is about sensible things and belongs to phantasy, and appetite is the desire for sensible things. In humans, however, it belongs to reason and will. Hence, as far as sensible things are concerned, brutes have the freedom of judging and desiring. But any beings having this kind of freedom can abstain or not abstain from pleasurable things. Brutes have this kind of freedom. Hence, brutes can abstain and not abstain. However, each abstinence from pleasurable things comes from reason, as Aristotle[9] says. Hence brutes have reason, which is wrong.

Moreover, any beings which can be moved based on abstinence or intemperance are susceptible to virtue and vice. Brutes can be moved in this way. Hence, they are susceptible to virtue and vice.

Moreover, any beings that are acted upon by an impulse of nature rather than acting do not have free choice. Brutes are acted upon by an impulse of nature rather than acting, as the Damascene[10] says. Hence, they do not have free choice.

Solution: We say that brutes neither have free choice nor free judgment nor free appetite. For choice is called 'free' because of the freedom of deciding about the good as such and the bad as such. This means to decide about them with regard to honourableness or dishonourableness rather than with regard to pleasantness or unpleasantness. Similarly, a free judgment is a decision about something honourable or dishonourable. This is proven by what is posited by all

---

[5] I.e. at the beginning of the first paragraph.

[6] The editors of the Latin edition provide a list of people to whom Albert might refer in this passage; see Albert the Great, *De homine*, eds. Anzulewicz & Söder (2008), 507.

[7] Unlike in other passages, the term *'arbitrium'* is translated with 'decision' instead of 'choice' to make the phrase less tautological.

[8] This definition actually appears in Peter Lombard's *Sententiae in IV libris distinctae*, b. II, dist. 24, ch. 3, ed. Brady (1971), 452, but was commonly (mis)attributed to Augustine.

[9] Aristotle, *De anima* III.9, 433a7f.

[10] John of Damascus, *De fide orthodoxa*, c. 41 ( = II.27), ed. Buytaert (1955), 153.

authors[11] regarding free choice at the beginning of the writings on ethics. The freedom of the appetite also consists in the fact that one has a faculty for turning oneself towards the thing judged, or for turning away from it. And these [i.e., free choice, free judgment, and free appetite] do not exist in brutes. For the judgment of brutes is only about something pleasant, and it is not at such a high level as a judgment about something honourable. And for this reason it is not absolutely free. For by being bound to matter, in which it exists as in an organ, it is forced to stay with the goodness of particulars and of sensible things. Likewise, by the organ in which it is, the appetite is bound to the good as it is now and the bad as it is now. And for this reason it is not entirely free.

1. Thus, to the first [argument] it must be said that this argument works well for anything having a power that is absolutely and entirely free.
2. To the other [argument] it must be said that, in brutes, the power of striving for something good or bad is not entirely free and without coercion – on the contrary, moved by something good that is sensible (because of the binding they have to matter), they are driven by an impulse and do not wait for a judgment about the honourableness or dishonourableness [of that sensible thing].

## Bibliography

### *Primary Sources*

Albert the Great. (2008). *De homine* (H. Anzulewicz & J. Söder, Eds.) (*Opera omnia* 27/2). Münster: Aschendorff.
Aristotle. (1957). *Metaphysica* (W. Jaeger, Ed.). Oxford: Clarendon Press.
Aristotle. (1961). *De anima* (W. D. Ross, Ed.). Oxford: Clarendon Press.
Bernard of Clairvaux. (1963). *De gratia et libero arbitrio* (J. Leclercq & H. M. Rochais, Eds.) (*Opera* III). Rome: Editiones Cistercienses.
John of Damascus. (1955). *De fide orthodoxa: Versions of Burgundius and Cerbanus* (E. M. Buytaert, Ed.). St. Bonaventure: The Franciscan Institute.
Peter Lombard. (1971). *Sententiae in IV libris distinctae, T. 1, P. 2, Liber I et II* (I. Brady, Ed.). Grottaferrata: Collegium S. Bonaventurae Ad Claras Aquas.

### *Secondary Sources*

Korolec, J. B. (1982). Free will and free choice. In A. Kenny, E. Stump, J. Pinborg, & N. Kretzmann (Eds.), *The Cambridge history of later medieval philosophy: From the rediscovery of Aristotle to the disintegration of scholasticism, 1100–1600* (pp. 629–641). Cambridge: Cambridge University Press.

---

[11] A list of possible references, including Augustine, John of Damascus, and Avicenna, is provided by the editors of the Latin text; see Albert the Great, *De homine*, eds. Anzulewicz & Söder (2008), 508.

# Chapter 22
# Free Choice (Bonaventure, *Commentarius in secundum librum Sententiarum,* Distinction 25, Single Article, Question 1)

**Abstract** In his commentary on the second book of the *Sentences*, Bonaventure discusses the nature of various creatures, including nonhuman animals. He provides an insightful approach to the question of whether or not 'free choice', 'decision' or 'judgment' (*liberum arbitrium*) – which he defines with Augustine as joint "faculty of reason and will" – is found in rational creatures alone. He clearly spells out what it means to be free or to ascribe freedom (*libertas*) to a being or to a cognitive power. Moreover, he discusses how the traditional denial of free choice to nonhuman animals is compatible with the observation that several of their behaviours give us the impression of being voluntary and free.

## Introduction

Bonaventure was no mere contemporary of Thomas Aquinas. He also shares with him the fame of ranking amongst the most important and influential thinkers of the thirteenth century.[1] Born in the small town of Bagnoregio, at some point between 1217 and 1221, he first went to Paris to study arts. One of his teachers was Alexander of Hales. He was not only the first Franciscan to hold a chair at the University of Paris, but also played a pivotal role for the reception of both Aristotle's newly translated writings and Peter Lombard's *Sentences*, the most important textbook during that time and for centuries to come.[2] In order to obtain a master's degree in theology, Bonaventure began commenting on the *Sentences* in 1250. In 1257, he got a chair in theology, just like Aquinas. Almost at the same time, he was elected minister general of the order of the Franciscans (which he had entered in 1238 or 1243). And so, in the following years he lived a life as clergyman and academic until he suddenly died in the summer of 1274, only one year after he had been made a cardinal by pope Gregory X.

---

[1] On his life and his writings, see Cullen (2006), 3–23.

[2] On the role and reception of the *Sentences*, see the introduction to Chap. 14.

© The Author(s), under exclusive license to Springer Nature Switzerland AG 2021
A. Oelze, *Animal Minds in Medieval Latin Philosophy*, Studies in the History of Philosophy of Mind 27, https://doi.org/10.1007/978-3-030-67012-2_22

Although his *Sentences* commentary fills four large volumes, it does not consti-tute even half of the total number of pages he wrote during his lifetime. Nevertheless, it is undoubtedly his most important text. The question translated in the following is part of a larger set of questions concerning the second book of the *Sentences*, which deals with creation. Given this context, it is rather unsurprising that it discusses the nature of various creatures, including nonhuman animals. Further, Bonaventure's use of authorities (Augustine, Anselm of Canterbury, John of Damascus) is in itself not particularly unconventional. However, he provides an insightful approach to the question of whether or not 'free choice', 'decision' or 'judgment'[3] (*liberum arbi-trium*) – which he defines with Augustine as joint "faculty of reason and will" – is found in rational creatures alone. He clearly spells out what it means to be free or to ascribe freedom (*libertas*) to a being or to a cognitive power. Moreover, he discusses how the traditional denial of free choice to nonhuman animals is compatible with the observation that several of their behaviours give us the impression of being vol-untary and free.[4]

## Bibliographical Note

The English translation is based on the following edition of the Latin text: Bonaventure. (1885). *Commentaria in quatuor libros Sententiarum magistri Petri Lombardi: In secundum librum Sententiarum* (*Opera omnia* 2) (pp. 592–594). Quaracchi: Collegium S. Bonaventurae. The Latin text has not yet been translated into English.

## Translation

Question I: Whether free choice is only in those having reason, or whether it is also in brute animals.

Regarding the first [question], we proceed as follows and ask whether free choice is only in those having reason, or whether it is also in brute animals. And it seems that it is in brute animals.

1. That power is called 'free' which is able to choose a good or to flee a bad thing. But we see that this power is in brutes, as is obvious with regard to the sheep that flees the wolf and seeks the shepherd. Therefore, etc.

---

[3] I translate '*arbitrium*' with 'choice' although it is not identical with the term '*electio*' that I also translate with 'choice' (see text 23). Yet, 'free choice' is the usual term for this subject and more common than 'free decision' or 'free judgment'.

[4] For a brief summary and analysis of the text, see Davis (2017), 112–115.

2. Similarly, a power which is capable of opposites possesses freedom. But brute animals have a power for doing opposed things, because sometimes they show friendliness, sometimes ferocity, sometimes they go away, sometimes they come. Therefore, freedom of choice belongs to such animals.

3. Similarly, a power which is the ruler of its acts is free. Yet, that is to say that it is capable of checking and restraining itself in its own act. But such a power is found in brute animals. This is obvious because by learning they are restrained from those things they desire, as is evident in pets and domesticated animals. Therefore, etc.

4. Similarly, a power possesses freedom regarding locomotion if its movement starts from an intrinsic origin. For this movement belongs to a power that is perfect in moving. But in brute animals it starts from an intrinsic origin. Therefore, etc.

5. Similarly, that power is particularly free to which it belongs to have foresight, not only with regard to present [things] but also with regard to future things. But such [an ability] is in brute animals, as is obvious with regard to ants[5] and other non-rational animals. Therefore, etc.

6. Similarly, that power which cannot be brought into a state of servitude participates in freedom more than the one which can. But humans can be brought into a state of servitude, while there are certain animals that can never be tamed, such as dragons and lions. Therefore, it seems that such [animals] have freedom of choice in the highest degree.

Yet, to the contrary: 1. Augustine defines free choice as follows: "Free choice is a faculty of reason and of will"[6] (as mentioned in the preceding distinction). But a faculty of reason is not in a [being] in which reason does not exist; and this exists only in rational beings, and hence free choice, as well.

2. Similarly, everyone who possesses free choice is praiseworthy or blameworthy. But only rational beings are worthy of praise or blame, punishment or reward. Therefore, etc.

3. Similarly, everyone who possesses free choice is capable of cogitating and deliberating. However, this [capacity] belongs to a rational being alone. Therefore, etc.

4. Similarly, free choice is the most excellent [faculty] that exists in humans. Thus, if free choice would be found in brutes, the most excellent [faculty] that exists in humans would also be found in them. Consequently, brute animals would be as excellent as rational beings. Since this is inappropriate, it is clear etc.

Conclusion: Free choice is found in rational substances alone.

I reply: It must be said that free choice is undoubtedly found in rational substances alone. – And the reason for this lies partly on the side of freedom, partly on the side of choice. On the side of freedom, [it is] because freedom is opposed to servitude. Therefore, only that power is said to be free that has full command with

---

[5] Ants were traditionally taken to act with foresight as they store food for the winter; see Chap. 11.

[6] This definition actually appears in Peter Lombard's *Sententiae in IV libris distinctae*, b. II, dist. 24, ch. 3, ed. Brady (1971), 452, but was commonly (mis)attributed to Augustine.

respect to an object as well as with regard to its own act. However, that power has command by being free with regard to an object, [when the power] is not bound to anything from the genus of desirable things, but is capable of desiring all desirable things and of rejecting everything that should be fled. Yet, there are three things in [the genus of] desired things, namely, good, useful, and pleasant [objects], while their opposites lie in flight. And there, the term 'good' means 'honourable'[7]; however, while the good, [insofar] as [it is] useful and pleasant, can be desired by non-rational beings, the good, [insofar] as [it is] honourable, can be desired by rational beings alone. And, therefore, the power that is not bound to anything from the genus of desirable things is found in them alone, and by means of this [power] they have freedom with respect to an object.

Further, the power which has freedom with respect to its own act is found in them alone. This is clear because, in rational beings, the will not only controls the hand or the feet, but also restrains itself, checks [itself], and frequently begins to hate what it has loved before; and this [it does] through its own order and command. In brute animals, however, some sort of command with respect to the external act can also be found, because sometimes they well restrain [from doing something], as is obvious regarding domesticated animals. Yet, with respect to the own internal act, that is, the appetite, there is no command. Hence, if they love something, they cannot not love it. That is, even when they are kept from striving for something, they love by the fear of a certain inflicting passion. And, therefore, the Damascene[8] says that "they are acted upon rather than acting". And for this reason, since they cannot restrain their own act, they do not have freedom, neither with respect to their own act nor with respect to the object. And, therefore, as freedom in them is deficient, they cannot participate in freedom of choice.

A reason [for the fact that free choice is found in rational creatures alone] lies also on the side of choice. For choice is the same as the judgment at the command of which the other powers move and obey. It is able to judge, however, in terms of full reason, to which it belongs to discern between just and unjust, proper and alien. No power, however, knows what is just and what is unjust except the one that is joined to reason and has been designed to cognise the highest justice, from which the rule of right derives in general. However, this [power] is only in the substance which is [created] in the image of God, and only a rational power is of this kind. For no substance discerns what is proper and what is alien, unless it cognises itself and its own act. But a power that is tied to matter never cognises itself or reflects on itself. So, if all powers, except the rational power, are tied to matter and the bodily substance, it is that [power] alone that can reflect on itself. And, therefore, it is that [power] alone in which there is full judgment and choice in discerning what is just and what is unjust, what is proper and what is alien. – And so, both in terms of

---

[7] I.e., the Good itself that is not desired for the sake of something else; see Davis (2017), 113.

[8] John of Damascus, *De fide orthodoxa*, c. 41 (= II.27), ed. Buytaert (1955), 153.

freedom and in terms of choice, free choice is found in rational substances alone. And the arguments which show this must be accepted.

1. The reply to the counter-arguments is clear from what has already been said. For to the first objection (that brutes favour the good over the bad) it must be said that it is true regarding the good [insofar] as [it is] useful or pleasant. But it is not true for the good [insofar] as [it is] honourable, with respect to which free choice exists in the proper sense.

2. The reply to the similar objection that brutes can move towards opposites is clear, because they cannot move toward all opposites but only toward those which are below the dignity of free choice.

3. To the objection that brutes control their acts since they can restrain themselves, it must be said that they do not control internal acts although they control external [acts]. For even though they refrain from an act they are, nevertheless, not withdrawn from the appetite. – Alternatively, it can be said that even though they are withdrawn from their act this, nevertheless, does not happen by their own command. For this happens by the imagination of some external, bad thing which terrifies [them] to such a degree that it restrains rather than attracts the appetite. And, therefore, as they are acted upon rather than acting when they strive for and seek something, they are also restrained rather than restraining when they refrain or withdraw from something.

4. And from this [reply] the reply to the other [objection] (which claims that the beginning of movement in brute animals derives from something intrinsic) is clear. For it can be said that even though the beginning of an external movement derives from something intrinsic, the internal appetite, nevertheless, originates from some external desired thing rather than from the order of the appetitive power. Thus, not any kind of movement [deriving] from something intrinsic makes a power [qualify as] free, but only that movement by which a power triggering movement moves itself. "For the will and free choice are tools that move themselves," as Anselm[9] says.

# Bibliography

## *Primary Sources*

Anselm of Canterbury. (1968). *De concordia praescientiae et praedestinationis et gratiae Dei cum libero arbitrio (Opera omnia* 1.2) (F. S. Schmitt, Ed.). Stuttgart/Bad Cannstatt: Friedrich Frommann.

Bonaventure. (1885). *Commentaria in quatuor libros Sententiarum magistri Petri Lombardi: In secundum librum Sententiarum (Opera omnia* 2). Quaracchi: Collegium S. Bonaventurae.

---

[9] Anselm of Canterbury, *De concordia praescientiae et praedestinationis et gratiae Dei cum libero arbitrio* III.11, ed. Schmitt (1968), 284. Bonaventure's quotation is imprecise insofar as Anselm does not mention free choice in that passage.

John of Damascus. (1955). *De fide orthodoxa. Versions of Burgundius and Cerbanus* (E. M. Buytaert, Ed.). St. Bonaventure: The Franciscan Institute.

Peter Lombard. (1971). *Sententiae in IV libris distinctae. T. 1, P. 2, Liber I et II* (I. Brady, Ed.). Grottaferrata: Collegium S. Bonaventurae Ad Claras Aquas.

## Secondary Sources

Cullen, C. M. (2006). *Bonaventure*. New York: Oxford University Press.

Davis, R. G. (2017). *The weight of love: Affect, ecstasy, and union in the theology of Bonaventure*. New York: Fordham University Press.

# Chapter 23
# Instinct and Deliberation (Roger Bacon, *Communia naturalium* Book 1, Part 2, Distinction 4, Chapter 1)

**Abstract**   In a passage of his *Communia naturalium*, Bacon distinguishes two types of agents: those who act *intentionally*, that is, by deliberation and will, and those who act *naturally*, that is, by instinct. One might assume that humans clearly fall within the first category, whereas nonhuman animals belong to the second. However, Bacon shows that even though nonhuman animals commonly act by nature, there are many cases in which humans do as well. His text, therefore, throws an interesting light not only on the interrelations of cognition, emotion, and volition, but also on the commonalities of human and nonhuman animals.

## Introduction

Of all of Bacon's works, the *Communia naturalium* has only very recently received scholarly attention.[1] Presumably written in the decade between 1260 and 1270, this text does not simply concern so-called 'natural things' (*naturalia*), that is, the four elements, inanimate beings, living beings (plants, animals, humans), and celestial bodies, since these things usually were the objects of particular sciences, such as physics (or natural philosophy) and astronomy. Rather, Bacon aims to examine what is 'common' (*communis*) to them. Therefore, he focuses, for instance, on what constitutes them, namely, matter and form, and on what causes their existence and activities, operations, or actions. Agency and causation are the general topics of the passage translated in the following. Since it is embedded within a broader discussion, it is presumably not as accessible as other texts. But with regard to the aspect of volition it is interesting to read because Bacon distinguishes two types of agents: those who act *intentionally*, that is, by deliberation and will, and those who act *naturally*, that is, by instinct. One might assume that humans clearly fall within the first category, whereas nonhuman animals belong to the second. However, Bacon shows that even though nonhuman animals commonly act by nature, there are many

---

[1] See the essays and introduction in Bernardini & Rodolfi (2014).

© The Author(s), under exclusive license to Springer Nature Switzerland AG 2021
A. Oelze, *Animal Minds in Medieval Latin Philosophy*, Studies in the History of Philosophy of Mind 27, https://doi.org/10.1007/978-3-030-67012-2_23

cases in which humans do as well. His text, therefore, throws an interesting light not only on the interrelations of cognition, emotion, and volition, but also on the commonalities of human and nonhuman animals.

## Bibliographical Note

The English translation is based on the following critical edition of the Latin text: Roger Bacon. (1909). *Liber primus communium naturalium: Partes prima et secunda* (*Opera hactenus inedita* 2) (R. Steele, Ed.) (pp. 108–111). Oxford: Clarendon Press. The Latin text has not yet been translated into English.

## Translation

In the second part of this first book of the [treatise on] *Those that Are Common to Natural Things*, we have spoken about matter in principle, its privation,[2] powers, and seminal reasons,[3] and also about the form which seemed to be necessary there.[4]

Now we must talk about the properties of all natural and non-natural causes, insofar as they refer to nature, in order to better understand the actions of natural things. Yet, there are two kinds of efficient causes[5] that work by themselves and not by accident, namely, nature and intellect. Here, however, the intellect is called a 'rational substance,' which works through the deliberation of reason and the choice of the will; and it is called an 'agent by intention and will' as the divine, the angelic, and the human intellect.

Everything, however, that does something without the deliberation of reason and without the choice of the will is called an 'agent by nature' because it acts by natural instinct. Yet, the intellect does not act by natural instinct but through its deliberation, in various ways and regarding various things, at the pleasure of the will; and it is called a 'rational power for doing opposite things'. In the created angelic and human intellect exists the power to do opposite things which are good and evil. This means that a rational creature taken as such can do both good and bad things; humans indeed do both by doing good and bad things. But since a rational substance does many things without deliberation and the choice of the will, it must, therefore, be called an 'agent by nature' with regard to such actions.

---

[2] I.e. the state in which form (*forma*) and matter (*materia*) do not yet form a compound (*compositum*).

[3] I.e., metaphorically speaking, the seeds which God planted during creation from which all things potentially grow. This theory, of which Bacon was a defender, aims to explain how divine creation and the development of new forms of life are compatible with each other.

[4] See Roger Bacon, *Communia naturalium*, lib. I, p. II, dist. 1–2, ed. Steele (1909), 50–92.

[5] I.e. an agent or a thing that brings a being about, such as the builder of a house.

These [actions] are of two kinds. Some happen without any cognition and voluntary appetite as, for instance, those operations that take place in the body for the
sake of existence, life, and well-being; they are jointly performed by the powers of
this substance working in the body. And such [actions] are natural because neither
are they based on the consideration of reason nor on voluntary appetite. Rather,
[they are based] on the natural power of its substance and on natural appetite. This
[appetite] is said to maintain the body, to which it is united, and the person which
consists of these two. And, likewise, any other operation that is performed by its
substance through a natural power, just as the flowing in of powers to the semen for
the generation of offspring, is natural. And, as I must briefly add, every operation is
natural that is performed neither by cognition nor by rational appetite but by its
active substance which alters the body or the body of the semen for the offspring; or
[which is performed] in a medium and by bodies in a medium through the flowing
in of powers (we have talked about that action in the first part of this book[6]).

The others, however, are operations of the soul together with cognition and
voluntary appetite. Yet, these can be performed with the deliberation of reason (and
then they are not called 'natural'); or they can be performed without deliberation
(and then they are called 'natural'), such as laughing and sighing and anything like
that. For human beings do not always and in every situation deliberate or use reason.
Infants, for instance, [don't], before [they are capable of] employing free choice.
Therefore, they lack [wilful] intent but act by nature.

Similarly, [humans do not deliberate] in sleep. This is why sleepwalkers perform
something naturally and not by deliberation, and [so do] mentally disabled people
or those who are mad, because they act as naturally as brute animals. But even
though some of the things they do resemble those things done by deliberation, they
do not have the capacity of employing free choice. This is not surprising because
healthy and careful human beings in their prime of life, in which they have the
freedom of choice, do many things without deliberation, as when something
unpleasant or pleasant is suddenly put before them. Then, in many cases, before
they have deliberated, they are sad or troubled or afraid or terrified or angry and so
forth, and because of what is pleasant they rejoice, jubilate, are astonished, or have
hope. And then they easily utter sounds that signify naturally and not arbitrarily, that
is, [sounds] that have not been deployed in order to signify something. Rather, they
express their emotions without deliberation, as it happens in brutes.

Likewise, with such sounds, a human being does many things before deliberating,
such as laughing, weeping, singing or sighing; and with others it drives something
off, flees, or seeks something. And the difference between those sounds that are
naturally produced and interjections[7] is that in [the production of] these [naturally
produced sounds] there is neither deliberation nor a deliberate, mental concept of
pleasantness or unpleasantness [involved]. Furthermore, they have not been given a
sound by convention. Therefore, such sounds do not form part of [conventional]

---

[6] See Roger Bacon, *Communia naturalium*, lib. I, p. I, dist. 2, ch. 1, ed. Steele (1909), 16–20.
[7] I.e. expressions which express a feeling (e.g. 'ouch!').

language, because nothing forms part of language unless it signifies a mental concept, as Priscian[8] says. But it must be understood that this concept is deliberate, although not always fully; and here the conception [in the mind] is the same as the apprehension of the soul which captures and understands a thing. However, a mental concept is twofold, namely, [first,] without any deliberation; and that is how it is in the sounds of both humans and brutes that signify naturally, for they conceive and apprehend or they capture, by virtue of a soul that cognises, what is unpleasant or pleasant. But they do not deliberate on this concept; rather, pain or joy or anything of this kind is immediately and through natural instinct aroused in them, and the emotion prevails over the concept. Therefore, they are emotionally affected rather than conceiving, because the concept is immediately transformed into an emotion. And in this respect, they are natural agents.

But, [second], when human beings deliberate on their concepts, they can do this in two ways, namely, either imperfectly, and then they bring forward interjections about feeling pain or enjoying something and so forth; or [they can do it] perfectly, and then they utter sounds from other parts of language. That is why sighing has three meanings: when one sighs feebly, and then this sound is not part of language; or by the interjection of sighing, or by this noun 'sighing' or this verb 'I sigh' or this participle 'sighing,' and in this way it is part of language. But insofar as it is an interjection it has a hidden, imperfect, and unformed sound, because the concept is imperfect and the deliberation is imperfect and the feeling is stronger than the concept. This is why they are said to signify in an emotional way because a human being is affected by pain, that is, feels pain before conceptualising pain or before devoting attention to conceptualisation because the concept quickly goes over into an emotion, although this does not happen immediately, as in sounds that signify entirely naturally. But insofar as it is a noun or a verb or a participle it has a clear and perfect sound because the deliberate concept is perfect. Therefore, they are said to signify by a pure concept. And in this case a human being is not affected by pain but by the concept that is deliberated.

And so, if the rational soul does many things naturally, as for instance when it does not deliberate, then brutes do whatever they do naturally because they do not deliberate. Therefore, those behaviours that most resemble behaviours [brought about] by reason are natural in brutes, as when a spider builds a web, a bee a hexagonal comb, a swallow a nest and things like that (and even other things). Also, all operations of the vegetative soul are natural in humans as well as in brutes and plants. These [operations] are nourishing, growing, propagating, digesting food, attracting what is useful, secreting what is superfluous by urine and the like, and keeping what is nutrient.[9]

---

[8] Priscian, *Institutiones grammaticae* XI.7, ed. Hertz (1855), 552.

[9] On these animal behaviours and their cognitive causes, see also Bacon's discussion in *Perspectiva* II.3.9 (= Chap. 10 in this volume).

Yet, in the second [book] of *On the Soul*,[10] Aristotle, says, by contrast, that nature operates only in one direction. For instance, fire [goes] upwards and earth downwards. But the soul [works] in all directions, because it sends nutriment to upper and lower parts and everywhere in the body. But this can be resolved because 'nature' can be employed in two ways: in one way as a power that works without the deliberation of reason and the choice of the will; in another way with a specific and narrow meaning as a power that works separately from the soul. And this is how Aristotle employs it in the second [book] of *On the Soul*.[11] But in the second [book] of the *Physics*[12] he employs it in the first way. And if the soul in plants and animals acts by nature, then the power working in the elements and mixtures and in all inanimate beings is even more natural, because nothing is deliberative nor similar to deliberation there.

## Bibliography

### *Primary Sources*

Aristotle. (1950). *Physica* (W. D. Ross, Ed.). Oxford: Clarendon Press.
Aristotle. (1961). *De anima* (W. D. Ross, Ed.). Oxford: Clarendon Press.
Priscian. (1855). *Institutionum grammaticarum libri XVIII, Vol. 1* (M. Hertz, Ed.). Leipzig: Teubner.
Roger Bacon. (1909). *Liber primus communium naturalium: Partes prima et secunda* (*Opera hactenus inedita* 2) (R. Steele, Ed.). Oxford: Clarendon Press.

### *Secondary Literature*

Bernardini, P., & Rodolfi, A. (Eds.). (2014). *Roger Bacon's Communia naturalium: A 13th century philosopher's workshop*. Firenze: SISMEL – Edizioni del Galluzzo.

---

[10] Aristotle, *De anima* II.4, 415b28–416a7.

[11] See note 10.

[12] Aristotle, *Physica* II.8, 199a20–30. For a more detailed discussion of this concept of nature, see the passage from Bacon's commentary on the *Physics* (= Chap. 11 in this volume).

# Chapter 24
# Choosing and Acting (Thomas Aquinas, *Summa theologiae*, Part I–II, Question 13, Article 2)

**Abstract** In question 13, article 2, of part I–II of the *Summa theologiae*, Thomas Aquinas addresses the question of whether nonhuman animals are capable of making a 'choice' (*electio*). Since he adopts Aristotle's definition of choice as the capacity to find the right means to an end, it seems, at first, as if various cases of animal behaviour show exactly that animals often do things on a means-to-end basis, and hence are capable of making a choice. However, Aquinas emphasises that we should be more careful in interpreting animal behaviour as voluntary, because even though animals seem to make rational choices – as he demonstrates with Sextus Empiricus' famous example of Chrysippus' dog – we should rather account for their behaviour by what he calls 'sensory appetite' (*appetitus sensitivus*). This does not mean that Aquinas considers animals to be simple machines (although he interestingly compares their behaviour to the behaviour of clocks and other artefacts). Rather, he wants to point out that (sometimes) even complex phenomena can be explained by simple processes.

## Introduction

In the *Summa theologiae*, Thomas Aquinas not only discusses the cognitive life of animals (see Chap. 12) and their emotions (see Chaps. 17, 18, and 19) but also volitional aspects of their behaviour. In question 13, article 2, of part I–II, which has been translated in the following, he particularly addresses the question of whether nonhuman animals are capable of making a 'choice' (*electio*).[1] Since he adopts Aristotle's definition of choice as the capacity to find the right means to an end, it seems, at first, as if various cases of animal behaviour show exactly that animals often do things on a means-to-end basis, and hence are capable of making a choice. However, Aquinas emphasises that we should be more careful in interpreting animal behaviour as voluntary, because even though animals seem to make rational

---

[1] For an analysis of this text, see Davids (2017), 191–193; Oelze (2018), 134–138.

© The Author(s), under exclusive license to Springer Nature
Switzerland AG 2021
A. Oelze, *Animal Minds in Medieval Latin Philosophy*, Studies in the History of
Philosophy of Mind 27, https://doi.org/10.1007/978-3-030-67012-2_24

choices – as he demonstrates with Sextus Empiricus' famous example of Chrysippus' dog – we should rather account for their behaviour by what he calls 'sensory appetite' (*appetitus sensitivus*). In this regard, his explanation resembles the argument of John Duns Scotus (see Chap. 13) who claims that a behaviour looking like a rational behaviour from the outside is not necessarily brought about by a rational and deliberate process. This does not mean that Aquinas considers animals to be simple machines (although he interestingly compares their behaviour to the behaviour of clocks and other artefacts). Rather, he wants to point out that (sometimes) even complex phenomena can be explained by simple processes.

## Bibliographical Note

The English translation is based on the following edition of the Latin text: Thomas Aquinas. (1891). *Prima secundae Summae theologiae, qq. 1–70 (Opera omnia* 6) (pp. 99–100). Rome. For an alternative English translation see, for instance, Thomas Aquinas. (1970). *Summa theologiae, Vol. 17: Psychology of human acts (1a2ae. 6–17)* (T. Gilby, Trans.) (pp. 127–129). London: Blackfriars.

## Translation

Article 2: Whether choice belongs to brute animals.

Regarding the second [article], we proceed as follows. It seems that choice belongs to brute animals. For [1.] choice is "a striving for things for an end," as is said in [book] III of the *Ethics*.[2] But brute animals strive for something for an end, because they do things for an end and because of an appetite. Hence, there is choice in brute animals.

2. Furthermore, the very term 'choice' seems to mean that something is favoured over something else. But brute animals favour one thing over another. This obviously occurs when a sheep eats one herb but rejects another. Hence, there is choice in brute animals.

3. Moreover, "it pertains to prudence that one carefully chooses those which are means to an end," as is said in [book] VI of the *Ethics*.[3] But prudence belongs to brute animals. Therefore, it is said at the beginning of the *Metaphysics*[4] that "some [animals], such as bees, are prudent without instruction although they cannot hear sounds." And this seems also clear through observation, because in the behaviour of such animals as bees, spiders, and dogs, occur astonishing cases of sagacity. For a

---

[2] Aristoteles Latinus, *Ethica Nicomachea* III.4, 1111b27, ed. Gauthier (1973), 414.

[3] Aristoteles Latinus, *Ethica Nicomachea* VI.13, 1144a8, ed. Gauthier (1973), 491.

[4] Aristoteles Latinus, *Metaphysica* I.1, 980a22f., ed. Vuillemin-Diem (1976), 7.

dog[5] that chases a deer, when it comes to a fork with three paths, inquires by smelling whether the deer entered the first or the second path. If it finds out that neither of them has been entered, it takes the third path straightaway, without exploration, as if using a disjunctive syllogism[6] by which it can infer that the deer escaped by this path from the fact that it did not escape through the other two, because there are no more paths. Hence, it seems that choice belongs to brute animals.

But against this is what Gregory of Nyssa[7] says [namely] that "children and non-rational beings do things somehow voluntarily but still without choosing." Hence, there is no choice in brute animals.

I reply by saying that, since choice is the preference for one thing in comparison to another, it is necessary that choice happens with respect to various things that can be chosen. And, therefore, in those beings which are entirely determined to one [object or behaviour], there is no place for choice. However, there is a difference between sensory appetite and will, because sensory appetite is determined by one particular thing, according to the order of nature, as is clear from what has been said before.[8] The will, however, is somehow determined by one common thing, which is the good, according to the order of nature, but it is indifferent with respect to particular things that are good. And, therefore, choosing in the proper sense of the term belongs to the will but not to the sensory appetite, which is the only [appetite] brute animals have. And for this reason, choice does not belong to brute animals.

Thus, to the first argument it must be said that not every sensory striving for something for an end is called 'choice', but [only] that with a certain discrimination between one thing and another. There is no place for this except where the appetite can be drawn to various things.

To the second argument it must be said that a brute animal favours one thing over another because its appetite is naturally determined by that thing. And so, as soon as something towards which its appetite is naturally inclined is represented to it (by sense or imagination), it moves only towards this thing without choice, just as fire moves upwards, not downwards without choice, as well.

To the third argument it must be said that "movement is the act of a movable thing [caused] by a mover," as is said in [book] III of the *Physics*.[9] And, therefore, the power of the mover appears in the movement of the moveable thing. And for this reason, the order of reason which moves appears in all things that are moved by reason even if they themselves do not possess reason. For in this way an arrow directly tends to a target by the movement of the shooter, as if it would have the rational capacity of aiming at something by itself. And the same occurs in the movements of clocks and all human inventions that have been produced by art. However,

---

[5] This famous example is known as 'Chrysippus' dog' (named after the Stoic logician Chrysippus). On its history see Floridi (1997). For a contemporary analysis see Rescorla (2009).

[6] I.e. an argument of the form 'Either A or B; if not A, then B'.

[7] This is a misattribution; see Dobler (2001), 70. The correct reference is Nemesius of Emesa, *De natura hominis* 32, eds. Verbeke & Moncho (1975), 126.

[8] I.e. in *Summa theologiae* I-II.1.2, ad 3.

[9] Aristoteles Latinus, *Physica* III.3, 202a13f., eds. Bossier & Brams (1990), 105.

artefacts relate to human art as all natural things relate to divine art. And, therefore, the order appears in those that are moved according to nature as well as in those that are moved by reason, as is said in [book] II of the *Physics*.[10] And from this it can be inferred that in the behaviours of brute animals certain examples of sagacity appear, insofar as they have a natural inclination towards certain processes which are highly ordered, that is, ordered by the highest art.[11] And for this reason – and not because there is some kind of reason or choice in them – also some animals are called 'prudent' or 'sagacious'. This is clear from the fact that all those [animals] having the same nature do things in the same manner.

# Bibliography

## *Primary Sources*

Aristoteles Latinus. (1973). *Ethica Nicomachea: Translatio Roberti Grosseteste Lincolniensis* (*Aristoteles Latinus* 26.1-3) (R. A. Gauthier, Ed.). Leiden/Brussels: Brill/Desclée de Brouwer.
Aristoteles Latinus. (1976). *Metaphysica, Lib. I-X, XII-XIV: Translatio Anonyma sive 'Media'* (*Aristoteles Latinus* 25.2) (G. Vuillemin-Diem, Ed.). Leiden: Brill.
Aristoteles Latinus. (1990). *Physica: Translatio vetus* (*Aristoteles Latinus* 7.1) (F. Bossier & J. Brams, Eds.). Leiden/New York: Brill.
Nemesius of Emesa. (1975). *De natura hominis: Traduction de Burgundio de Pise* (G. Verbeke & J. R. Moncho, Eds.). Leiden: Brill.
Thomas Aquinas. (1891). *Prima secundae Summae theologiae, qq. 1–70* (*Opera omnia* 6). Rome.
Thomas Aquinas. (1970). *Summa theologiae, Vol. 17: Psychology of human acts (1a2ae. 6–17)* (T. Gilby, Trans.). London: Blackfriars.

## *Secondary Sources*

Davids, T. (2017). *Anthropologische Differenz und animalische Konvenienz: Tierphilosophie bei Thomas von Aquin.* Leiden/Boston: Brill.
Dobler, E. (2001). *Falsche Väterzitate bei Thomas von Aquin: Gregorius, Bischof von Nyssa oder Nemesius, Bischof von Emesa? Untersuchungen über die Authentizität der Zitate Gregors von Nyssa in den gesamten Werken des Thomas von Aquin.* Freiburg (Schweiz): Universitätsverlag.
Floridi, L. (1997). Scepticism and animal rationality: The fortune of Chrysippus' dog in the history of western thought. *Archiv für Geschichte der Philosophie, 79*(1), 27–57.
Oelze, A. (2018). *Animal rationality: Later medieval theories 1250–1350.* Leiden/Boston: Brill.
Rescorla, M. (2009). Chrysippus' dog as a case study in non-linguistic cognition. In R. W. Lurz (Ed.), *The philosophy of animal minds* (pp. 52–71). Cambridge: Cambridge University Press.

---

[10] Aristoteles Latinus, *Physica* II.5, 196b22f., eds. Bossier & Brams (1990), 68.

[11] I.e. God.

# Chapter 25
# Freedom and Free Choice (Thomas Aquinas, *Quaestiones disputatae de veritate*, Question 24, Article 2)

**Abstract** In his *Disputed Questions on Truth*, Thomas Aquinas discusses the question of whether nonhuman animals are endowed with free choice (*liberum arbitrium*). The treatise consists of two major sets of questions. The second one is concerned with the good, that is, with one of the ends, if not the end, of human actions. But what about nonhuman animals? Are they not also striving for something good when they, for example, try to reach a portion of food? And are they not also avoiding something bad when they flee a harmful object, as when the sheep runs away from the wolf? Apparently, there are many cases in which the behaviour of nonhuman animals resembles human actions. However, the question is whether their behaviour is based on a deliberate decision. In question 24, article 2, Aquinas addresses this problem, and he is quite original in developing a strategy that allows him, on the one hand, to preserve the peculiar character of human actions based on free will, while leaving room for at least some sort of freedom and voluntariness in the actions of nonhuman animals, on the other.

## Introduction

In the *Summa theologiae*, Thomas Aquinas clearly rules out that nonhuman animals are capable of making a rational choice (*electio*) (see Chap. 24). Nevertheless, he discusses the question of whether nonhuman animals are endowed with free choice (*liberum arbitrium*) in his *Disputed Questions on Truth*. This treatise was written at the end of the 1250s, when Aquinas was teaching in Paris.[1] It consists of two major sets of questions. The second one is concerned with the good, that is, with one of the ends, if not *the* end, of human actions. But what about nonhuman animals? Are they not also striving for something good when they, for example, try to reach a portion of food? And are they not also avoiding something bad when they flee a harmful object, as when the sheep runs away from the wolf? Apparently, there are many

---

[1] On his biography, see the introduction to Chap. 12.

A. Oelze, *Animal Minds in Medieval Latin Philosophy*, Studies in the History of Philosophy of Mind 27, https://doi.org/10.1007/978-3-030-67012-2_25

cases in which the behaviour of nonhuman animals resembles human actions. However, the question is whether their behaviour is based on a deliberate decision. In question 24, article 2, Aquinas addresses this problem, and he is quite original in developing a strategy that allows him, on the one hand, to preserve the peculiar character of human actions based on free will, while leaving room for at least some sort of freedom and voluntariness in the actions of nonhuman animals, on the other.[2]

## Bibliographical Note

The English translation is based on the following edition of the Latin text: Thomas Aquinas. (1973). *Quaestiones disputatae de veritate, qq. 21–29 (Opera omnia* 22.3.1) (pp. 684–687). Rome. There is an older English translation based on this edition: Thomas Aquinas. (1954). *Truth, Vol. 3: Questions 21–29* (R. W. Schmidt, Trans.) (pp. 144–148). Chicago: Henry Regnery.

## Translation

The second question is whether there is free choice in brutes. And it seems that this is the case. For [1.], based on the fact that our acts are voluntary, we are said to be endowed with free choice. But according to the philosopher in [book] III of the *Ethics*,[3] children and brutes participate in the voluntary. Hence, there is free choice in brutes.

2. Furthermore, according to the philosopher in [book] VIII of the *Physics*,[4] in everything that moves itself exists [the capacity] to move or not to move. But brutes move themselves. Therefore, [the capacity] to move or not to move exists in them. Yet, we are said to be endowed with free choice based on the fact that there is in us [the capacity] of doing something, as is clear from [the words of] Gregory of Nyssa[5] and the Damascene.[6] Consequently, there is free choice in brutes.

3. Moreover, free choice entails two things, namely, judgment and freedom. Both of them are found in brutes, for they have some judgment over what is to be done. This is clear from the fact that they pursue one thing but flee another. Moreover, they

---

[2] For an analysis of parts of this text, see, for instance, Gallagher (1994), 251–256; Davids (2017), 195–201; Oelze (2018), 106–111.

[3] Aristotle, *Ethica Nicomachea* III.4, 1111b8f.

[4] Aristotle, *Physica* VIII.4, 255a7f.

[5] This is a misattribution. Aquinas actually refers to a passage in Nemesius of Emesa, *De natura hominis*, c. 39, eds. Verbeke & Moncho (1975), 146f. Dobler (2001), 88, thinks he refers to c. 40, 150.

[6] John of Damascus, *De fide orthodoxa*, c. 40 (= II.26), ed. Buytaert (1955), 150.

possess freedom because they can move or not move. Hence, there is free choice in them.

4. Moreover, when a cause has been placed an effect is placed [as well]. Yet, the Damascene[7] places the cause of the freedom of choice in the fact that our soul begins from a change, because it is from nothing and, therefore, it is changeable and relates to many things in a potential manner. But the soul of a brute also begins from a change, and hence there is free choice in them.

5. Moreover, if something is not obliged to anything, it is called 'free'. But the soul of a brute has no obligation towards either side of [two] opposites because, unlike the power of natural things that always do the same, its power is not determined by one thing. Therefore, the soul of a brute possesses free choice.

6. Furthermore, punishment is not due to anybody who lacks free choice. But in the Old Law[8] one can frequently find penalties inflicted on brutes, as is evident with regard to the beast touching the mountain, [mentioned] in *Exodus* 19,[9] with regard to the cow hurting somebody with its horns, [mentioned] in *Exodus* 21,[10] and with regard to the animal with which a woman has intercourse, [mentioned] in *Leviticus* 20.[11] Therefore, brutes seem to be endowed with free choice.

7. Furthermore, as the saints[12] say, a sign that human beings are endowed with free choice is the fact that, by commands, they are encouraged to [do] something good and restrained from [doing] something bad. Yet, we see that brutes are induced by rewards, moved by commands, or terrified by threats to do or dismiss something. Thus, brutes are endowed with free choice.

8. Moreover, a divine command is not given to anyone not possessing free choice. But a divine command is given to a brute. This is why, in another version of *Jonah* 3, it is said that "God commanded a worm, and it struck the ivy".[13] Therefore, brutes possess free choice.

Yet, on the contrary, [1.] humans seem to have been created in the image of God insofar as they are endowed with free choice, as the Damascene[14] and also Bernard[15] say. But brutes have not been created in the image of God. Consequently, they are not endowed with free choice.

---

[7] Ibid., c. 41 (= II.27), ed. Buytaert (1955), 152. As Dobler (2000), 151, shows, John of Damascus relies on Nemesius of Emesa, *De natura hominis*, c. 40, eds. Verbeke & Moncho (1975), 150.

[8] I.e. the Old Testament, in particular the books of Moses.

[9] In Ex. 19:13, God tells Moses that neither humans nor animals must touch mount Sinai, otherwise, they will be punished.

[10] Ex. 21:28 mentions that a cow which mortally injures a human being must be stoned to death.

[11] Lev. 20:15–16 imposes the death penalty on both humans and animals involved in sodomy.

[12] E.g. Augustine, *De gratia et libero arbitrio*, c. 2, ed. Migne (1845) (= PL 44), 882f.

[13] Jon. 4:7. Aquinas seems to refer to an older Latin translation of the Bible, the so-called *Vetus Latina*.

[14] John of Damascus, *De fide orthodoxa*, c. 26 (= II.12), ed. Buytaert (1955), 113.

[15] Bernard of Clairvaux, *De gratia et libero arbitrio* IX.28, ed. Winkler (1990), 213f.

2. Furthermore, everything that is endowed with free choice acts and is not only acted upon. But "brutes do not act but are acted upon," as the Damascene says in book II.[16] Consequently, brutes are not endowed with free choice.

Reply: It must be said that brutes are in no way endowed with free choice. For the proof of this, it must be known that even though three things concur for our action, namely, cognition, appetite, and the action itself, the whole concept of freedom depends on the mode of cognition. For appetite follows cognition, because appetite is only about something good that has been proposed to it by a cognitive power. And the fact that sometimes appetite does not seem to follow cognition is because appetite and the judgment of cognition do not concern the same thing. For appetite concerns a particular relating to an action, whereas the judgment of reason sometimes concerns some universal which is sometimes opposed to appetite. Yet, a judgment about this particular thing that relates to an action as it is [here and] now can never be opposed to appetite. For someone who wants to fornicate generally knows that fornication is bad, but, nevertheless, judges this present act of fornication to be something good for himself and chooses it under the aspect of [its being] good. For nobody acts intending something bad, as Dionysius says.[17]

Yet, as long as there is nothing in the way, a movement or an action follows an appetite. And so, if the judgment of the cognitive [faculty] is not in the power of somebody but is determined by something else, the appetite will not be in his power either and, consequently, neither the movement nor the action absolutely. The judgment, however, is in the power of the one who judges insofar as he can judge about his own judgment, for we can judge about what is in our power. However, [the capacity of] judging about one's own judgment belongs to reason alone; it reflects upon its act and cognises the appearances of things about which it judges and by which it judges. Therefore, the root of all freedom is situated in reason. And so, something relates to free choice as it relates to reason. However, reason is fully and perfectly found in human beings alone. Hence, only in them free choice is found to a full degree. Brutes, however, possess some likeness of reason inasmuch as they possess a certain natural prudence, [and] insofar as an inferior nature somehow adjoins what is of a superior nature.[18] The likeness exists with regard to the fact that they possess an orderly judgment about certain things. Yet, in their case this judgment derives from natural estimation, not from some [cognitive] gathering, because they do not know the reason for their judgment. Therefore, unlike the judgment of reason, this kind of judgment does not extend to all things, but only to some particulars. And, similarly, there is in them some likeness of free choice inasmuch as they can do or not do one and the same thing according to their judgment, and in this way there is in them some sort of limited freedom. For they can do something when they judge that something is to be done, or not do

---

[16] John of Damascus, *De fide orthodoxa*, c. 41 (= II.27), ed. Buytaert (1955), 153.

[17] Dionysius Areopagita, *De divinis nominibus* IV.32, ed. Suchla (1990), 177.

[18] See ibid. VII.3, ed. Suchla (1990), 198.

something when they do not judge [that something is to be done]. But since their judgment is determined to one particular thing, the appetite and the action are consequently determined by one particular thing, as well. Therefore, according to Augustine in [book] XI of *On the Literal Meaning of Genesis*, "they are moved by things they have seen"[19] and, according to the Damascene,[20] they are controlled by emotions, because it is clear that they naturally judge about this visual perception or that emotion. Thus, by the sight of a particular thing or by an emotion that is aroused they must necessarily move and flee or seek something, as a sheep must necessarily be terrified and flee when it has seen a wolf. And when the passion of anger is aroused in a dog it must necessarily bark and pursue to harm [that thing or being that causes the anger]. But human beings are not necessarily moved by the things that occur to them, or by passions that have been aroused, because they can accept or reject them. And, therefore, human beings are endowed with free choice, whereas brutes are not.

1. To the first [argument] it must be said that the voluntary is placed in brutes by the Philosopher not insofar as it comes from the will, but insofar as it opposed to [what is done by] coercion. And in this sense, it is said that the voluntary is in brutes or children because they do something of their own accord, not by the employment of free choice.

2. To the second [argument] it must be said that the moving faculty of brutes, taken as such, does not tend to one side of [two] opposites rather than to another side. And in this sense, it is said that they can move or not move. But the judgment, based on which the moving power goes for one side of [two] opposites, is determined. And so, they are not endowed with free choice.

3. To the third [argument] it must be said that even though there is in brutes a certain indifference of actions, it, nevertheless, cannot be said in the proper sense that there is in them freedom of actions or [freedom] of doing or not doing something. For actions – since they are performed by the body – can be suppressed or prohibited, not only in brutes but also in humans, so that not even a human being is said to be free in her action. And, in addition, even though there is, taking the action in itself, an indifference towards doing or not doing something, the superordinate role of the judgment from which it derives, which is determined to one particular thing, still needs to be considered. And from this derives a certain obligation for the actions themselves, so that freedom in the full sense of the term cannot be found in them. Even if one took for granted that they have a certain freedom and a certain judgment, it would still not follow that they have freedom of judgment, because their judgment is naturally determined to one particular thing.

4. To the fourth [argument] it must be said that the Damascene does not identify beginning from change or being created from nothing as the cause of free choice, but as the cause of the flexibility of free choice with regard to evil. However, the

---

[19] Augustine, *De Genesi ad litteram* IX.14, ed. Migne (1887) (= PL 34), 402.

[20] John of Damascus, *De fide orthodoxa*, c. 62 (= III.18), ed. Buytaert (1955), 254.

Damascene[21] as well as Gregory of Nyssa[22] and Augustine[23] assign reason as the cause of free choice.

5. To the fifth [argument] it must be said that, even though the moving faculty of brutes is not determined by one particular thing, their judgment about the things that are to be done is, nevertheless, determined by one particular thing, as has been said.

6. To the sixth [argument] it must be said that brutes have been created as being obedient to humans insofar as brutes are employed for whatever serves humans, for the sake of which they have been created.[24] Thus, brutes are punished on the basis of divine law – not because they have sinned themselves, but because the human beings who are their owners are punished by their punishment, terrified by the severity of this punishment, or even instructed by the meaning of the mystery.

7. To the seventh [argument] it must be said that both humans and brutes are motivated by rewards and rebuked by beatings, or by orders and prohibitions. Yet, [they are motivated] in different ways, because it is in the power of humans to choose or reject the same things that are shown to them in a similar way, no matter whether they are orders or prohibitions, rewards or whippings, by the judgment of reason. Yet, in brutes the natural judgment is determined by the fact that what is proposed or occurs in one way, is accepted or fled in the same way. However, it happens that brutes, by memory of previous rewards or beatings, apprehend one thing as something friendly and desirable or something that is to be hoped for, and another thing as harmful, repulsive, or terrifying. And, therefore, by the feeling of fear that is aroused in them after they have been beaten, they are led to obeying the commands of their trainer. Yet, it is not necessary that such things are done by brutes out of free choice but because of an indifference of actions.

8. To the eighth [argument] it must be said that, according to Augustine in [book] IX of *On the Literal Meaning of Genesis*, a divine order given to brutes "must not be understood as having been given in such a way that they are capable of understanding and obeying a voice by which an order is coming out of a cloud in the form of words that rational souls hear; for beasts and birds have not been endowed with this capacity. Nevertheless, they obey God in their own way, [that is,] not by the choice of a rational will. Rather, as he moves all things in time without being moved in time himself, brutes move in time to fulfil his orders".[25]

---

[21] John of Damascus, *De fide orthodoxa*, c. 41 (= II.27), ed. Buytaert (1955), 153.

[22] Once more (see note 5), the correct reference is: Nemesius of Emesa, *De natura hominis*, c. 40, eds. Verbeke & Moncho (1975), 150.

[23] E.g. Augustine, *De libero arbitrio* II.6, ed. Green (1970), 246f.

[24] This is based on Gen. 1:26–28.

[25] Augustine, *De Genesi ad litteram* IX.14, ed. Migne (1887) (= PL 34), 402.

# Bibliography

## *Primary Sources*

Aristotle. (1894). *Ethica Nicomachea* (I. Bywater, Ed.). Oxford: Clarendon Press.
Aristotle. (1950). *Physica* (W. D. Ross, Ed.). Oxford: Clarendon Press.
Augustine. (1845). *De gratia et libero arbitrio* (J.-P. Migne, Ed.) (PL 44). Paris.
Augustine. (1887). *De Genesi ad litteram libri XII* (J.-P. Migne, Ed.) (PL 34). Paris.
Augustine. (1970). *De libero arbitrio: Libri tres* (W. M. Green, Ed.) (CCSL 29). Turnhout: Brepols.
Bernard of Clairvaux. (1990). *De gratia et libero arbitrio* (G. B. Winkler, Ed.) (*Sämtliche Werke* 1). Innsbruck: Tyrolia.
Dionysius Areopagita. (1990). *De divinis nominibus* (B. R. Suchla, Ed.) (*Corpus Dionysiacum* 1). Berlin/New York: De Gruyter.
John of Damascus. (1955). *De fide orthodoxa: Versions of Burgundius and Cerbanus* (E. M. Buytaert, Ed.). St. Bonaventure: The Franciscan Institute.
Nemesius of Emesa. (1975). *De natura hominis: Traduction de Burgundio de Pise* (G. Verbeke & J. R. Moncho, Eds.). Leiden: Brill.
Thomas Aquinas. (1954). *Truth, Vol. 3: Questions 21–29* (R. W. Schmidt, Trans.). Chicago: Henry Regnery.
Thomas Aquinas. (1973). *Quaestiones disputatae de veritate, qq. 21–29* (*Opera omnia* 22.3.1). Rome.

## *Secondary Sources*

Davids, T. (2017). *Anthropologische Differenz und animalische Konvenienz: Tierphilosophie bei Thomas von Aquin*. Leiden/Boston: Brill.
Dobler, E. (2000). *Indirekte Nemesiuszitate bei Thomas von Aquin: Johannes von Damaskus als Vermittler von Nemesiustexten*. Freiburg (Schweiz): Universitätsverlag.
Dobler, E. (2001). *Falsche Väterzitate bei Thomas von Aquin: Gregorius, Bischof von Nyssa oder Nemesius, Bischof von Emesa? Untersuchungen über die Authentizität der Zitate Gregors von Nyssa in den gesamten Werken des Thomas von Aquin*. Freiburg (Schweiz): Universitätsverlag.
Gallagher, D. M. (1994). Free choice and free judgment in Thomas Aquinas. *Archiv für Geschichte der Philosophie, 76*(3), 247–277.
Oelze, A. (2018). *Animal rationality: Later medieval theories 1250–1350*. Leiden/Boston: Brill.

# Glossary

**Accident** (*accidens*)  Non-essential property of an object, such as its place, size, or colour (e.g. Socrates' whiteness). It inheres in a thing without altering its →substance (i.e. Socrates' rational nature).

**Appetite** (*appetitus*)  Power which makes a being strive for something. Depending on the object it is either sensory or intellective (in which case it is called →will).

**Cogitative power/Cogitation** (*vis cogitativa/cogitatio*)  Internal sensory power for gathering and comparing several individual →intentions. Its thought-like process is a preliminary stage to concept-formation or the cognition of →universals.

**Common sense** (*sensus communis*)  Internal sensory power for bundling cognitive information deriving from the external senses. It plays a crucial part in forming →phantasms.

**Estimative power/Estimation** (*vis aestimativa/aestimatio*)  Internal sensory power for apprehending individual →intentions (e.g. harmfulness) and for triggering an appropriate reaction (e.g. flight or avoidance).

**Imaginative power/Imagination** (*vis imaginativa/imaginatio*)  Internal sensory power for storing and, according to some theories, also for separating and (re-) combining →phantasms.

**Intellect** (*intellectus*)  Highest power of the rational or intellective soul, usually used in conjunction or synonymously with →reason. Unlike sensory powers, it apprehends and operates on so-called 'intelligibles' or →universals.

**Intention** (*intentio*)  Observer-relative feature of a sensory object (e.g. harmfulness) (in the context of medieval theories of cognition). It is linked to matter, yet non-material, and hence cannot be grasped by the external senses but only by the →estimative power.

**Memory** (*memoria*)  Internal sensory power for storing individual →intentions. It is a necessary prerequisite for the recognition of objects and, if linked to →intellect and →reason, for recollection.

A. Oelze, *Animal Minds in Medieval Latin Philosophy*, Studies in the History of Philosophy of Mind 27, https://doi.org/10.1007/978-3-030-67012-2

**Phantasm** (*phantasma*)   Bundle of cognitive information (e.g. a flavour or an odour) deriving from the external senses which is then further processed by the →imaginative power, for example.

**Reason** (*ratio*)   Highest power of the rational or intellective soul, usually used in conjunction or synonymously with the →intellect. Its most crucial operation is reasoning.

**Sensible** (*sensibilium*)   Object that can be apprehended by an external and/or internal sensory power. If it can be perceived only by one specific sense (e.g. sight), it is a so-called *proper sensible* (e.g. colour); if by all senses, it is a *common sensible* (e.g. size).

**Species** (*species*)   (Mental) representation which is either sensitive or intellective. According to medieval defenders of the so-called species theory of cognition, without such representations one could not have cognitive access to any object in the world.

**Substance** (*substantia*)   Basic entity and constituent of reality. An individual substance (e.g. Socrates) cannot be predicated of anything else (but Socrates), yet it can have various →accidents (e.g. whiteness).

**Universal** (*universale*)   Most general type of abstraction or general concept (e.g. the general concept of house, contrary to individual houses) which is apprehended (or formed) and processed by →intellect and →reason.

**Will** (*voluntas*)   Rational power which is usually linked to →intellect and →reason. Unlike natural instinct, it causes an action based on rational deliberation or decision-making.

# Author Index

# Subject Index

© The Author(s), under exclusive license to Springer Nature
Switzerland AG 2021
A. Oelze, *Animal Minds in Medieval Latin Philosophy*, Studies in the History of
Philosophy of Mind 27, https://doi.org/10.1007/978-3-030-67012-2

Printed in Great Britain
by Amazon

44192326R00126